Prehistory

AN INTRODUCTION

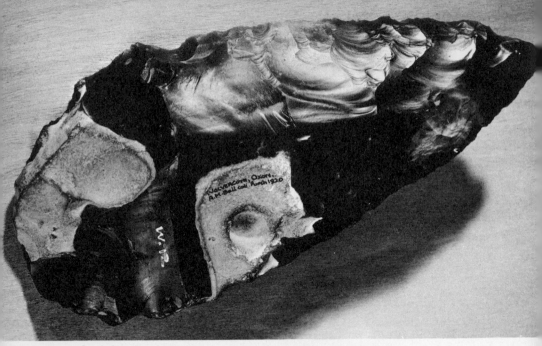

1 A fine handaxe: late Acheulian, from Wolvercote, Oxford; length 22 cm. Pitt Rivers Museum, Oxford.

Prehistory

AN INTRODUCTION

DEREK ROE

MACMILLAN

© Derek Roe 1970

First published 1970 by
MACMILLAN AND CO LTD
Little Essex Street London WC2
and also at Bombay Calcutta and Madras
Macmillan South Africa (Publishers) Pty Ltd Johannesburg
The Macmillan Company of Australia Pty Ltd Melbourne
The Macmillan Company of Canada Ltd Toronto
Gill and Macmillan Ltd Dublin

Library of Congress catalog card no. 70-81799

SBN 520-01406-5

Printed in Great Britain by
FLETCHER AND SON LTD
Norwich

Contents

LIST OF MAPS

Preface

The purpose of this book is to offer a first introduction to the subject of prehistory, to the sequence of events in prehistoric times, and to some of the ways in which they are studied. No attempt is made to deal with these subjects exhaustively, and indeed it would require many books this size to achieve that.

Since the account has to be highly selective, it has been necessary to omit, usually without much explanation or apology, whole subjects, whole parts of the archaeological sequence, and whole geographical areas. This has caused me just as much anguish as it may cause to any senior scholars of prehistory who may happen to look at this book, even though it was not really intended for them. Again, I am bound to have adopted in good faith long-established views about certain events of prehistory, which will soon be completely disproved when some researcher has time to take a fresh look at all the evidence, using modern methods of study, instead of accepting old and perhaps hasty conclusions based upon some small fraction of it. The aspiring prehistorian might well be excused for feeling that there are no facts in prehistory—only a kaleidoscope frequently shaken, in which the same pieces resolve themselves into a new and different pattern each time.

I hope, however, that the task of selection for this book has not been carried out in such a way as to give a false impression of the whole picture. Although this is not intended to be an account of British prehistory, the principle has been to write in most detail of the British sequence, endeavouring however to place it firmly in its context and to describe other areas within the Old World as fully as necessary. For some periods, the context is wider than others: thus, the nature of the British Lower Palaeolithic sequence demands reference to, for example, east

Africa and the Far East, but these areas are hardly directly relevant to, say, the British Bronze Age or Iron Age.

To confine one's attention to Britain would, of course, be to give a seriously incomplete account of Man's prehistoric past, because Britain is at all times during the prehistoric period a peripheral area in terms of human occupation, and not everything that was important is represented there. Thus, the early Neolithic period in Britain is remote both in time and distance from the occurrence of the so-called 'Neolithic Revolution' itself, which was so vital to the course of human events; or again, to base an account of the Upper Palaeolithic period on the handful of finds of that date from Britain, would be to miss out almost everything of importance about the first appearance of *Homo sapiens* in the archaeological record. So, even if this is an account of prehistory as seen from Britain, it is not intended that the British local sequence should overwhelm the rest of the story.

The book is arranged so that the narrative is as continuous as possible within each chapter, and notes are placed at the end of each chapter. These notes are designed to fulfil two needs: first, they indicate that certain points in the text are not as simple and straightforward as what I have written there may make them seem—though even with the addition of the notes, there is no space for properly exhaustive discussion of controversial matters. Secondly, the notes are intended to assist the reader's further and fuller study of the points to which they refer. Usually they indicate relevant literature.

In recommending literature for further study, I have had particularly in mind the reader who has access to an archaeological library, though I realise that there will be many who have no means and perhaps no inclination to follow up some of the less easily obtainable references. But very much of the most important archaeological literature, especially of recent years, is contained in periodicals rather than books, and it would have been a grave omission not to have quoted such references. I have not often referred to really obscure periodicals, or to foreign books and journals rarely seen in England, though on one or two occasions it has been necessary. For the rest, the reader may be pleasantly surprised to find how many large public libraries receive such periodicals as *Antiquity* and the *Proceedings of the Prehistoric Society*. Where I know of any relevant work of a more popular nature that is both sound and up to date, I have listed it with the other references. I have not normally been able to include material published after the first half of 1967, except to bring a very few important points up to date.

There are few prehistorians who could hope to write with equal knowledge and authority on all periods of prehistory even in a short introductory book, and I am certainly not one of them. I am therefore much indebted to the authors of all the books or papers on prehistoric subjects quoted, and many others, on whose scholarship, original work and specialist knowledge I have drawn deeply. The best specific acknowledgement I can pay to those to whom I owe most has been to recommend their works as sources of further reading, and this I have done, but it must be realised that the list is by no means complete.

I am also particularly grateful to Professor C. F. C. Hawkes, to Mr Dennis Britton, and to my wife Fiona Roe, for their kindness in reading the draft versions of various chapters, particularly those concerning the later periods of prehistory. They have both supplied me with much up-to-date information, and also removed a considerable number of inaccuracies; if any errors of fact remain, however, it is entirely my fault and in no way theirs. Mr E. W. MacKie and Miss Joanna Close-Brooks have also given me helpful advice on specific points, for which I am grateful to them.

8

It is perhaps worth adding that no new book on prehistory is now ever likely to be wholly up to date even at the moment of its publication, thanks to the magnificent acceleration of research and discovery in the subject. But all any author can do about that is to await with interest and perhaps trepidation the new facts which are bound to emerge while his book is in the press.

Oxford   D. A. R.
January 1968

Acknowledgments

The publishers acknowledge with thanks the help given by the following in connection with the illustrations of which the figure numbers are quoted:

Aerofilms, Ltd 90, 96; American School of Prehistoric Research 14; L'Anthropologie (Masson et Cie) 7 a, b, 45, 47; The Society of Antiquaries of London: Archaeologia (1890) 128, (1943) 98; Musée des Antiquités Nationales, Saint-Germain-en-Laye 27 a, b, 115; Archives Photographiques, Paris 80; Dr Jean Arnal (Préhistoire 14, Presses Universitaires de France) 65; Ashmolean Museum, Oxford 84, 88, 91, 138 (figures 84 and 138 are the copyright of Major G. W. G. Allen); Bedford Museum 113; F. Bordes: Typologie Paléolithique Ancien et Moyen (Imprimeries Delmas) 16 a–d, 17 a–d; British Museum 8, 12 a, b, 23, 31 a, b, 78, 94, 130, 134; British Museum (Natural History) 13 a, b, 41; Cambridge University Museum of Archaeology and Ethnology 103, 127; J. Allan Cash 120; Central Office of Information 77; Centre National de la Recherche Scientifique 116; Centre des Recherches Préhistoriques Français de Jérusalem 51; Professor J. Desmond Clark 3; J. G. D. Clark and others: Excavations at Star Carr (C.U.P.) 39 a, 40 a, b; Colchester and Essex Museum 118; Glyn Daniel: The Megalith Builders of Western Europe (Hutchinson University Library) 81, 82; Danish National Museum 42; Denise de Sonneville-Bordes: Le Paléolithique Supérieur en Périgord (Imprimeries Delmas) 20 a, b, d, e, 21 a–e, 22, 24 a, b, 25 a–d, 28 a–c, 43, 44 a–d; Edinburgh University (Dept. of Archaeology) 89; Herbert Greer 140; D. A. E. Garrod and D. M. A. Bate: The Stone Age of Mount Carmel (Clarendon Press) 50;   General Electric Company, New York 136; Journal of Geology, 1955 (University of Chicago Press) 137; Germania XL, 1962 (Gebr. Mann) 102; The Green Studio, Dublin 83; Prof. W. F. Grimes and the London University of Archaeology 117; W. F. Grimes: The Prehistory of Wales (National Museum of Wales) 100 b, c, 104a; Controller of H.M.S.O., from Archaeological Report No. 1, Excavations at Jarlshof, Shetland 131; Biologisch-Archaeologisch Instituut, State University, Groningen 62, 63, 64 a–c;

Heinemann Educational Books, Ltd 2; G. Henri-Martin: La Grotte de Fontéchevade (Masson et Cie) 20 c; Hirmer Fotoarchiv, Munich 92; National Museum of Ireland 106 a, b; Israel Academy of Sciences and Humanities 7 c, d; Dr Kathleen Kenyon 52, 54; Dr B. Klíma 32, 33; O. Klindt-Jensen: Denmark before the Vikings (Thames & Hudson) 39 b; Jericho Excavation Fund 55; R. Lacam, A. Niederlender et H. V. Vallois: Le Gisement du Cuzoul de Gramat, Archives de l'Institut de Paléontologie Humaine, Mémoire 21, 1944 (Masson et Cie) 46; L. S. B. Leakey: Olduvai Gorge (C.U.P.) 4 a–d, 6; Dr C. B. M. McBurney 141 a; C. B. M. McBurney and R. W. Hey: Prehistory and Pleistocene Geology in Cyrenaican Libya (C.U.P.) 19 a, b; Paul MacClintock 135; Magyar Nemzeti Museum, Budapest 87; Mansell Collection 30 a, b; James Mellaart 56 a, b, 58, 59; James Mellaart: Çatal Hüyük, A Neolithic Town in Anatolia (Thames & Hudson) 57; V. Milojčić: Chronologie der Jüngeren Steinzeit Mittel- und Südeuropas (Gebr. Mann) 60; H. Müller-Karpe: Handbuch der Vorgeschichte (Beck'sche Verlagsbuchhandlung) 15, 18 a–h, 21 f; National Geographic Society 5; Naturhistorisches Museum, Vienna 112; Neue Ausgrabungen in Deutschland (Gebr. Mann) 110; Ordnance Survey (Crown Copyright) 123; C. D. Ovey (editor): The Swanscombe Skull (Royal Anthropological Institute of Great Britain and Ireland) 10, 11; Panstwowe Muzeum Archaeologiczne, Warsaw 101 a–c; University Museum, University of Pennsylvania 139; M. and St. J. Péquart: Hoëdic (De Sikkel, Antwerp) 48; S. Piggott: Ancient Europe from the Beginnings of Agriculture to Classical Antiquity (Edinburgh University Press) 111; S. Piggott: The Dawn of Civilisation (Thames & Hudson) 49; S. Piggott: The Neolithic Cultures of the British Isles (C.U.P.) 70; Pitt Rivers Museum, Oxford (Photographs by V. P. Narracott) 1, 79, 85, 108, 142; Proceedings of the Prehistoric Society: (1937) 9 a–d; (1940) 122; (1955) 26, 133; (1956) 53; (1963) 99 a, b, d; (1964) 100 d, 105; (1965) 132 a, b; Ministry of Public Buildings and Works (Crown Copyright) 72, 125, 126; Rheinisches Landesmuseum, Bonn 114; Robert J. Rodden 61; Dr Gianni Roghi 107; Dr Andrée Rosenfeld 141 b; Dr J. K. S. St Joseph 71, 73, 121; H. Schwabedissen: Die Federmesser-Gruppen des Nordwesteuropäischen Flachlandes zur Ausbreitung des Spät-magdalénien (Karl Wachholtz Verlag) 34, 35, 36, 37; Isobel Smith (ed.): Windmill Hill and Avebury: Excavations by Alexander Keiller 1925–39 (Clarendon Press) 74 b, c, 76; J. F. S. Stone: Wessex before the Celts (Thames & Hudson) 124; Swiss National Museum, Zürich 67, 68, 69; Stanley Thomas 95; Institut für Vor- und Frühgeschichte (Tübingen) 109; J. D. van der Waals: Prehistoric Disc-Wheels in the Netherlands (J. B. Wolters) 66, 86 a–c; National Museum of Wales 97; Walker Studios, Scarborough 38; Wiltshire Archaeological and Natural History Society, Devizes (from F. K. Annable and D. D. A. Simpson (compilers): 'Guide Catalogue of the Neolithic and Bronze Age Collections in Devizes Museum') 74 a, 75 a–c, 93, 99 c, 100 a, 104 b; R. E. M. Wheeler: Maiden Castle, Dorset (Society of Antiquaries of London) 119 a, b; Yan, Toulouse 29.

These are in no sense archaeological period maps, or distribution maps of any kind: they are intended only to help the reader locate sites, places or features mentioned in the text, in relation to present physical geography. No allowance has been made for the gradual evolution of the present coastlines, drainage and relief, which continued throughout the prehistoric period but especially of course during the Pleistocene. Site or place names mentioned only in the picture captions have not been included.

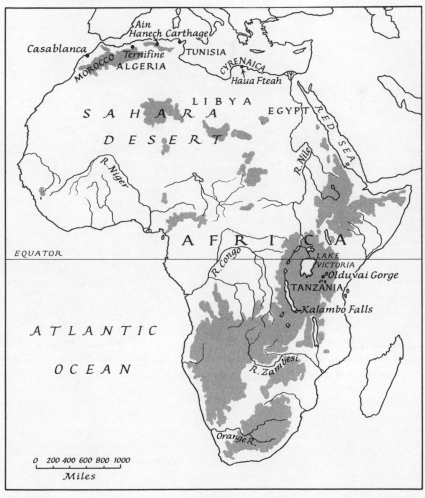

1. Africa

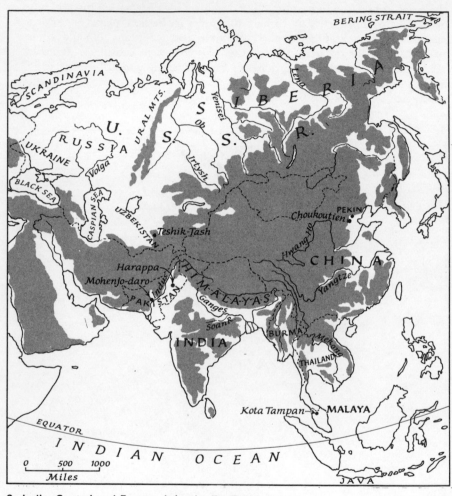

2. India, Central and Eastern Asia, the Far East

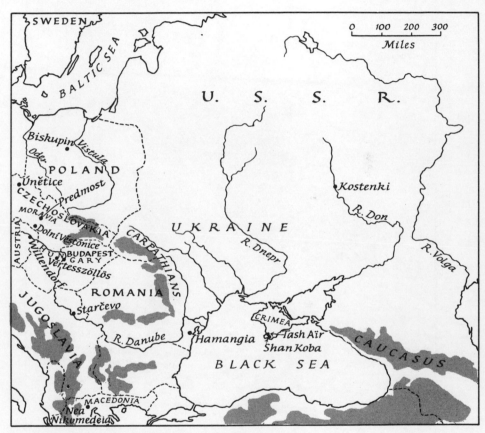

3. Eastern Europe and the Western U.S.S.R.

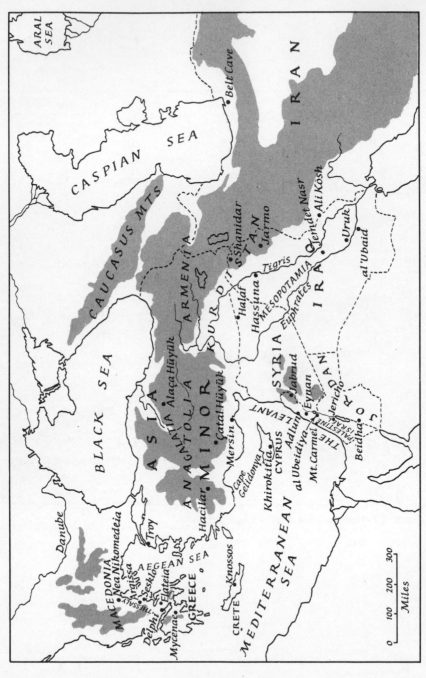

4. Greece and the Middle East

5. Southern, Western and Central Europe

15

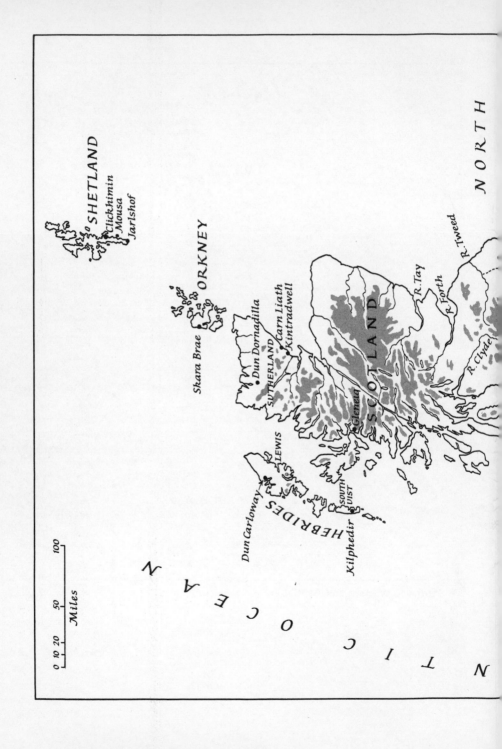

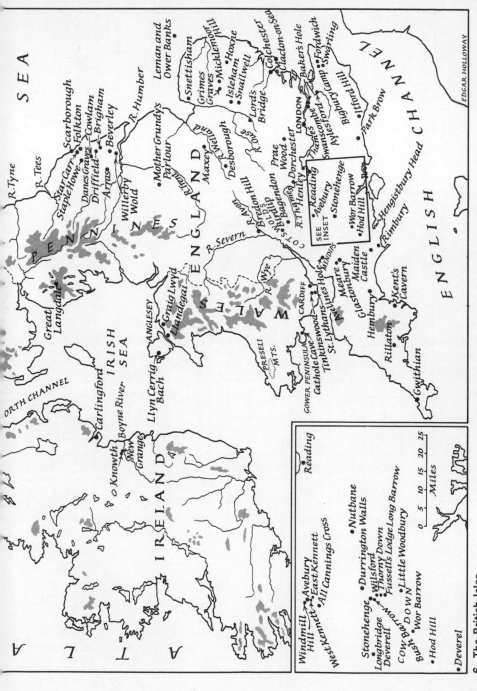

SEA

R. Tyne

R. Tees

IRISH SEA

NORTH CHANNEL

ATLANTIC

IRELAND

WALES

ENGLAND

PENNINES

Great Langdale

Carlingford

Boyne River
New Grange
Knowth

Llyn Cerrig Bach
ANGLESEY
Craig Lwyd
Llandegai

PRESELI MTS.

GOWER PENINSULA
Cathole Cave
Tinkinswood
St. Lythans

CARDIFF

R. Wye

R. Severn

COTSWOLDS
MENDIPS

Aveline's Hole

Meare
Glastonbury
Hembury
Maiden Castle

Rillaton

Kent's Cavern

Gwithian

Rimbury

Hengistbury Head

ENGLISH CHANNEL

Scarborough
Star Carr
Staple Howe
Folkton
Danes Graves
Driffield
Arras
Cowlam
Brigham
Beverley

R. Humber

Willerby Wold

Mother Grundy's Parlour

R. Derwent

Maxey
R. Wells
Desborough

Bredon Hill
R. Avon
WOLDS
Birdlip
Bagendon

R. Thames
Henley
Reading
Avebury

Stonehenge
Wor Barrow
Hod Hill

Leman and Ower Banks

Snettisham
Grimes Graves
Isleham
Hoxne
Snailwell
Mickle moor Hill

Lord's Bridge
R. Ouse

LONDON
Prae Wood
Dorchester

Colchester
Clacton-on-Sea
Swanscombe
Aylesford
Baker's Hole
Fordwich
Swarling
Bigbury Camp
Ilford Hill
Park Brow

SEE INSET

EDGAR HOLLOWAY

Reading

Windmill Hill
West Kennett
Avebury
East Kennett
All Cannings Cross

Stonehenge
Longbridge
Deverel
Wilsford
Durrington Walls
Thorny Down
Fussell's Lodge Long Barrow
Little Woodbury
Nutbane

COW BOTTOM DOWN
BUSH DOWN
Wor Barrow

Hod Hill

Deverel

0 5 10 15 20 25
Miles

6. The British Isles

TABLE I: *Breakdown of prehistory, based on the original three age system*

Original Three Ages	Subdivisions	Transitional Phases		Notes on Further Subdivisions, etc
STONE AGE	OLD STONE AGE (PALAEOLITHIC)		LOWER PALAEOLITHIC	Cultures often extending over huge areas, with comparatively little local variation. The main cultures are usually divisible into broad stages to some extent.
			MIDDLE PALAEOLITHIC	Cultures extending over wide areas, with some local variations, and internally divisible into stages almost everywhere.
			UPPER (OR ADVANCED) PALAEOLITHIC	The cultural sequence varies according to area. Some cultures occur over wide areas; others are purely local. Most have well-defined stages, sometimes numerous.
		EPI-PALAEOLITHIC		Not a valid phase everywhere: various cultures locally recognisable, and occasionally forming a short sequence.
	MIDDLE STONE AGE (MESOLITHIC)			Local cultures and culture-sequences, making up a period of very variable duration and importance according to geographical position.
		PRE-POTTERY OR 'ACERAMIC' NEOLITHIC		A phase of variable duration, only locally recognisable and only occasionally subdivisible.
	NEW STONE AGE (NEOLITHIC)			'Early', 'Middle' and 'Late', or 'Primary' and 'Secondary' phases have been distinguished in some areas, but are not synchronous between different territories. Local cultures differ widely, and local chronology depends on the spread and development of the first farming cultures.
		'COPPER AGE' (CHALCOLITHIC)		A locally recognisable phase of variable duration and importance, sometimes subdivisible, preceding in some areas the introduction of bronze working.
BRONZE AGE				'Early', 'Middle' and 'Late' phases are encountered in certain areas, but such terms no longer have much validity as general subdivisions of the Bronze Age. Where they are used, they are usually defined on grounds of the technology and typology of the bronze implements. Local cultures occur, and their names are also sometimes loosely used as subdivisions of the Bronze Age in their own areas. Chronology of the inception and development of the Bronze Age is locally much influenced by the very variable extent and directness of contacts between the barbarian and civilised peoples.
IRON AGE (Pre-Roman)				As with the Bronze Age, there are no general synchronised 'Early', 'Middle' and 'Late' Iron Age phases, although such terms as 'Early Iron Age' or 'Late Pre-Roman Iron Age' are sometimes used in specific areas for specific purposes. The dating of the first spread of iron-working varies considerably between areas according to their geographical position and relations with the higher cultures, while the expansion of the Roman Empire brings the Iron Age in some areas to a premature end. The spread of the major Iron Age cultures of Hallstatt and La Tène over much of Europe offers the best means of establishing local sequences and phases, but is not directly effective everywhere.

1 Introduction to Prehistory

History, whatever else may be said about it, is generally agreed to begin with the earliest written records. But writing does not start until a very long time after the appearance of Man himself, and it is the function of prehistory to fill in the gap, by tracing the story of human development backwards in time, as far and as completely as possible.

The very nature of prehistory makes the subject's limits in time extremely flexible. On the one hand, writing was not invented simultaneously all over the world, so that the prehistoric period may end some thousands of years earlier in one region than in another. It is perfectly true to say that some primitive tribes in, for example, Africa or Australia were living a fully prehistoric life well into the last century. On the other hand, the beginnings of the prehistoric period are still barely discernible in the mists which shroud the other extreme of the time-scale, and it is only now beginning to be generally accepted that the first true men began to make implements nearer to two million years ago than one million.[1] Again, large parts of the world, such as the American Continent, evidently remained uninhabited until what would elsewhere be regarded as late in the prehistoric period, so that the beginning of prehistory is no more a unified affair all over the world than is its ending.

Within these vague limits of time and space lies the whole exciting province of prehistory, spread out like a huge jigsaw puzzle, which anyone may help to solve. Here and there, a few of the pieces have been fitted together, and the picture is beginning to take shape, but there remains a long way still to go.

Anyone more used to ordinary history, with its relatively short duration and precise dates, will find it hard to comprehend at first the immense stretches of time which prehistory involves. A simple experiment may help to show just how vast these periods are. Take a large number of pennies, and imagine that the thickness of each one represents a hundred years. So, if you pile four of them on top of each other, you have got back almost to the beginning of the reign of Queen Elizabeth I, while the addition of a further five extends to the Battle of Hastings almost exactly. A pile of twenty pennies represents approximately the time which has elapsed since Caesar landed in Britain, and it will serve well enough for the moment to represent time in Britain since the end of prehistory.

But now take a conventional date for the first appearance of Man in north-west Europe—say 500,000 B.C. (He certainly appeared a good deal earlier elsewhere, and later on some account will be given of how dates of this kind are established, and how accurate they are likely to be.) To reach this date with the pennies, one would need five thousand of them—over £20 worth, and the column, if it could ever be made to balance, would be something like 28 feet high. Even then, such a column would only represent the full length of the prehistoric period in this particular part of the world according to present knowledge, and the first beginnings elsewhere may be three or four times as long ago. But the lifetime of one man—one modern man, that is—is represented by only about three-quarters of the thickness of a single penny.

Prehistory, then, is the immensely long period of Man's existence before written records, and in the absence of writing, there are various special kinds of evidence, with which the prehistorian, the student of prehistory, has to concern himself.

He is concerned with finding, identifying and explaining the solid and visible traces left by prehistoric man, the most obvious ones being structures, living sites and burial places and implements and manufactured items of all kinds. To the latter is given the general name 'artifacts', whether the objects concerned be weapons, tools, ornaments, receptacles, or anything else that is 'made'—or even the waste-products of manufacture, like, for example, the flakes of flint struck off in the shaping of an axe or an arrowhead. All these things are artifacts, and the occurrence of artifacts is definite evidence for the presence of Man. Whether or not the prehistorian can go further than this, and say what sort of man, and when he lived and how his life was spent, will depend on a great deal of study and background knowledge, which enables him to recognise the artifacts as belonging to such and such a period. He may even be able to assign some sort of date to the objects themselves, based upon their type. (See Chapter 7 for a discussion of typology as a dating method.)

The prehistorian is also concerned, less directly, with the natural background to prehistoric human existence. He must therefore study such things as the long-term changes of climate in the Pleistocene period, which produced the various glaciations and the warm periods which separated them.[2] These climatic events had a profound effect on the vegetation of vast areas, on the animal populations, and on the relative distribution of land

and sea over the whole earth. Such matters naturally dictated what areas were available for human habitation, what were the sources of food, and hence what kind of life was to be lived; these things in turn are, of course, reflected in the distribution and nature of the human artifacts belonging to the period concerned. All these matters are bound up very closely together, and the prehistorian must concern himself with them all. In studying Man's past, he is merely one of a number of specialists all working together: among the others will be geologists, physicists, botanists, zoologists, physical anthropologists, and many more. The present tendency is for the written report on a prehistoric site or discovery to be really a symposium of complementary specialist reports on all the different aspects; the detailed knowledge required is now far too great for anyone to cover all the relevant sciences himself at a high enough level.

So far, deliberately, no mention has been made of archaeology. To some people, 'archaeologist' and 'prehistorian' would be identical terms: after all, do they not both study Man's ancient past? But some definition of prehistory has already been offered, and archaeology covers both the prehistoric period and almost all the time that has elapsed since the advent of written records. An archaeologist is as at home on a Roman, Dark Age or Medieval site as he is excavating a Bronze Age barrow, an Iron Age farmstead, an Old Stone Age hunting camp—or, for that matter, the capital city of an ancient civilisation—though individual archaeologists naturally have their own particular periods or interests. And now even 'Industrial Archaeology' (the study of sites mainly of the Early Industrial Age by fieldwork and recording and sometimes even by excavation) is no longer a new and outlandish term.[3]

So the prehistorian may be an archaeologist, and *vice versa*, but the two terms are not completely synonymous. Archaeology is best regarded as the science which concerns itself with re-covering and studying the relics of Man's past; it has its own techniques, of which excavation is only one, though a highly specialised and important one. Prehistory, on the other hand, is to be thought of as the discipline of recounting coherently the events of Man's past before written records. The archaeologist in his element is usually a field worker, the prehistorian not necessarily so. But most prehistorians are archaeologists as well.

The Prehistoric Period itself is much too long and varied to be studied without divisions. The original and classic division was eminently simple: a good deal too simple, as it has turned out. It divided prehistory into three parts, successive technological stages, which are not by any means of equal length, thus:

THE STONE AGE
THE BRONZE AGE
THE IRON AGE

There is at the moment a good deal of discussion as to the value or otherwise of retaining this outmoded Three Age System, as it is called. However, it has wormed its way so deeply into the literature, especially the earlier books and the more popular works, that to destroy it completely and replace it with a new terminology may prove almost impossible; even if archaeologists accomplish this amongst themselves, they may find it hard to make themselves understood afterwards outside their own world.

Provided one accepts the limitations of the Three Age System at the outset, it makes an adequate first introduction to the break-down of prehistory. The main limitations are easy to see. The system is an over-simplification; it is not of world-wide applica-tion: for example, a bronze-using phase is not found everywhere. The change-over from one 'age' to the next is not a simple quick event, taking place everywhere at the same moment. The names, taken literally, can also be misleading, by implying, for example, that in the Bronze Age stone was no longer used, or that iron in its turn replaced all other raw materials. Nor do the names Stone Age, Bronze Age and Iron Age tell us anything about the way of life of the periods to which they are applied. If they tell anything at all, it is merely to give some hint of the nature of the material from which some tools or weapons were made at the time, and of the broad technological stage which certain contemporary craftsmen had reached—interesting, but not in itself an outstanding piece of information.

The account of prehistory in this book will, however, keep to the general framework of the Three Ages, bearing in mind these weaknesses, and taking due note of the various subdivisions which have been added, rather than attempting to suggest new names. As a first step, it is worth while glancing at the origin of the Three Age System—since this will both cast some light on the system's shortcomings, and also touch briefly upon the origins of the study of prehistory itself.[4]

It is clear enough that Man's interest in his own past dates back a long way: Greek and Roman authors indulged in speculation about origins, and at all times the outstanding visible ancient monuments (Stonehenge, for example) attracted endless wonder and various hypotheses about their origins. But it is one thing to indulge in free speculation, and quite another to explore scientifically, and scientific exploration of the past ages before written history had made no significant progress at all by the beginning of the nineteenth century, although individuals such as William Stukeley (1687–1765) had made important contributions (if of somewhat variable quality) to antiquarian studies.[5] It was customary to believe literally in the Old Testament account of the Creation as unfolded in the Book of Genesis, and, if one sought a date for this in years, there was the figure of 4004 B.C. calculated by Archbishop Ussher (1581–1656), and widely accepted. The length of ancient civilisation as then known (again mainly in Biblical or classical terms), obviously occupied a very large amount of the time which had elapsed since that date, so the free-thinkers who dared to suggest a prehistoric period proper were left with very few years into which to crowd it, let alone any vast stretches of pre-human geological time. It was this kind of barrier which rendered impossible the establishment of a proper prehistoric chronology; in Britain, one could only write off objects and monuments which were evidently pre-Roman as belonging to the Druids or to the Ancient Britons—the native population encountered and mentioned by Caesar himself. Since Ancient Britons were mentioned by such a reputable historical source, their existence could scarcely be denied.

It is not a purpose of this book to describe in detail how this Genesis-minded attitude was attacked and overthrown. Geologists, notably Sir Charles Lyell (1797–1875), demonstrated the immensely long periods of time required for the formation of geological strata, and therefore the very high antiquity of the fossils they contained; archaeologists (in England, notably William Pengelly (1812–94)), showed beyond doubt that actual skeletal remains of man, and undoubted implements of human manufacture, were contemporary with the fossilised remains of long-extinct animals. Darwin (1809–82), Wallace (1823–1913) and the Evolutionists placed the study of human origins on a totally new footing, by showing what was the biological context of human 'Creation'—what, in fact, the biological mechanisms of Genesis' Six Days of Creation were. But all this took the first six decades of the nineteenth century, and won only gradual acceptance. Nevertheless, the slow triumph of these views extended beyond all comparison the available space in the time-scale into which prehistory was to be fitted. But how was the fitting in to be arranged?

The Three Age System was an early attempt to divide and order the prehistoric period. It had its origins in Denmark on a limited scale, and made its own headway in the new climate of free scientific thought created by the work of the geologists, archaeologists and evolutionists; its spread was contemporary with the spread of their work, and closely related, but its origin was completely independent, and it was certainly not something devised later to make sense of the newly expanded chronology.

The invention of the Three Age System is usually attributed to C. J. Thomsen (1788–1865) of Copenhagen, and took place in 1816–19.[6] He was engaged on the task of sorting and arranging collections of miscellaneous antiquities for the new Danish National Museum, and he sorted the prehistoric tools not by type, but by the material of which they were made—Stone, Bronze and Iron; it soon became evident to him that his groups must succeed each other chronologically, and this was later borne out by excavations (especially those of his pupil, J. J. A. Worsaae (1821–85)) in Danish burial mounds and peat-bogs, where the vertical sequence Stone, Bronze, Iron could be physically demonstrated. This new idea immediately introduced depth into prehistory, and made possible at least some ordering of prehistoric objects and sites: for example, one could now hope that the excavation of, say, a British site would reveal it as belonging to the Bronze Age of Britain, or whatever the case might be, rather than to the Ancient Britons in general. It still remained of course to develop and subdivide the Three Age System, and to assign to the divisions accurate dates in years. This process made good headway in the rest of the nineteenth century, and in a sense all modern prehistoric archaeology is merely the continuation and refinement of it.[7]

The nature of the main subdivisions of the original Three Age System which are so often encountered is also important, because these still necessarily form the framework of any account of prehistory. It seems to be a standard archaeological habit to divide things into three, and the usual names are Early, Middle and Late. However, the divisions of the Stone Age were called Old, Middle and New, though Palaeolithic, Mesolithic and Neolithic are terms in more general use in this particular case. (Greek: *palaios*, ancient or old, *mesos*, middle, and *neos*, new, with *lithos* stone.) Another form of the usual tripartite division used in certain cases is Lower, Middle and Upper. This is an echo of geology, for in an undisturbed sequence of geological strata, the lowest stratum must always be the oldest, simply because it was formed first, with the next one on top of it, and so forth. So, Lower corresponds to Early or Old, and Upper to Late or New. As will be described later, archaeological strata work in the same way, so the use of Lower, Middle and Upper as archaeological terms is entirely appropriate. All three versions are commonly found in one context or another.

The other kind of subdivision which most often occurs is the cultural one. For an explanation of this, a few simple definitions are necessary.

It was stated earlier that an artifact was any implement or other object made by man. Where the archaeologist uncovers a whole group of artifacts of different sorts, which were plainly all made at the same time by the same people, he calls the group an industry. Then, maybe, his researches and those of his colleagues eventually reveal a number of such industries, which seem to belong closely together in type, time and space—that is to say, their content is apparently similar, the dating of the series is consistent, and they share a common geographical location within greater or smaller limits. Where these conditions are fulfilled, the whole group of industries receives the title of a culture.[8]

Ideally, of course a culture will consist of far more than just so many groups of artifacts. Burial practices and settlement types, means of livelihood, artistic motifs, and evidence for ritual and religion, social organisation and outside contacts—these and other such things are all very much part of what an archaeologist or prehistorian may mean when he refers to a prehistoric culture. On occasion there may even be evidence for correlation between a culture and some specific human physical type.

Even so the archaeologist must make do with what he can find, and what he can fairly deduce from it, and he is therefore dependent on the survival of his evidence. For example, except in certain rare conditions, particularly waterlogging, desiccation or freezing, it is unusual for organic materials to survive very long: these would include objects of bone, wood, leather, textiles and so forth. Yet, in the absence of such favourable conditions, one could perhaps infer say woodworking or leatherworking from the nature of the inorganic tools which did survive, or reconstruct the approximate appearance of a building from the post-holes and beam-slots traceable in the ground, although the actual timbers had completely vanished.

Cultures are frequently named after the site where they were first recognised in typical form (the type-site). Thus, in the Palaeolithic Period, there is the Acheulian Culture, called after Saint-Acheul, a French site, or the Clactonian Culture, first recognised at Clacton-on-Sea, Essex, or there is the Neolithic Windmill Hill Culture, which takes its name from a Wiltshire site near Marlborough. Sometimes cultures are called after some object or structure which is highly typical of them, as in the names Beaker Culture or Tumulus Culture.

These cultures are important in the present context, because their names have often come to be used to represent periods of prehistoric time, in other words to break up still further the subdivisions of the Three Age System which have already been mentioned. This is admittedly a somewhat loose usage of the culture names, but it has the advantage of permitting such reasonable shorthand expressions as 'during Acheulian times' or 'by the end of the Beaker period'.[9]

It has been necessary to dwell at such length on the rather obscure business of the divisions and subdivisions of prehistory, because the dull list of names and stages forms the essential framework into which must be fitted all the sites or objects found, so that their relationship to each other is clear. To illustrate this, and to summarise the various subdivisions of the original Three Age System, this chapter includes a table (page 18) showing how the framework is achieved for the whole Prehistoric Period, in so far as this book covers it. This is a very simplified and generalised table, because one which listed all the possible subdivisions in full would become hopelessly complicated, and in any case cultures are by nature local phenomena, so that the various local sequences differ a great deal from each other in detail, even where they remain similar in general outline. Besides, as knowledge increases and names change, diagrams of this kind soon acquire a very out-of-date look—like the tables of human evolution drawn up not at all so long ago which included the famous or infamous Piltdown Man, whose remains were subsequently proved to have been a deliberate fake.[10]

NOTES

1. Until recently the conventional date for the beginning of the Pleistocene Period (see p. 35) was one million years ago, but it has now become clear that this figure must be hopelessly too low. The age determinations of around 1.75–2.2 million years obtained for Bed 1 at Olduvai Gorge (see p. 41) are the best and most often quoted illustration of this; the deposit in question belongs

to by no means the beginning of the Pleistocene. The full length of the Pleistocene may even be as great as three or four million years, though estimates still differ considerably. See also Ch. 2, n. 7.

2. This is the best illustration of the point, but smaller climatic changes, locally often of considerable importance, can be demonstrated at many points in the prehistoric period, and even in more recent times: there is evidence for periods of increased rainfall or other climatic deterioration which had some economic effect in Britain during the Roman and medieval periods, for example.

3. See, for example, Hudson, 1963.

4. The history of prehistory is a subject in its own right, and the reader who wishes to follow it up can readily do so, using as a starting point such works as Daniel, 1943, 1950a, 1962, 1967a; Bibby, 1957 and Ceram, 1952. Most of the more popular books on archaeology also contain further information on the subject, though it is regrettable that a few have concerned themselves only with the more lurid details.

As further general reading in connection with the subject-matter of the present chapter as a whole, the following are especially recommended: Clark, 1957; Piggott, 1959; Childe, 1951a; Pyddoke, 1964.

5. See Piggott, 1950.

6. Some doubt, however, must remain as to whether Thomsen really was the originator, since scholars in other countries were undoubtedly working on the same lines at much the same time, and similar ideas had been expressed, if not applied, previously. See the works quoted in n. 4 above for further discussion.

7. Another way of looking at this would be to say that modern studies are concerned with replacing the old system and substituting a more viable set of basic hypotheses. The acceptance of the Three Age System in Britain during the nineteenth century was lamentably slow, and not anything like complete until well into the second half of the century. A fascinating reminder of this conservatism occurs in the title of the British Museum's Department of British and Medieval Antiquities—where 'British' means 'Ancient British' in the pre-Three Age System sense. One hastens to add that the Department's magnificent prehistoric collections have long been ordered on more up-to-date lines!

8. The terms 'culture' and 'industry' are unfortunately used by different writers in different senses, and often far too loosely, so that the reader must always approach them with caution. In the present book, the terms are used as here defined.

9. There are undoubtedly far too many supposed 'cultures' in the textbooks, especially if a rigid definition of 'culture' is maintained. The validity of many

(even some of those whose names are used here as examples) is open to doubt, and it may be that the term 'culture' will in due course vanish from archaeological literature, though it has certainly not done so yet. Meanwhile, it would not be hard to find at least one archaeologist, and often many more, opposed to the validity of almost any culture name that has ever been used.

10. For an excellent account of the Piltdown affair, including how the hoax was eventually revealed, see Weiner, 1955.

2 The Old Stone Age

It is in many senses true to say that less happens in the Old Stone Age, for all its vast length, than in any of the other major periods of prehistory. There are many reasons for this, of which the most obvious is the low level of man's intellect and ability at this stage of human development. This should not only be thought of in terms of his having a small or inefficient brain; limbs and hands too were probably clumsy enough in the earliest stages to inhibit cultural advance, just as much as lack of inventiveness. And the deficiencies in the diet of primitive hand-to-mouth hunters and gatherers, who knew nothing for example of bread, were a constant brake on physical and mental development.

What does happen in the Old Stone Age, however slowly, is this: Man, by his toolmaking ability, emerges from an animal background and assumes higher status than any other animal. He becomes a hunter, using artificial weapons, and his hunting methods and equipment slowly but constantly improve; he learns to build himself shelter, to use fire, to clothe himself, to transmit ideas presumably by speech though not in writing. By the later part of the period, he is burying his dead with ceremony, and has created art of both a decorative and a magical character. All these things, but most strikingly the last two, show just how far he had advanced in the use of conceptual thought, which is a peculiarly human ability, and how far indeed he had become human. But throughout the period he remains at the mercy of his environment.

This then is the framework of cultural advance during the Old Stone Age. Alongside it goes physical development: this is an enormous and complicated subject, and little more than a general note on it can be included here.[1] The various human physical types of the Lower Palaeolithic, as known from the extremely sparse surviving fossil remains, were more or less primitive in the ways suggested above, while the Middle Palaeolithic was dominated by Neanderthal Man, whose brain was large but whose skeletal structure was still unrefined, with thick, heavy bones. With the Upper Palaeolithic, however, comes *Homo sapiens*, man of physically modern type, in all essentials skeletally the same as ourselves.

From the steadily growing but still pitifully weak volume of human fossil evidence of Palaeolithic date, it is comparatively easy to pick out standard types of man, representing generalised stages of human development: *Australopithecus*, *Pithecanthropus*,[2] *Homo neanderthalensis* and *Homo sapiens*. These main types can also be subdivided to varying degrees. But it must be stressed at once that there is no clear linear development from one to the other. In other words, *Pithecanthropus* does not demonstrably evolve into *Homo neanderthalensis*, nor the latter into *Homo sapiens*. The generalised types are perhaps more like branches off a main stem of development, some of them more important than others. Some of the individual human fossils, too, belong to different parts of their own branch; some stand near to the main stem

2

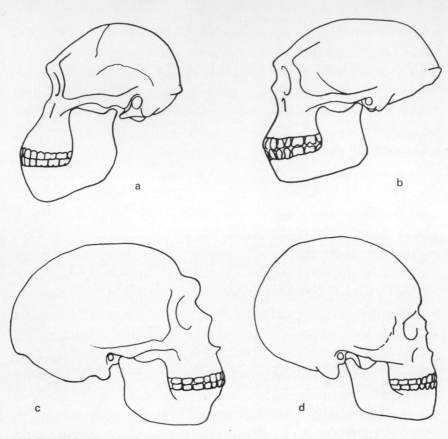

2 Skulls of:
    a. *Australopithecus*
    b. *Homo erectus (Pithecanthropus)*
    c. *Homo neanderthalensis*
    d. *Homo sapiens*

of development, and others in more remote, less influential positions. The old music-hall joke about a missing link between man and the great apes is long dead, it being now well known that man and the apes are both descended from a remote common ancestor. But there are very many 'missing links' still to be supplied before the pattern of human development during the Old Stone Age becomes clear.[3] And then there is the incompleteness of the accompanying cultural pattern; the solving of these problems is what Old Stone Age archaeology and prehistory are all about. This is not a dull period at all: it is the slow, vital formative phase which laid the foundations of everything that followed.

Perspective and chronology for the Palaeolithic period are supplied by a series of vast climatic changes. This whole series is sometimes loosely called the Ice Age, but it is far too complicated for such a simple title. There were in fact four main ice ages or glaciations, of by no means equal lengths, with certainly some earlier cold phases which have not left such clear evidence. The glaciations were divided from each other by warm periods called interglacials, and the improvement of climate which has followed the last of the four glaciations, and which persists today, is often called the postglacial period ('neothermal' is an alternative name).

The great glaciations themselves were not periods of unbroken cold. Within them, substantial oscillations of temperature can be detected, including periods of milder conditions to which the name of interstadials is given. An interstadial lacked the intensity and duration of an interglacial, but nevertheless left its traces in the geological record, and is naturally of importance from the point of view of human settlement, because interstadials could make land inhabitable which was not so during fully glacial conditions.

Correspondingly, the warm interglacial periods are not unbrokenly warm—signs are beginning to be recognised of quite sharp cold spells within them, but the extent of these is not yet fully understood.

The geological epoch which contains the glaciations and interglacials, and the Old Stone Age, is known as the Pleistocene Period. The glaciations themselves are named; there are several sets of names, according to various local sequences. In Table 2, they are named according to the sequence first worked out in the

TABLE 2: *The major cold and warm periods of the Pleistocene*

Period	Glaciations and Interglacials	Major Subdivisions
Upper Pleistocene	Würm Glaciation	Würm III (Late Würm): Cold, with two short interstadials (Bølling and Allerød) Würm II (Middle Würm or 'pleniglacial'): Very cold, with two interstadials (perhaps merging into one in some areas) Würm I (Early Würm): cold: with two minor interstadials
	Last Interglacial (often called Eemian)	(Probably included one or more colder spells)
Middle Pleistocene	Riss Glaciation	Riss II: Interstadial (sometimes called Inter-Riss) Riss I
	'Great' Interglacial (often called Hoxnian)	(certainly included at least one colder spell)
Lower Pleistocene	Mindel Glaciation	Mindel II: Interstadial (sometimes called Inter-Mindel) Mindel I
	First Interglacial	
	Günz Glaciation	Günz II: Interstadial Günz I
Basal Pleistocene	(Various Pre-Günz cold phases can be detected in parts of the northern hemisphere, but are not yet known or understood in detail)	
Pliocene Period		

Alpine area—still the set of names most commonly encountered.[4] As the table shows, the Pleistocene in fact begins a long time before the onset of the first major (Günz) glaciation, which used to be its conventional starting point; this has only become widely recognised comparatively recently. The designation Basal Pleistocene is given to this earliest part of the epoch, to distinguish it from the Lower Pleistocene, a term already in use which referred to the period from the beginning of Günz to the end of Mindel. It now appears that this Basal Pleistocene phase occupies at least half the length of the whole Pleistocene Period. The divisions are not shown to scale in the Table.

The Pleistocene climatic changes were referred to above as vast, and this should perhaps be stressed, as it is important to understand something of their magnitude and the way in which they affected the life and movement of the Palaeolithic hunters, whose existence was at best precarious, even in favourable conditions. It is hard enough in temperate Europe today to picture such things as a wall of ice, anything up to a mile thick, advancing extremely slowly but quite relentlessly across the landscape, and to realise that for example in England the actual ice sheet and accompanying fully arctic conditions reached on occasion as far south as the Thames valley. Conversely, at the height of an interglacial, animals which one would today not expect to find outside the tropical and subtropical zones, could flourish even quite far north in Britain; their remains occur there in interglacial deposits.

A glaciation or an interglacial would therefore, over a long period, utterly change the fauna and flora of an area, but there were other equally profound changes. If all the present polar ice were to melt, the sea level of the world could be expected to rise by at least a hundred feet, and a glance at any physical map of the world will give some idea of the kind of effect this would have on existing coastlines. It follows of course that during the interglacial maxima of the Pleistocene, when mean temperatures considerably exceeded those of the present, the sea-level was higher than that of today; the evidence for this is plain to see in the form of old cliff lines now some way inland, or traces of marine beaches high up the faces of present-day sea cliffs—phenomena found all over the world.

Similarly, when the glaciations were at their height, and so much water was locked up in the ice-sheets, the worldwide sea-level fell accordingly, sometimes by several hundred feet. Thus land-bridges came into existence where seas had been; at such times, Britain was a mere peninsula of Europe. The importance of such conditions in terms of human and animal movements across the land-bridges is obvious.

As the sea-level gradually rose or fell, so too there were drastic changes within the major river valleys, and indeed in whole drainage systems. Rivers responded to the rise or fall of sea-level by building up the deposits in their valleys, or cutting deeply down into them, and traces of this activity survive in the form of 'river terraces' intermittently preserved in the present topography of many valleys of sufficiently ancient origin.

All these vast climatic events of the Pleistocene period have left their traces in the geological record, as is only to be expected, and it is the task of the Pleistocene geologist to identify and interpret them, assigning this or that deposit or phenomenon to 'warm' or 'cold' conditions first, and then if possible to a specific warm or cold phase in the Pleistocene sequence. This is no easy matter, especially when one reflects that on the one hand there should be several sets of superimposed deposits belonging to different phases, and on the other that each glaciation tends to obliterate or badly to damage the traces left by its predecessors. It is not within the scope of this book to examine the ways in

3 Acheulian artifacts, including handaxes, *in situ* on an excavated working floor, Kalambo Falls, Tanzania. The dark objects are wood remains, consolidated ash and charcoal. Scale in inches.

which the geologists approach their task.

For the prehistorian and archaeologist, the point of all this is a simple one: during the times when occupation was possible, and in the favourable areas that could be reached, Palaeolithic man lived and hunted. His artifacts and industries are therefore to be found *in the appropriate contemporary Pleistocene deposit*. And with luck, that deposit can be recognised and interpreted, and assigned to a specific Pleistocene climatic event—to the Great Interglacial for example, or perhaps to a particular interstadial of the Würm Glaciation. Different cultural traces will be found to belong to other specific Pleistocene events and slowly a sequence will emerge. This is what was meant by saying that perspective and chronology for the Palaeolithic Period are supplied by the climatic changes. There is, alas, no magic method of finding out exact dates from the flint implements themselves which make up such a high proportion of the archaeological material of the Old Stone Age. (A number of archaeological dating methods relevant to the period are briefly discussed in the closing chapter of this book.)

Not all the phenomena of the Ice Ages are of world-wide occurrence. The high and low sea-levels are, of course, because it is not possible to have an altered level in one part of the sea only. However, all those direct effects which depend on the actual presence of the ice-sheet are not to be found in, for example, Africa, since Africa was never glaciated—and Africa is a vital area as regards the earliest Palaeolithic industries, and indeed the origins of man himself. There are still climatic changes, however, which can be used as a framework for the Pleistocene Period in Africa, and instead of glacial and interglacial phases these take the form of periods of wetter or drier climate, known as 'pluvials' and 'interpluvials'.

Unfortunately, there is not yet any general agreement as to whether a pluvial period in Africa corresponds to a glacial or to an interglacial period in Europe. If this matter can be satisfactorily settled, there is an attractive prospect of correlating the two archaeological sequences more closely than can yet be done. One would imagine that the long-term climatic fluctuations in Africa could hardly be independent of the expansions and contractions of the ice-masses which can be traced in the northern hemisphere. The onset of a glaciation must profoundly affect the normal rainfall patterns of all areas, but it is easier to say that than to interpret exactly what the effects would be, and whether they would be immediate.

But although the African and European sequences of Old Stone Age industries cannot yet be closely correlated, there are plenty of reasons for supposing that the first African industries are older than anything found in Europe.

First, they are old geologically—that is to say, they occur in deposits of very early Pleistocene age, accompanied by remains of a primitive fauna to which the name of Villafranchian has been given. Many of the animals of the Villafranchian group are survivals from the preceding geological epoch, the Pliocene period, and they become extinct everywhere by the Middle Pleistocene.[5]

Secondly, these earliest industries are archaic typologically. They consist of what are called pebble-tools and allied forms— simple pebbles very roughly worked by the removal of flakes to make a range of crude implements with points or with edges that could be used for chopping, cutting or scraping. Some of the flakes were also roughly trimmed for use. There is nothing in these pebble-tool industries as refined as the more carefully made handaxe tools of the succeeding Acheulian Culture, which will be described later on.[6]

Thirdly, at the famous east African site of Olduvai Gorge, a date in years has been calculated by the potassium-argon method (see page 235), which suggests that the earliest pebble-tool industry there was being made at least as long ago as one and three-quarter million years and perhaps even two million. This remarkably high figure has only gained acceptance slowly, perhaps mainly because there is so far so very little else with which to compare it, since the special conditions required for the use of the method are rare in association with archaeological remains. But little doubt can now reasonably remain as to the very high

5

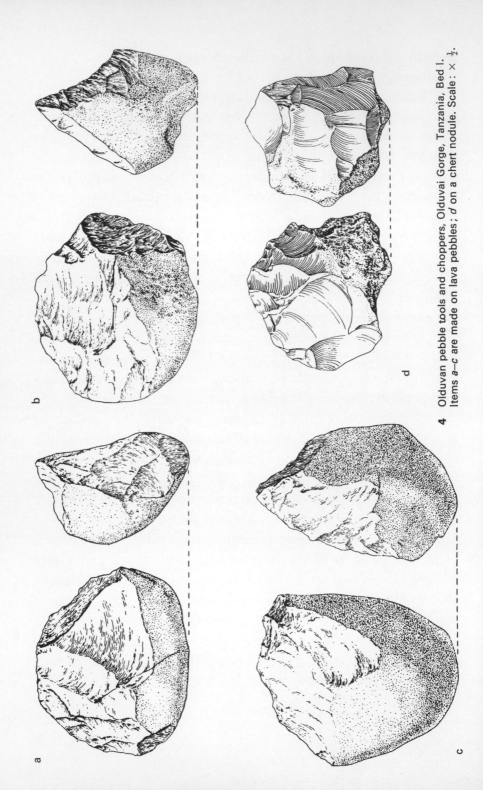

4 Olduvan pebble tools and choppers, Olduvai Gorge, Tanzania, Bed I. Items *a–c* are made on lava pebbles; *d* on a chert nodule. Scale: × $\frac{1}{2}$.

antiquity of the base of the Olduvai sequence.[7]

Olduvai Gorge itself is one of the most important prehistoric sites in the world.[8] The Pleistocene sequence revealed there in the walls of a rift valley incorporates various expansions and contractions of a lake, in response to wetter and drier climatic phases over an extremely long period of time, and there were also important periods of volcanic activity. The camp sites of Palaeolithic man, with abundant tools, are found on ancient land-surfaces throughout the deposits, whose combined maximum thickness runs into hundreds of feet. There are four main divisions of the sequence, called Beds I, II, III, and IV, and it is from Bed I, the lowest and oldest, that the first pebble-tool industries have come, associated with abundant remains of animals of the Villafranchian fauna, including numbers of bones split open by the hunters to obtain marrow. These industries of Bed I are called Olduvan, after the name of the Gorge, and they continue into Bed II, in the upper part of which, however, they begin to give way to somewhat improved implement types. Bed II is

5 Olduvai Gorge, Tanzania: a general view. In the foreground are Dr L. S. B. Leakey and one of his sons. National Geographic Society.

6
Skull of *Australopithecus
(Zinjanthropus) boisei:*
reconstruction, incorporating
the cranium found in 1959

divided into two parts with a break between them: the faunal
remains from the upper part make it clear that the Villafranchian
fauna had given way to one of Middle Pleistocene type. The
remainder of the sequence, notably in Bed IV, contains a magnificent series of Acheulian handaxe industries, gradually gaining in
refinement.

To return however to the pebble-tool industries: the next
question must be, who was their maker? The deposits of Bed I
at Olduvai, beside their yield of implements and animal remains,
have also produced some of the earliest known primitive hominid
remains in the world. Several of these certainly belong to the
genus *Australopithecus.*

At the moment, however, the evidence is not strong enough to allow the very obvious conclusion that *Australopithecus* was the maker of the Olduvan pebble-tool industries, even though his remains have been found *in situ* on a living floor; the alternative is that he was merely an item of the prey of the tool-making hunters, rather than himself being the hunter. The difficulty is that his brain is very small and his general status of evolution low; also, though a considerable number of Australopithecine remains have now been found at other African sites, there is hardly ever any reason for thinking that they were associated with stone implements. Was *Australopithecus* in fact capable of being a tool-maker?

Further discoveries will no doubt eventually settle this question, but at Olduvai a small number of hominid remains have been found at the same levels as *Australopithecus* and the pebble-tool industries, which have been interpreted as belonging to a more advanced hominid. Dr L. S. B. Leakey, the excavator of Olduvai Gorge, has called this more advanced creature *Homo habilis*. These finds are still very much under discussion, and the proposed classification of them is not yet accepted by everyone, but one view would certainly be that *Homo habilis* and not *Australopithecus* was the maker of the Olduvan pebble-tools.

This point must be set aside for the moment, however, as undecided, and meanwhile there are other occurrences of pebble-tool industries at other sites to be noted. In the African continent, they have also been found in early deposits on the Moroccan coast, and at a site called Ain Hanech in Algeria. In the former area, a dating which would be older than that of Olduvai has been claimed for the earliest stages, while at Ain Hanech a Villafranchian fauna is again present.

Two comparatively recent finds of pebble-tool industries further north are of great interest. One is at the site of al 'Ubeidiya in the Jordan valley, where the dating is apparently somewhat later than most of the African sites—perhaps near the very beginning of the Middle Pleistocene. Very fragmentary hominid remains were found with the industry, but their nature and age (and even their contemporaneity with the artifacts) are open to doubt, although they have been claimed as Australopithecine. The other site is in Hungary, at Vértesszöllös near Budapest: a find pebble-tool industry was found, with abundant environmental evidence to show that it is of Mindel Interstadial age (see Table 2). Once again there was a hominid fossil, part of a skull, but this time it belonged not to *Australopithecus*, but to a more advanced human type. The first descriptions attributed it to *Pithecanthropus* (*Homo erectus*), but it has since been reclassified as an early *Homo sapiens* form, and given the name *Homo sapiens palaeohungaricus* (see note 11 to this chapter).

Remains certainly attributable to *Homo erectus*, in association with early industries, are to be found in a completely different part of the world—China. The most prolific finds come from a group of caves at Choukoutien, about forty miles south-west of Pekin, where remains of over forty individuals of this human type have been found in deposits which represent occupation over a long period of time, which may not however begin much before the Middle Pleistocene. The accompanying implements are crude, simple choppers and pebble tools, with flakes trimmed to form points, knives and scrapers of a rough kind. Broadly similar industries have come to light in Thailand, Burma, Malaya and Java. *Homo erectus* remains too are known from Java, though not yet in association with the implements.

It seems probable that the origins of this Far Eastern group of pebble-tool industries must lie ultimately in Africa, rather than implying a second and separate area where primitive tool-making came into being independently. The Himalayan mountains, which are the major barrier on any likely route from Africa to the Far East, seem not to have felt the effects of the Günz glaciation, though the Mindel cold phases certainly left traces there. A human migration from Africa should thus perhaps have taken place before the Mindel glaciation, after which the way may have been closed. Pebble-tool industries seem certainly to have reached the Soan river valley in north-west India by Mindel times, and a pebble-tool site in Malaya called Kota Tampan offers an early enough date to support the idea of a pre-Mindel spread from Africa all the way to the Far East.[9]

In the Far East, there seems to have been little further development from the pebble-tool stage during the whole of the Middle Pleistocene, perhaps because there was no chance of contact with the more progressive industries which now began to develop further west. Certainly there are no undoubted handaxe industries in the Far East, and it is these which in Africa form the next stage of the Lower Palaeolithic sequence.[10]

Handaxes are more refined implements than the coarse pebble-tools so far mentioned. Technically, they may be described as 'bifacially worked core-tools'—that is to say, they are implements made from selected blocks of raw material by the removal of flakes from both sides to achieve the desired shape. At their best (see Fig 1 (Frontispiece)), handaxes can be most beautifully and delicately made, a pleasure to look at and handle. In the earliest stages, however, they are still thick and rough; between these two extremes of roughness and refinement there lies a considerable range of variation, which can be interpreted as a series of evolutionary stages, the evolution taking place slowly and offering prehistorians a series of generalised cultural stages, and thus some sort of relative chronology of a typological kind (see pages 225–229). However, there is no doubt that in the past there has been a tendency to subdivide handaxe development into far too

7 Implements from early handaxe industries: *a, b,* Ternifine (Algeria); *c, d,* 'Ubeidiya (Jordan Valley). Scale: × $\frac{3}{10}$.

many numbered stages, some of which have little or no meaning. It is also becoming apparent that some of the variations between industries may be of a functional nature and hence have no chronological implications.

The earliest handaxe industries, so far as is known, seem to be the work of men who can still be called *Pithecanthropus* or *Homo erectus*. Hominid remains of this broad type have been found at a similar level to the earliest handaxe industries at Olduvai Gorge itself, near the top of Bed II, and at Ternifine, near Oran, in north-west Africa. Various other early handaxe industries are known, though without hominid fossil association, for example at Casablanca and also at al 'Ubeidiya, where they follow the pebble-tool industry already mentioned.

It does not seem possible at the moment to prove that there was any penetration of Europe by handaxe makers at this very archaic cultural stage, although there may well have been, on a small scale. The main culture of the handaxe makers, of immensely long duration, is known as the Acheulian culture, often just referred to as 'the Acheulian'. The name Abbevillian, after Abbeville, which like Saint-Acheul is in the valley of the river Somme, has been given to the earliest handaxe stage; Chellean, after Chelles, is an older name for the same stage, still sometimes found. But although there are certainly very old river terrace deposits in the Somme valley, in which a very ancient fauna has been found, it has not been shown conclusively that implements constituting an archaic handaxe industry come from the same levels. Nor is there much reliable evidence for an Abbevillian stage in England; supposedly ancient deposits containing implements in the Thames valley between Reading and Henley have now been shown to be much younger. There is certainly a series of very crude handaxes from Fordwich, near Canterbury in Kent, and they are likely to be of a high antiquity, but

49

unfortunately the geological evidence for their age is at the moment far from clear.

This leads to the question of what are the earliest industries in Europe, aside from Vértesszöllös and the sites just mentioned. Several important discoveries have been made over the last ten years or so. At the Vallonet cave in the Alpes Maritimes in south-eastern France, a few rather generalised and inconclusive artifacts have been recovered in association with a fine Villafranchian fauna, and are of Lower Pleistocene date, perhaps contemporary with a phase of the Günz glaciation. At the Escale cave, Saint-Estève-Janson (Bouches-du-Rhône), another early fauna and a few flakes have been found, in a deposit perhaps of early Mindel age; there are clear traces of hearths, and therefore of human occupation. Neither of these sites has produced any handaxes, and no clear cultural attribution of the artifacts, such as they are, can be made. At Torralba and Ambrona in Spain, north-east of Madrid, fine early Acheulian industries with handaxes and cleavers have been discovered, associated with the remains of partially dismembered carcasses of hunted animals, notably elephants. These sites, recently meticulously re-excavated by Professor F. C. Howell, are evidently of late Mindel age.[11] The industries are of somewhat less archaic appearance than those of Ternifine or 'Ubeidiya, or the earliest handaxe industries from Olduvai or Casablanca.

But if there is only limited evidence in Europe for the earlier stages of handaxe manufacture, there are abundant traces of the more developed stages of the Acheulian Culture. The deposits of the Somme and Thames valleys especially have produced tens of thousands of handaxes, and the waste flakes which are by-products of their manufacture, not to mention the simpler implements, particularly scrapers, which Acheulian man used in great numbers to supplement the all-purpose tools which is what

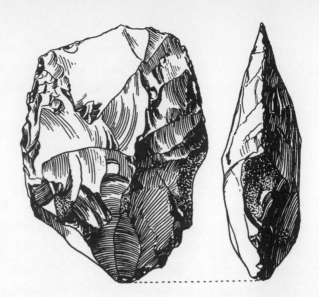

8
Cleaver of
Middle Acheulian type,
north-east London,
length 15·5 cm. (× ⅓).
British Museum.

his handaxes probably were. A handaxe could offer a very sharp cutting edge, a hammer-like butt, and a point, or, as an alternative, the special axe-like edge of the cleaver types. The uses of all these are readily imagined, but not so easy to determine scientifically.

So little is known, of course, of the life of Acheulian man; the vast length of time that has passed since he lived, and the scale of the climatic disturbances of the Pleistocene period, mean that few Acheulian objects have survived apart from the imperishable flint tools. But it is clear that the Acheulians were nomadic hunters and gatherers, who formed probably quite small bands. No buildings are associated with their sites, but they were evidently capable of erecting at least simple wind-break shelters.

There are about three thousand places in Britain alone where traces of the Acheulian culture have been found—all over southern England, just into Wales, and as far north as Yorkshire. The density in France is of course comparable, and the culture is also represented in Spain, western Germany and Italy, though only a single typical handaxe has so far been recorded from Greece. The Acheulian is also known from much of the land bordering the Mediterranean on the south side, and on the east side even as far north as Turkey and Armenia. It is abundant over most of Africa, and well represented in India, but no further east.

It does not penetrate, however, except very sporadically indeed, into Europe and Asia away from the Atlantic and Mediterranean coasts, and the river valleys draining to them. No doubt the lands and conditions here were less favourable, but there is also some reason for thinking that these areas were occupied by a rather different culture—though 'occupied' and 'culture' are perhaps too strong words in view of the sparse nature of the evidence. Such as they are, the finds seem to represent industries that did not use the handaxe form. The tools consisted of large plain or slightly trimmed flakes, struck from crude irregular or roughly spherical cores, and the cores themselves may sometimes have offered a useful jagged edge for chopping or cutting.

'Flake industries' of this kind, as opposed to handaxe industries, can be found in eastern England and have been claimed in the Netherlands, and at various places across the European plain, and even, though not very satisfactorily, in Russia; it has even been suggested that they have their ultimate origin in the Far Eastern group of pebble-tool cultures. However, the Vértesszöllös find in Hungary, mentioned on page 46 above, may perhaps be interpreted as indicating activity of the right type and date, much better placed geographically to provide their origin. They are obviously not too dissimilar in style from the early pebble-tool industries, which certainly contain a proportion of flake tools.

Of these flake industries of Europe, the clearest group is provided by the English Clactonian series. That the Clactonian really is something distinct from the Acheulian, because Clacton is of course far enough west to fall within the handaxe area, is

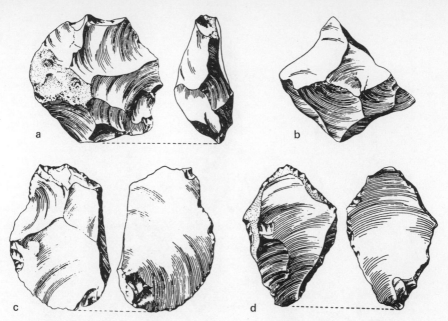

9 Clactonian artifacts, from Clacton-on-Sea, Essex. Scale: × ⅓.

a. core, Lion Point
c. retouched flake, Jaywick Sands

b. core, Jaywick Sands
d. retouched flake, Lion Point

suggested by the fact that several thousands of the typical cores and flakes have been found at Clacton and in Clactonian levels elsewhere, notably at Swanscombe, Kent, without any sign of a true handaxe in proper association with them.

It also seems likely that in England the Clactonian is present earlier than the Acheulian; as suggested above, there is little evidence for an Abbevillian stage of handaxe manufacture in England, except perhaps at Fordwich and possibly one or two other sites, none of them very satisfactory. One site, the most famous of all English Palaeolithic sites, the Barnfield Gravel Pit at Swanscombe in north Kent, provides an admirable picture of the British Lower Palaeolithic sequence.[12]

The gravels at this pit consist of successive deposits laid down by the river Thames, when it flowed into a sea whose level was about a hundred feet higher than the sea-level of today. This is a

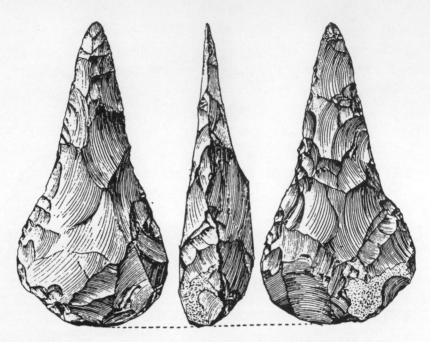

10 Pointed Middle Acheulian handaxe from the Lower Middle Gravels at Barnfield Pit, Swanscombe. This type, with its characteristic ogival outline, is called a *ficron*. Length 22 cm.; scale: × ⅓. British Museum.

well-known Middle Pleistocene height, which is firmly associated with the Great or Mindel-Riss Interglacial.

The various deposits at Barnfield Pit offer the following succession of industries, from the base upwards, i.e. the oldest first:

1. CLACTONIAN—plenty of the typical cores and flakes, and no handaxes at all.
2. ACHEULIAN—a rich industry, with many pointed, rather triangular-shaped handaxes, often well made. The cultural stage may be simply called Middle Acheulian, to indicate its fairly advanced nature within the whole Acheulian tradition, even though no 'Early Acheulian' is to be seen at Swanscombe.

3. ACHEULIAN—another level of Middle Acheulian, more or less identical, but this time accompanied by the fragments of the famous Swanscombe Skull. This important human fossil is tantalisingly incomplete: it certainly seems to be more advanced than a Pithecanthropine, and suggestions have been made that it represents an early type of *Homo sapiens*, ancestral to both Neanderthal man and *Homo sapiens* of Upper Palaeolithic date (see below, and see also note 14 to this chapter).

4. ACHEULIAN—this time a more advanced stage, dominated by flat, refined ovate handaxes rather than the pointed type. It may be called 'Late Middle Acheulian', or simply 'Evolved Acheulian'.

The evidence from the rest of Britain, and France, is in broad general agreement with the sequence that can be observed at Swanscombe. The Middle Acheulian stage, dominated by pointed handaxes, is widely represented—another of the many places where it occurs is Hoxne in Suffolk, which is an important site because there is again abundant evidence of a Great Interglacial date. The subsequent stage with the refined ovate handaxes can also be paralleled many times in the Thames and Somme valleys and elsewhere, and handaxes of this type continued to be made after the close of the Great Interglacial. There are some signs that the very end of the Acheulian culture in Europe produced a resurgence of the pointed types of handaxe, of specialised form and considerable refinement, a phase which has been called

11
Late Middle Acheulian ovate handaxe, with twisted profile, from Barnfield Pit, Swanscombe. Length about 10 cm.; scale: × ⅓. National Museum of Wales (Stopes Collection).

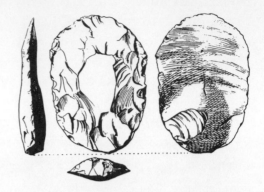

12a Two views of Levalloisian 'tortoise' core from Northfleet, Kent, showing the large scar left by the removal of a Levalloisian flake. Length of core 16·5 cm. British Museum.

12b Four views of a Levalloisian flake, also from Northfleet, struck from a core similar to the one illustrated. Length 13·4 cm. British Museum. Scale of both : × ¼.

Micoquian after a French site, La Micoque. But it is questionable whether this final stage is at all widely represented, and in England handaxe industries of Last Interglacial date seem rather rare. The continental Micoquian industries may even date from as late as early Würm times.

A tool-type which in north-west Europe assumes considerable importance after the close of the Great Interglacial, to the gradual exclusion of the handaxes, is the Levalloisian flake, the name again being taken from a French type-site. This tool is a large, flat, sharp-edged flake, produced by elaborate shaping and preparation of a core before the blow was struck which removed the flake itself as a finished implement. Often the core would produce only a single Levalloisian flake, and would then have to be thrown away, so the method was rather wasteful of raw material. The technique seems first to have been used as something like a quick way of producing a tool whose proportions, and also probably function, were those of a thin ovate handaxe, but a Levalloisian flake was not usually bifacially worked, and therefore remained a flake tool and not a handaxe in any strict typological sense.

This 'Levalloisian technique' seems to have been used on rare occasions even before the end of the Great Interglacial, and it is reasonable enough to suppose that the Acheulians invented it, so far as north-west Europe was concerned; the idea seems to have been independently invented in more than one area at about the same time, and there is no need to try to make a direct cultural connection between the Early Levalloisian sites in, for example, England and north Africa. It is only after the end of the Great Interglacial, and in a few areas, that the technique was adopted to form the basis of whole industries or a proper 'Levalloisian culture'.

Southern England and northern France form such an area, perhaps because there were abundant supplies of raw material very suitable for the use of the Levalloisian technique, namely the large flint nodules from the chalk hills. At a quarry called Baker's Hole, near Northfleet, Kent, a fine Early Levalloisian working site was discovered. It seems to date from an interstadial of the Riss glaciation, which means that it follows on quite closely in time from where the sequence at nearby Swanscombe ended. A few true handaxes are said to have been found with the Levalloisian flakes and cores.[13]

The Levalloisian technique continues to be used in this area throughout the Last Interglacial, and industries based upon it may even survive as late as the beginning of the Würm glaciation. After the large, heavy, oval flakes which characterise the early

12b sites like Baker's Hole, the tendency is for the flakes to become smaller, thinner and more blade-like. Unfortunately, no human fossil remains have yet been found in association with a pure Levalloisian industry.

The Levalloisian technique makes a considerable contribution to the next major culture, the Mousterian, although most Mousterian tools are made on flakes struck not from Levalloisian cores but from 'disc' cores (see Fig. 19a)—flat, roughly circular cores, whose shape permitted them to produce a large number of useful flakes and therefore to be more economic of flint than Levalloisian cores. The few pure Levalloisian industries are more or less on the border-line between Lower and Middle Palaeolithic, but the Mousterian is to be regarded as fully Middle Palaeolithic. In certain areas, it can be shown to begin before the end of the Last Interglacial (Riss-Würm), and it lasts generally speaking until the spread of *Homo sapiens* and the first Upper Palaeolithic cultures, an event which varied in time according to area, but in general took place between about 40,000 and about 30,000 B.C., that is to say, about the middle of the Würm glacial complex. The Mousterian culture takes its name from Le Moustier, a cave in southern France in the area where so many classic Middle and Upper Palaeolithic cave sites are situated.

Because the main Mousterian occupation is often of caves rather than open sites, it has been possible to learn more about the culture than any of those so far described. The brief sketches given of the Acheulian, Clactonian, Levalloisian and Pebble-Tool cultures were little more than lists of vague types of stone tools. For example, for somewhat more than a hundred thousand English stone artifacts of Lower Palaeolithic age in museums and private collections in Britain, there is barely a handful of supposedly worked bone tools from various sites, and one single

13 sharpened wooden spear tip from Clacton!

13 The wooden spear tip from Clacton-on-Sea, Essex (length 76 cm.; scale × ¼) with a close-up view of its sharpened point (scale × ½). British Museum (Natural History).

Another important point is that Mousterian man quite often buried his dead in the caves in which he lived—the first time this practice, of such value to the archaeologist, is encountered. There are limited traces of ceremonial or ritual in connection with the burials, for example the several goat-horns which were carefully placed with a Mousterian child-burial at Teshik-Tash **14** in Uzbekistan, and there are a few signs of possible cannibalism which might be of a ritual kind, where skulls seem to have been deliberately broken open as if for the extraction of the brain, as at Monte Circeo in Italy. **15**

Apart from the rather vague but invaluable light it casts on human ideas at this time, the Mousterian practice of burial is important for providing an amount of human skeletal material for study which must be regarded as abundant by comparison with what has survived from the whole of the Lower Palaeolithic put together. These finds, taken together, confirm that the Mousterian culture belongs to Neanderthal Man, *Homo neanderthalensis*. The latter was endowed with a brain larger on occasion even than the present-day average (though that is not to say that it was as

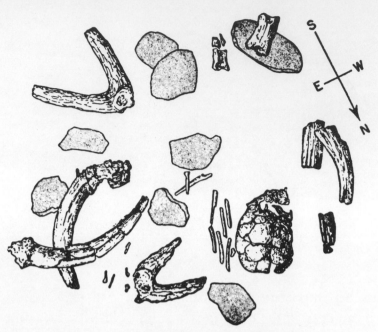

14 Mousterian burial from Teshik-Tash cave, Uzbekistan : goat horns accompany the human bones

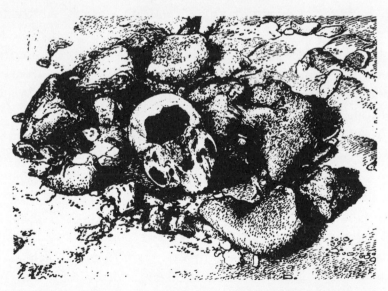

15 Neanderthal skull deliberately broken open at the base, possibly in ritual cannibalism, Monte Circeo, Lazio, Italy

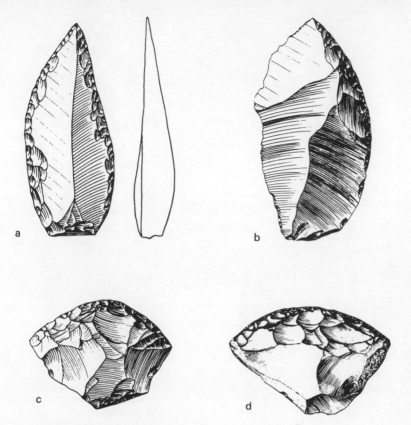

16 Mousterian flint artifacts. Scale: × ½.

    a. point made on flake, cave of Abou-Sif (Jordan)
    b. convex side-scraper, Pech de l'Azé Bed 4 (Dordogne)
    c. transverse scraper with convex working edge (Ain Meterchem, Tunisia)
    d. similar transverse scraper (Combe Grenal level N 1, Dordogne)

highly developed), but his limb bones and his skull retained a number of 'primitive' features. Within the Neanderthal range there are many variations, from forms much closer to *Homo sapiens* in appearance, to others in which the more primitive characteristics seem exaggerated. These latter 'extreme Neanderthalers' are mostly to be found in western Europe.[14]

17 Mousterian handaxes (West Mousterian) from France: *a*, Saint-Jacques-sur-Darnétal (Seine-Maritime); *b–d*, Pech de l'Azé Bed 4 (Dordogne). Scale: × ⅓.

16 The stone tools of Neanderthal man are very consistent, with neatly made flake points and scrapers predominating, and the Levalloisian technique playing a variable part in the different industries. Handaxe tools are also present in certain Mousterian **17** industries, but they are typically rather more squat in shape than most of the Acheulian forms. Broad, flat ovate or 'cordiform' types are the commonest, sometimes with finely worked squared butts which offer an almost axe-like cutting edge.

Three main variants of the Mousterian culture can be detected, and each of these has its own subdivisions, sometimes numerous.[15] Geographically, in general terms, the West Mousterian includes western Europe, notably France, Spain, Belgium and England, with some slight penetration of western Germany; the East Mousterian includes Italy, the Alpine area, most of Germany, eastern Europe, northern Iran and the U.S.S.R. right across at least to Siberia, and perhaps even extending into China, a vast spread. The third variant, the Levalloiso-Mousterian, extends along the southern shore of the Mediterranean, and up the eastern shore. The differences between these three main divisions of the Mousterian lie partly in the presence of different tool-types, and partly in the different degrees of importance which various standard implements and manufacturing techniques assume in each. For example, the Levalloisian technique is particularly important to the Levalloiso-Mousterian variant, as the name suggests, **19** or again, handaxes are more or less confined to certain industries of the West Mousterian, while the East Mousterian has its own particular types of bifacial implement, often of rather plano- **18** convex section and worked in a characteristic style.

The origins of the Mousterian cultures are still very imperfectly understood. It may be that, in Europe at least, apart from the Levalloisian influences, later members of the Lower Palaeolithic flake-industries group were an important contributory factor— that is, successors of the Clactonian and its more easterly neighbours, of which a few traces have been found. But both the Mousterian culture and Neanderthal man burst upon the scene fully evolved and alarmingly unheralded; exactly where and when their evolution took place is simply not known. Nor can it easily be shown that the three main Mousterian variants had a common immediate origin.

As regards dating, the East Mousterian can be shown to have begun well back in the Last Interglacial; at the site of Ehringsdorf in Germany, animal and plant remains of fully interglacial character are associated with East Mousterian implements. According to the evidence of fauna and the interpretation of

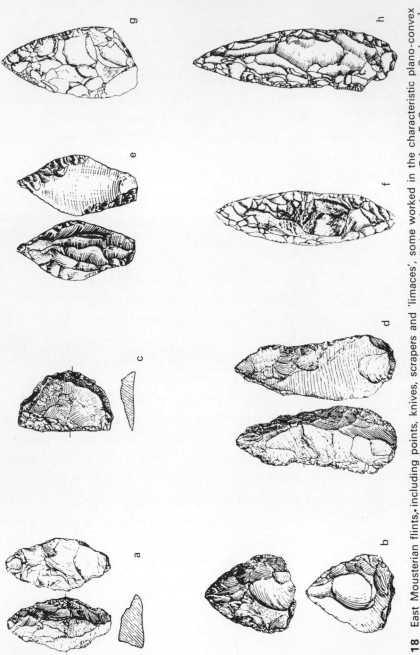

64

18 East Mousterian flints, including points, knives, scrapers and 'limaces', some worked in the characteristic plano-convex manner: *a–d*, Schulerloch, Kelheim, Bavaria, W. Germany; *e–h*, Weimar-Ehringsdorf, near Erfurt, E. Germany. Scale: × ½.

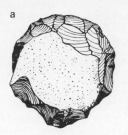

a

b

19 Levalloiso-Mousterian flints from Hajj Creiem, Cyrenaica: *a*, three
views of disc core; *b*, point and/or double-sided scraper made on a
Levalloisian flake. Scale: $\times \frac{3}{10}$.

raised beaches on the Mediterranean coasts attributed to phases of
the Last Interglacial, the Levalloiso-Mousterian variant may also
have begun in some places before the end of the Eemian. The
evidence in the case of the West Mousterian is less clear, and it
may not have begun in typical form before the earlier part of the
Würm glaciation, though a few isolated industries may be
earlier.

The Mousterian cultures appeared rather suddenly; their
departure from the scene is even more abrupt. In western Europe
especially, the Mousterian vanishes with barely a trace at the
arrival of *Homo sapiens* and the earliest Upper Palaeolithic cultures.
The same is true in south-west Asia, and a sharp transition is also
seen in Cyrenaica on the north African coast; in the U.S.S.R.,
the picture is less clear, partly at least because of the vast areas
of land involved.

The arrival of the first Upper Palaeolithic cultures is thus
every bit as sudden as that of Neanderthal man and the Mousterian.
The Upper Palaeolithic cultures use implements manufactured
from blades rather than flakes; blades *are* flakes, but very refined
flat narrow ones, struck from a core of fluted or prismatic appear-   **31**
ance, with the aid of a punch rather than by direct percussion.[16]

Fully evolved early blade-using cultures first appear during a
somewhat milder part of the Würm glaciation, which occurred

65

between about 40,000 and 29,000 B.C. or a little after—these are generalised dates which must have varied considerably at different latitudes, and perhaps also at different longitudes in the northern hemisphere. This milder phase does not seem to have been unbrokenly mild, and it is not at the moment clear whether it can be properly described as a single interstadial;[17] it may represent two minor warm oscillations with a colder spell between them, and doubtless its structure was different in different places.

The first occurrences of the early blade-using industries are in south-west Asia and north Africa (Cyrenaica), and the Upper Palaeolithic influences had reached western Europe quite by the beginning of the next cold phase; even the earliest Upper Palaeolithic is thus comfortably within the range of the radio-carbon dating method (see page 232). In the U.S.S.R., the earliest finds of Upper Palaeolithic character are not yet soundly dated, but they may well prove to be of comparable age. So far, the place of origin of the first Upper Palaeolithic cultures is simply not known, and the same goes for the area, which may well be the same, where the evolution took place of the first true *Homo sapiens* forms (cf. note 14). The solving of these two problems will be among the most important future contributions to Palaeolithic studies.

It seems likely that the area or areas in question must lie somewhere between the Levantine coast and the Himalayas, and much of this territory is archaeologically unexplored, or else contains desert of comparatively recent origin. One important hint that this is the right area is the presence of intrusive blade-using industries at sites on or near the Mediterranean coast, as far back as the Last Interglacial—at Mount Carmel (Tabun Cave), Jabrud and Adlun on the eastern side, and on the southern side at the Haua Fteah cave in Cyrenaica. This Pre-Aurignacian or Amudian culture, as it has been called, makes only a brief appearance, at

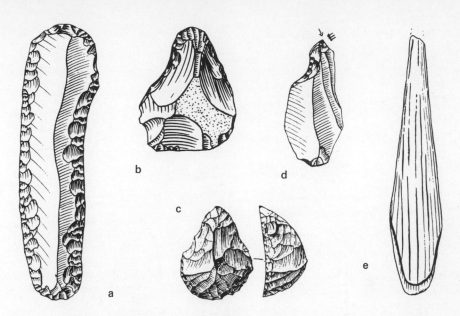

20 Aurignacian implements from the Périgord, France: *a*, peripherally trimmed blade, La Ferrassie level F; *b*, nosed steep scraper, Abri Castanet lower bed; *c*, carinated steep scraper, Grotte de Fontéchevade level B2; *d, burin busqué* (a specialised engraving tool), La Ferrassie level H; *e*, split-based bone point, Abri Lartet. Scale: × ½.

a time when the area in question was still occupied by Lower Palaeolithic people. The next time blade industries appear, after an interval of perhaps 50,000 years, they are fully Upper Palaeolithic and are brought by *Homo sapiens*.[18] No remains of whatever human type was associated with the Pre-Aurignacian industries have yet been found, unfortunately.

There is a simple but basic division which can be made in the Upper Palaeolithic proper, between the cultures which make regular use of the very obvious tool-form known as the 'backed blade', which is just a blade one of whose edges has been blunted for holding or hafting, much after the style of a modern penknife blade, and the one which does not. The latter is called the Aurignacian, and its special tool-types include 'steep' and 'nosed'

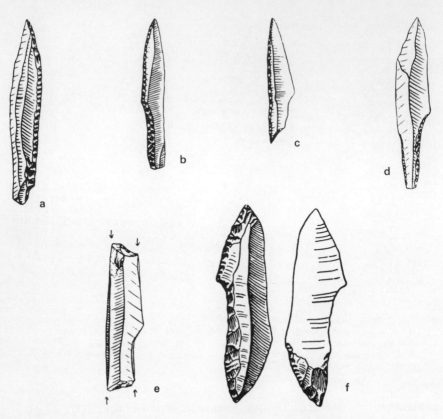

21 Gravettian flint implements: *a–c*, backed blades ('Gravette points');
b, with single-shouldered tang; *c*, with truncated base, all from La Ferrassie
level J; *d*, double-shouldered tanged point ('Font-Robert point'), same source;
e, multiple burin or graver, La Roque Saint-Christophe; *f*, East Gravettian
shouldered point from Kostenki Site I level 1, Don Valley, U.S.S.R.
Scale: × ½.

scrapers, and large blades with rather flat trimming (see Fig. 20).
Of the cultures which use backed blades, the one in which they
appear most frequently is the Gravettian (Fig. 21). Certain tool-
types are, of course, common to all the Upper Palaeolithic
cultures. These include various scraping or piercing tools made on
flint blades, and special engraving tools called 'burins', of which
there are many kinds: their common feature is a short, sharp

working edge somewhat like that of a modern chisel of a very small size, and they were clearly much used in the working and carving of bone.

Both Aurignacian and Gravettian are widely represented in Europe, especially in the classic cave area of southern France, where most of the early work on the Upper Palaeolithic was done, and where the sites occur from which the cultures have taken their names. Both can also be traced back for a considerable way over the very long but reasonably clear routes by which they seem to have reached western Europe. The trail of the Aurignacian leads back eastwards, keeping mainly north of the Alps, through Germany and Hungary, round the Black Sea by way of the Crimea, but then turning away from central Russia and leading south to the Levantine caves of Mount Carmel, Jabrud and several others. The Gravettian trail also passes back across Europe, taking in Italy, Austria and Czechoslovakia, and then leading to the heart of the U.S.S.R., where there are clear traces, for example, in the Don valley, notably in the Kostenki area, and also a good deal further east. This general picture offers an apparently reliable indication of where the Aurignacian and Gravettian cultures originated, in the sense of what were the areas from which they spread to western Europe, and also of the routes by which they came.[19]

There is also a third and much more restricted early Upper Palaeolithic spread, which involves the brief appearance in the Levant of a culture called the Emiran, making use of backed blades and certain other rather specialised tool-types, at about the same time as the earliest Aurignacian there, but apparently separate from it. Another culture, the Dabba Culture, evidently closely related to the Emiran, also appears, in Cyrenaica, but it begins several thousand years earlier than the Emiran on present dating, and certainly lasts a great deal longer: the Emiran is

TABLE 3: *Cultures and stages in the French Upper Palaeolithic sequence*

Culture	Subdivisions
MAGDALENIAN	VI (B) ⎫ VI (A) ⎬ Upper Magdalenian V ⎪ IV ⎭ III Middle Magdalenian II ⎫ Lower Magdalenian I ⎭ (Industries classed as proto-Magdalenian have occasionally been found)
SOLUTRIAN	Upper Solutrian Middle Solutrian Lower Solutrian (Proto-Solutrian industries occasionally occur)
GRAVETTIAN	Up to five stages or variants can be distinguished
AURIGNACIAN	Up to four successive stages have been observed, but few sites show more than two
CHATELPERRONIAN	Two stages have been claimed, but only one is present at most sites

(MOUSTERIAN)

ephemeral, but the Dabba culture continues, in a developed form, for perhaps twenty thousand or twenty-five thousand years. This Emiran-Dabban spread does not affect Europe, while the Aurignacian Culture for its part never spread along the north African coast to Cyrenaica.

It is in France that the best sequence for the whole Upper Palaeolithic Period can be obtained. Almost all the important stages occur at two famous cave sites, La Ferrassie and Laugerie

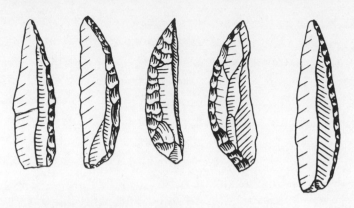

22 Chatelperronian points, Roc de Combe-Capelle, Périgord, France. Scale: × ⅔.

Haute in the Périgord region, and there are numerous other sites nearby to fill in what gaps remain.[20] The richness of the French sequence can be attributed to the favourable habitat which the classic cave area provided, and also to the fact that, when the ice-sheets were extended, southern France was a logical terminus for most possible cultural spreads originating in the east.

The French Upper Palaeolithic sequence (see Table 3) begins with a short and rather vague phase called the Chatelperronian, in which blade tools first appear, including curved and pointed backed blades not unlike some Gravettian types. Whether the Chatelperronian is a real early Upper Palaeolithic culture of a rather generalised kind, is not clear; another explanation would be that it comprises the traces left by small bands of hunters representing the advance elements of both the main Aurignacian and Gravettian spreads from their different sources, perhaps with an admixture of final Middle Palaeolithic elements of local origin; hunting bands of such diverse origins could share the area without necessarily uniting, and their archaeological record might give a false appearance of unity.[21]

Soon, however, the Chatelperronian gives place to the Aurigna-cian, of which a number of subdivisions can be made according to variation of tool-types. As many as four Aurignacian levels occur at La Ferrassie, characterised by different types of bone spearhead, as well as by variations of emphasis on different parts of the lithic industry. In the succeeding Gravettian Culture, there are again several possible subdivisions. It should perhaps be emphasised here that the Gravettian of France is by no means identical to the Gravettian of east Europe or the U.S.S.R., but that there is a general underlying unity throughout the vast area of the Gravettian culture as a whole.[22]

The next culture in the French sequence, the Solutrian, is something rather different from its predecessors. Its most striking tool-types are beautifully made, flat, bifacially worked 'leaf-shaped points', often of superb workmanship (see Figs. 23 and 24b). The origins of the Solutrian are not easy to understand, and certainly there is no long clear trail leading away to the east

a b

24 Solutrian flint implements from the Périgord, France. Scale: × ½.

a. 'laurel leaf point',
Laugerie Haute, level H'''

b. 'willow leaf point' (Late Solutrian),
Pech de la Boissière

23 Solutrian 'laurel leaf point', length 18·5 cm., Saône-et-Loire, France

and out of Europe, as there was for the Aurignacian or Gravettian. The Solutrian proper is in fact strictly a west European phenomenon, confined in its developed form to England, France and Spain, and of these there is only very poor representation in England, mainly of the earlier phases. It seems likely that the Solutrian origins lie in contact between the incoming Aurignacian elements, and the native Mousterian population they met in eastern and central Europe; such contact could well have produced the leaf-shaped points with flat retouch, and certain other aspects of Solutrian flintwork. Hunting bands bearing this hybrid tradition of flint-working may have passed into the open land of the north European plain, where, cut off from the main Upper Palaeolithic spread, they gradually worked their way westwards to Britain, before the severity of the last major Würm cold phase drove them southwards into France and Iberia, where the full Solutrian culture developed, in more congenial conditions.[23] Reasonably well defined Early, Middle and Late stages can be distinguished.

All the Upper Palaeolithic cultures so far mentioned produced objects of bone as well as stone, especially projectile heads, often finely made, and the types varied according to the culture. But it is in the culture which succeeds the Solutrian in France, the Magdalenian, that the bonework really reaches its height, especially during the later stages. Simple bone points give way to a **25** fine series of elaborate barbed harpoons, and there are such **26** objects as spear-throwers, rods and batons, beautifully decorated **27** with carved or incised patterns, or representations of animals. Small, delicately worked bone needles are another example of Magdalenian skill in this medium. Magdalenian flintwork, on the other hand, is of much less interest, and the aesthetically fine achievements of the Solutrians in this respect seem to leave scarcely an echo, although the Magdalenians made certain specialised engraving tools and other implements which show

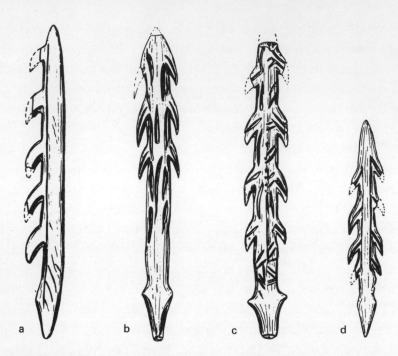

25 Upper Magdalenian 'harpoons' (barbed bone points), from La Madeleine, Dordogne: *a*, Magdalenian V, uniserially barbed, level B; *b–d*, Magdalenian VI, biserially barbed, level C. Scale: × ½.

great skill in both design and manufacture (Fig. 28). This lack of continuity is enough in itself to suggest that the origins of the Magdalenian culture do not lie in the Solutrian, and the probability is that it arose from the Gravettian background somewhere outside the classic French cave area, during the period when the latter was occupied by the Solutrians. The Magdalenian is essentially French in its development, and only in its evolved stages does it seem to spread outwards to certain adjacent areas, notably parts of Spain and Germany but perhaps also to Britain.

Space does not permit any fuller account of the crowded and often fascinating French Upper Palaeolithic sequence, nor any analysis of the local sequences in other areas. But one important

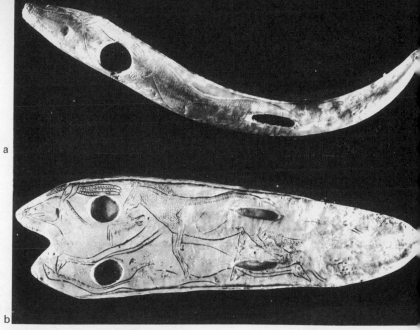

27 Magdalenian decorative art:
a, animal engravings on perforated antler object from
Abri Mège à Teyjat, Dordogne, France, length 30 cm.;
b, cast of the same artifact, flattened out to show
the whole of the decoration.
Musée des Antiquités Nationales, Saint-Germain-en-Laye.

26 Magdalenian decorated spear-thrower (Magdalenian IV),
Mas d'Azil, Ariège, France. Length 27·5 cm.
Musée des Antiquités Nationales, Saint-Germain-en-Laye.

aspect of the Upper Palaeolithic remains to be considered, namely
its art. This is the first art of the world, and represents an achievement far beyond the intellectual range of *Homo erectus*, and even of
Homo neanderthalensis, so far as is known. It has two main aspects:
the decoration of everyday, utilitarian objects, like the Magda-

28 Magdalenian flint-work
from the Périgord, France:
a. 'parrot beak burin', a
specialised engraving tool,
Abri du Soucy
b. small finely pointed awl,
Grotte des Eyzies
c. dihedral burin or graver,
same source
Scale: × $\frac{2}{3}$.

29 Upper Palaeolithic cave art: bison and ibex painted in black, at Niaux, Ariège, France. Magdalenian. Some of the animals are apparently shown pierced by spears or arrows. The larger bison figures are a little over a metre long.

lenian spear-throwers, and the painting or engraving on cave walls of careful and often beautiful pictures, mainly of animals. The general nature of these, and the fact that many of the animals are deliberately shown as wounded, dying or dead, suggests that the cave painting may have been connected with sympathetic hunting magic and fertility ritual. Certainly, anyhow, this aspect of Palaeolithic art was not purely decorative, since the pictures were usually hidden away in obscure parts of the caves, often where daylight could never possibly have penetrated.

In the matter of ritual art, mention should also be made of the

Upper Palaeolithic carved and sculptured statuettes, mostly anthropomorphic and female (the so-called Venus figurines), but a few of animals. These belong especially to the Gravettian culture, though not quite exclusively, and are incidentally one of the best pieces of evidence for its underlying unity, since they occur in Gravettian contexts of one sort or another from Siberia to the south of France. Their exact use remains unknown, although their general nature has often given rise to the conclusion that they were part of some kind of fertility cult; figurines of such a kind occur from time to time in other periods of prehistory, the earlier Neolithic of the east Mediterranean being a good example. Human figures also occur from time to time in the art of the Magdalenians, usually in engravings.

Upper Palaeolithic art begins somewhat tentatively in the Aurignacian culture, gathers strength in the Gravettian and Solutrian, and blossoms forth in the Magdalenian, both in the splendid decoration of ordinary objects, and in the superb polychrome cave paintings like those at the north Spanish cave of Altamira, and several of the French caves. To describe all its variations even in outline would require a whole book.[24]

30
Upper Palaeolithic art:
two views of female figurine
('Venus figure') from
Dolní Věstonice, Moravia.
Height: 11·4 cm.

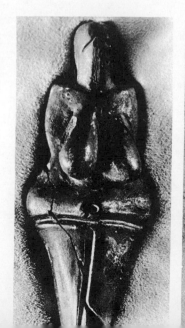

The flourishing and brilliant Magdalenian culture, of which some seven stages can be distinguished in France, ends not through any invasion of a new and superior people, but because the cold conditions, to which its hunting methods and way of life were so closely adapted, were brought to an end by the gradual withdrawal of the last Würm ice-sheets, and the consequent changes in environment and fauna. The impoverished Mesolithic cultures which succeed it sometimes contain a lingering echo of Magdalenian art or bonework, but no more. *Homo sapiens*, although he had raised the life of a hunter to a totally new plane during the Upper Palaeolithic Period, could not yet control his environment or quickly adapt himself to momentous climatic change, without cultural impoverishment. Is it too fanciful and too irrelevant to the understanding of prehistoric events, to reflect that twentieth-century *Homo sapiens* is perhaps fortunate not to have been put to a similar test?

NOTES

1. The study of fossil man is a subject of increasing complexity and technicality, as indeed is the study of prehistory itself. A useful and easily obtainable starting point for further reading is Le Gros Clark, 1958, in which further references are quoted. A classic work on a larger scale is Boule and Vallois, 1957; this contains a mass of important information, but is no longer wholly up-to-date, and some of the archaeological terminology is rather archaic. Two very useful works of more recent date are von Koenigswald, 1962 and Day, 1965.

2. Now more commonly referred to as *Homo erectus*.

3. Much is quite rightly made of every fragment of Lower and Middle Pleistocene hominid skeletal material that is found. But it is necessarily always difficult to draw wide general conclusions from such a small body of evidence; it would be rash for example to assume that each surviving bone or skull fragment belonged to an individual wholly typical of his kind and period. For two recent highly detailed and technical studies of hominid fossil fragments, see Tobias, 1967a, and Ovey, ed., 1964 (the appropriate chapters). With regard to *Homo sapiens* and *Homo neanderthalensis*, see also n. 14 to this chapter.

4. The studies of glaciology and Pleistocene geology are again specialist disciplines, but anyone interested in Palaeolithic studies must be prepared to learn their rudiments in theoretical outline at the very least. The different kinds of deposit associated with the warmer and colder phases, and the main events of the Pleistocene sequence, will be found clearly set out in such works as Zeuner, 1958, Zeuner, 1959 and Flint, 1957. The latter work is perhaps the easiest of the three as a starting point, although some of the terminology is American; in the two books by Zeuner, both the chronological scheme and some of the cultural diagnoses are open to criticism and should be approached with caution. A more recent work which is also useful and relevant is Butzer, 1964, and an important and comprehensive source book on a larger scale is Charlesworth, 1957.

5. For example, various primitive types of elephant and pig, and archaic carnivores and bovids. Such primitive elephants as *Deinotherium* are a good example. Many of the extinct types are giant forms of the animal in question. In Europe, the Villafranchian fauna includes such forms as *Mastodon, Elephas meridionalis* and *Machairodus* (the sabre-toothed tiger).

6. For the basic information about the laws of fracture which apply to flint, and about flint tool types and their manufacture in the Palaeolithic and other periods, see Watson, 1956 and Oakley, 1965; both are small and inexpensive handbooks, the second of which, incidentally, also incorporates a useful outline account of various aspects of the Palaeolithic and Pleistocene Periods.

7. More recently, a date of the same order of magnitude has been obtained for the same bed at Olduvai by another method, 'fission track dating' (see p. 239).

Dates have also been worked out for past reversals of the earth's magnetic field. Such reversals leave their traces in certain contemporary rock formations, notably those of volcanic origin. A 'normal' interval (i.e. with the magnetic field as it is today) during an epoch of reversed magnetic field took place about 2,000,000 years ago, and this is represented in volcanic deposits at Olduvai Gorge itself. A useful reference here is Cox et al., 1967.

The same fluctuations in the magnetic field have been recognised in sedimentary deposits on the ocean bed. Their use in conjunction with the presence or absence of certain tiny marine fossils, in long cores extracted from such deposits, has recently made possible an estimate of the date of the boundary between the Pliocene and the Pleistocene Periods, at about 1,850,000 years ago. See Berggren et al., 1967, quoting further references.

For all these reasons, the high potassium-argon dates for Olduvai Bed I seem much more easily acceptable than they did to many prehistorians when they were first announced.

8. Archaeological research at Olduvai Gorge began as long ago as 1931; in 1951 Dr L. S. B. Leakey published a monograph (Leakey, L. S. B., 1951) on the finds made up to 1947. This work has been made manifestly out of date in several respects by further discoveries at the site and continued study of the finds, but the first two volumes of a new several-volume work, designed to present the results up to at least 1961, have now appeared (Leakey, L. S. B., ed., 1966–7) and others will follow shortly. One more at least should have appeared while this book is in the press. Even these are intended only to comprise an interim report, and the completion of a definitive account is awaited by pre-historians all over the world with feelings ranging from mere eagerness to noisy impatience. Another recent work which contains literature on, or highly relevant to, Olduvai is Bishop and Clark, J. D., eds., 1968; this includes an important paper by Mrs M. D. Leakey (Leakey, M. D., 1968). The question of whether *Australopithecus* was a tool-maker, referred to in subsequent paragraphs, is discussed in Tobias, 1967*b*.

9. See Walker and Sieveking, 1962. For Choukoutien, an accessible reference which quotes further sources is the chapter concerned with the Palaeolithic Period in Chêng Tê-K'un. 1959.

10. The post-Acheulian sequence in Africa south of the Sahara is not described in this book. Outline accounts for most of the territory can readily be obtained from Clark, J. D., 1959 and Cole, 1964. It is worth noting that in east Africa a late Acheulian industry at Kalambo Falls has been dated by the radiocarbon method (see p. 232) to as late as *c*. 55,000 B.C. Since the top of Bed II at Olduvai, containing the earliest Acheulian industries, seems likely to date from around 600,000 B.C., it can be seen that the time span of the Acheulian culture is immense in this area, in spite of the almost negligible cultural and technological advance. For Kalambo Falls, and many other sites of interest and importance, see Howell and Clark, J. D., 1963. Another source book for the African sequence is Alimen, 1957.

11. Only interim reports are yet available on the sites mentioned in this paragraph. All are referred to in what is the most recent extensive survey and evaluation of Lower Palaeolithic sites in Europe, a paper by Professor F. C. Howell of the University of Chicago (Howell, 1966) in a volume entitled *Recent Studies in Paleoanthropology* which contains many articles of interest to those who wish to study the Palaeolithic Period. It can be obtained at certain large or specialist libraries in Britain. For the early handaxe industry from 'Ubeidiya, and also the pebble-tools there, see Stekelis, 1966. The latest account of the Ternifine handaxe industry is Balout *et al.*, 1967. Vértesszöllös is included in Howell, 1966, but for the reclassification of the hominid fossil found there,

mentioned on p. 46 above, see a paper by A. Thoma in the French periodical *L'Anthropologie* LXX, 1966, p. 495.

It should be noted in passing that up-to-date full-scale textbooks for the Palaeolithic Period are badly needed. Such works as *The Old Stone Age* by M. C. Burkitt, or *Adam's Ancestors* by L. S. B. Leakey, are now more or less out of date. K. P. Oakley's *Frameworks for Dating Fossil Man* (1966) will be found helpful, and contains useful references. Another recently published small book is Clark, J. G. D., 1967. C. B. M. McBurney's *The Stone Age of Northern Africa* (McBurney, 1960) is also important, and is of wider scope than its title suggests. A short and inexpensive general book on the Palaeolithic, *The Old Stone Age* by Professor F. Bordes, will be published in 1968 by Weidenfeld and Nicolson in their World University Library series. For those who read German, there is also Müller-Karpe, 1966, a large and encyclopaedic work: even for those who can't cope with the text, the large collection of line drawings will be a very valuable reference source.

12. The fullest and most recent account is contained in the *Swanscombe Skull* volume (Ovey, ed., 1964) already referred to.

13. This is not absolutely certain, although it is sometimes stated without qualification. The main finds were made early this century, and were not recorded very scientifically. Plenty of handaxes were recorded from the pit, which was very large, but other deposits were present besides the one which contained the Levalloisian industry, and the handaxes may have come from one of these; few closely resemble the Levalloisian flakes and cores in condition. For the original report, see Smith, 1911.

14. For simplicity, I have here retained the designations *Homo sapiens* and *Homo neanderthalensis*, and emphasised the physical differences between the two, which are quite in keeping with the cultural differences between Middle and Upper Palaeolithic. But the physical differences must not be over-stressed, and recent opinion has been increasingly in favour of regarding the two forms as sub-species of the same species, *Homo sapiens*: in other words, they should properly be called *Homo sapiens sapiens*, and *Homo sapiens neanderthalensis*. Which hominid fossils represent the common ancestor stage for these two remains a matter of doubt and dispute; the Swanscombe, Steinheim and Vértesszöllös fossils must be relevant in this connection, but both are incomdlete. Of course, the evidence has not necessarily yet been found, a point well worth keeping in mind. It was always difficult, if not impossible, to argue that *Homo sapiens* 'evolved directly' from *Homo neanderthalensis*, since the differences between them seemed sufficient for such a process to have required some hundreds of thousands of years. The whole question of the ancestry, immediate origins and relationships of the hominids of the Middle and Upper Palaeolithic

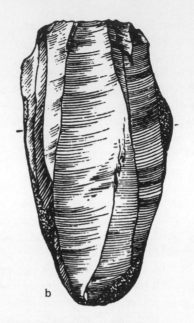

31 'Prismatic' cores from which flint blades have been struck with the use of a punch: *a*, find-spot unknown; *b*, La Madeleine, Dordogne, France. Scale: × ⅔.

is extremely complicated, and it would be quite wrong to put forward any facile explanation here.

15. Space does not permit a proper examination of such cultural and geographical overlaps as can be discerned between the main Mousterian variants, or of the various subdivisions suggested for the different major facies. The distinction between East and West Mousterian was first drawn by Dr C. B. M. McBurney, and is explained with a quantity of relevant information in a paper by him (McBurney, 1950). A scheme of subdivisions for the West Mousterian in France has been put forward by Professor F. Bordes in several articles e.g. Bordes, 1953 and 1961. Work carried out over the past few years at recently discovered cave sites in Greece, by an expedition from Cambridge University directed by Mr E. S. Higgs, may well eventually considerably increase our knowledge of both the East Mousterian and Levalloiso-Mousterian variants and their subdivisions. The works quoted in n. 18 below are useful for the Levalloiso-Mousterian, and further references are listed in them. In quite another direction, some recent studies have suggested that some at least of the observed variations between different Mousterian industries may be of a

functional rather than a cultural or temporal nature: see for example two papers in the special 'Paleoanthropology' volume already referred to in n. 11 above, namely Binford and Binford, 1966 and Freeman, 1966.

16. Such a method permits great accuracy in striking blades of the required size and shape, and is very economical of raw material. It also leaves recognisable traces on the blade itself—e.g. a characteristically minute striking platform and diffuse bulb of percussion, besides a typical pattern of elongated primary dorsal scars on the vast majority of blades struck from any particular blade core. The cores themselves typically assume a 'prismatic' appearance. (See the works quoted in n. 6 above.)

17. This interstadial, or composite warm oscillation, will be found in much of the comparatively recent literature as the Göttweig Interstadial, but the latest views do not favour this nomenclature, recognising the deposits in question from which the name had been taken as belonging to an earlier warm phase. An admirable recent account of the Würm sequence, based upon deposits in the Netherlands, with many radiocarbon dates and a good bibliography is that of van der Hammen et al., 1967; see also Vogel and van der Hammen, 1967. Both these papers are written in English, and the periodical which contains them is obtainable in this country at specialist libraries.

18. The Amudian industries are discussed in Professor Dorothy Garrod's Huxley Memorial Lecture of 1962 (Garrod, 1962). A monograph on the Haua Fteah cave site by Dr C. B. M. McBurney has recently been published (McBurney, 1967). Two other important sources of information on the initial Upper Palaeolithic of the Levant are Higgs, 1961 and Brothwell, 1961.

19. However, much of the information on which these 'trails' are based is rather out of date, and a complete and unified reappraisal of the material from some of the central and east European sites is badly needed, with a modern classification of the artifacts and a host of fresh radiocarbon dates to help decide the chronological order of the various industries. On balance, the picture briefly sketched here remains the best and most likely present interpretation. An important step in the required direction was taken by Hallam L. Movius Jr (Movius, 1960).

20. Details of all the leading sites, and most of the rest, from this classic area, have been assembled with numerous illustrations in a magnificent book by Madame Denise de Sonneville-Bordes (de Sonneville-Bordes, 1960), but this is almost impossible to obtain in England outside a specialist library. The cultures and their various subdivisions are discussed. Most of the other literature is in French archaeological journals.

21. The problem has been recently discussed in Lynch, 1966, a paper which includes a very full bibliography. In France the Chatelperronian is usually

called 'Lower Perigordian' and the Gravettian is called 'Upper Perigordian'.

22. This general unity is best seen in the consistent occurrence of the main backed-blade tool-types, and of various kinds of flint tanged or shouldered points, which were projectile or arrow tips (though actual archery cannot be proved at this stage). Another striking feature which tends to unite the whole Gravettian spread is the occurrence of the so-called 'Venus figures', small anthropomorphic (female) figurines of various shapes and styles, not usually beautiful to modern eyes and often interpreted, from the frequent emphasis on sexual characteristics, as likely to belong to some form of fertility cult. (See pp. 76–7 and Fig. 30.)

23. Leaf-shaped implements were a not infrequent feature of certain East Mousterian industries, while the Aurignacians often used a flat, invasive retouch in their flintwork. An apparently hybrid Upper/Middle Palaeolithic culture, the Szeletian, existed in and around Hungary at about the time when the first Aurignacians were reaching France. It must be remembered that this Szeletian culture therefore flourished some 10,000 years or so before the Solutrian of France, so that if there really were development from one to the other, it was a slow process. However, a few industries not dissimilar to the Szeletian, but apparently a few thousand years later in date, are known, which helps to fill the wide chronological gap and make the whole notion much more reasonable. And there is certainly some sort of a 'Proto-Solutrian' phase in Britain, with only a very few signs of more evolved Solutrian material to follow it. An excellent source book for the French Solutrian is Smith, P. E. L., 1966.

24. There are indeed many books, large and small, on Palaeolithic art, all with abundant illustration usually of a very high standard. Among the larger volumes, see for example Breuil, 1952, and Graziosi, 1960, or, more recent and rather more controversial in its interpretation of the art's significance, Leroi-Gourand, 1968. The most recent of the smaller books is Ucko and Rosenfeld, 1967, which contains an important evaluation of previous work on the subject, and of various interpretations of the significance of the art. It also has copious references.

3 Final Palaeolithic Cultures and the Middle Stone Age

The Middle Stone Age or Mesolithic Period has lost something
of the meaning originally attributed to it. With the close of the
Würm glaciation, the west European area which dominated
much of the last chapter loses its importance for the moment, and
the centre of interest shifts to south-west Asia, where the human
groups and the special circumstances existed which were to
produce probably the most important breakthrough of the whole
of prehistory—the change from a hunting economy to one of
controlled food production. The development of the vital new
ideas of crop-growing and animal husbandry is, by the standard
definition, the work of the earliest Neolithic communities; it
therefore follows that the actual inventions were those of Mesolithic man. This splitting of hairs shows as well as anything the
uselessness of adhering rigidly to the old concepts of Mesolithic
and Neolithic, and indeed of trying to draw a sharp dividing
line between any two consecutive archaeological periods.

The Mesolithic Period, then, comprises the cultural activity
which in any area fills the hiatus between the end of the established

Upper Palaeolithic hunting cultures (ending because the climatic conditions which supported them were withdrawn), and the arrival of the first farming, food-producing peoples. By its very nature, therefore, the Mesolithic Period is of different duration and significance in different areas. In south-west Asia it is short and dynamic, while in north-west Europe it is longer and rather uninspired; for example, it was not until the latter half of the fourth millennium B.C. that Neolithic farmers began to arrive in Britain—that is, some five thousand years or so after the first crop growing and animal herding began in south-west Asia.

So it is in western and northern Europe that there is most time for a Mesolithic period to develop, and here various cultures can be distinguished. On the other hand, it could be argued that the name Mesolithic is not really properly applicable in south-west Asia at all, because there is little time-lag and comparatively little difference between the industries of the Palaeolithic hunters of the very end of the Pleistocene, and the ones which accompany the first traces of the growing or at least the reaping of cereals.

In western Europe the end of glacial conditions cut short the brilliant Magdalenian culture which had flourished at a safe distance from the actual ice sheets, in an area which offered an admirable terrain for cave-dwellings and open sites, and abundant supplies of game—the large cold-climate species such as mammoth, woolly rhinoceros, bison and especially reindeer, as well as many smaller animals. The Magdalenian, it will be remembered, was distinctively French, with only a limited outward spread. It will be useful to summarise the other final Upper Palaeolithic Cultures of adjacent areas, because, with the Magdalenian, they must supply all the immediate origins of their Mesolithic successors.

Most of the inhabited areas not affected by the Magdalenian remained broadly Gravettian—that is, occupied by cultures using such typical Gravettian tool forms as the backed blade. Italy is a

32
Mass of discarded mammoth
bone and ivory left by
Upper Palaeolithic hunters
at Dolní Věstonice, Moravia,
as excavated in 1950

good example of such areas, but the finest development of the
Gravettian is to be seen in the East, in the open-site hunting
cultures of Russia and east Europe. Here mammoth-hunting
stations like those at Predmost, Dolní Véstonice, Willendorf or
Kostenki have left enough discarded mammoth bone and ivory
to cover several acres of ground; the game herds must have been
vast, and the quarry provided not only meat and clothing, but
much of the raw material of tool-making, and even of building,
since the huge mammoth tusks and bones played a part in some
of the rare traces which have been found of the dwellings of the
hunters which consisted of semi-permanent tent-like structures. **33**
In the flint work, backed blades and shouldered or tanged points of
one sort or another are recurrent features, and certain very small
('microlithic') tool types are intermittently present.[1]

A prominent item of the later Magdalenian hunting equipment
was the harpoon or barbed bone spearhead. This tool type offers

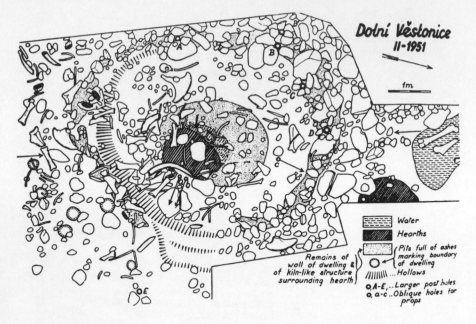

33 Plan of circular hut-dwelling of Upper Palaeolithic hunters
at Dolní Věstonice, Moravia, as excavated in 1951

a possible connection between the Magdalenian and a contemporary culture in which the harpoon is also found, the Hamburgian of north Germany and Holland, for early phases of which radiocarbon dates of around 13,500 B.C. have been obtained.[2] The Hamburgians were reindeer hunters who occupied open sites in the summer season. Apart from their use of harpoons, they share one or two other tool forms or techniques with the Magdalenians, but just how close the links between the two cultures were is uncertain. Doubtless the Hamburgian also had roots in the late Eastern Gravettian, which included a wide variety of industries, and it may be here that the origins lie of the flint

34 tanged points much used by the Hamburgians, and only comparatively rarely found in the Magdalenian. The Hamburgian is

88

very well represented at the site of Meiendorf in Schleswig-Holstein, where waterlogged conditions preserved traces of a reindeer hunters' summer encampment in considerable detail.[3]

The Magdalenian, the later East Gravettian and the Hamburgian can all be shown to have flourished during the last main phase of the Würm glaciation. This and its aftermath in the climatic record comprise a complicated series of stages covering the final withdrawal of the Würm ice sheets and the coming of warmer post-glacial or neothermal conditions. The ice sheets did not withdraw evenly, and there are marked warmer and colder oscillations. These major Late-Glacial and early Post-Glacial climatic phases are summarised in the accompanying table, which carries on from where the Pleistocene table on page 36 left off. It is of course much more detailed than the Pleistocene diagram, because the evidence is much more complete and accessible. A comparable

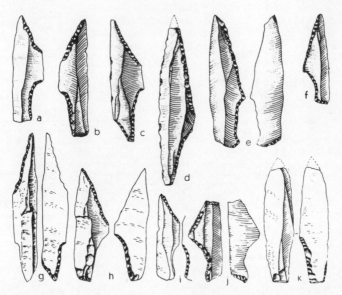

34 Hamburgian shouldered points from north German sites: *a, i, k*, Meiendorf; *b*, Kl. Vollbüttel; *c, j*, Pennemoor; *d*, Glaner Heide; *e, f*, Stade-Campe; *g, h*, Stellmoor. Scale: × c. ½.

TABLE 4: *The major Late-Glacial and Post-Glacial Climatic phases in North-west Europe*

Note: this table is based on the sequence in Jutland, although it is here used to represent north-west Europe as a whole. Local sequences differ considerably in detail and chronology, and in many areas subdivisions of some of the main stages have been introduced. Different systems of zone numbering are also sometimes used.

Period	Dating	Pollen Zone	Climatic Stage	Climate	Vegetation	
POST-GLACIAL	c. 500 B.C.	IX	Sub-Atlantic	Decline from optimum temperatures to the conditions of today	'Artificial' effects on vegetation from increasing agriculture	Beech forests
	c. 3000 B.C.	VIII	Sub-Boreal			Mixed oak forests, with ash and some beech.
	c. 5000 B.C.	VII	Atlantic	Warmth slowly increasing to reach an optimum in Atlantic times (zone VII), when mean temperatures were higher than those of today	Mixed oak forests (elm, lime and alder frequent)	
	c. 6000 B.C.	VI	Boreal (Late)		Hazel, with oak, elm, lime and alder	
	c. 6800 B.C.	V	Boreal (Early)		Pine, giving way to hazel	
	c. 8300 B.C.	IV	Pre-Boreal		Birch, giving way to pine	
LATE-GLACIAL	c. 8800 B.C.	III	Younger Dryas	Sub-Arctic. (Final spell of renewed cold conditions)	Mainly open landscape with Dryas flora, grasses and sedges; some willow, birch and pine	
	c. 10000 B.C.	II	Allerød	Warm oscillation (minor interstadial)	Birch forests, with some pine	
		I	Older Dryas	Arctic. Subdivisible into two colder periods (Oldest Dryas and Older Dryas), separated by a minor phase of amelioration (Bølling interstadial)	Mainly treeless landscape, but with some willow and birch. Arctic Dryas flora, grasses and sedges	

series of events doubtless followed each earlier glaciation, but in those cases few of the characteristic deposits can have survived; nor is the necessary background knowledge available to interpret in such detail what evidence does remain. The story of the Late-Glacial and Post-Glacial climatic events has been revealed by various techniques, of which one of the most fruitful has been that of recognising and interpreting climatically the pollen grains which survive in the successive deposits. (See Chapter 7.)

Just as the Late-Glacial and Post-Glacial climatic periods grade into each other, so do the late Palaeolithic and post-Palaeolithic cultural stages, which represent man's successive adaptations of his equipment and means of livelihood to the climatic changes and everything they brought. This time there is no dramatic arrival upon the scene of new people bringing drastically different tool types—no 'marker horizon' for the beginning of the Mesolithic Period like the sudden appearance of blade-tools at the start of the Upper Palaeolithic. In fact between the fully Upper Palaeolithic Cultures mentioned above, and the fully Mesolithic ones to be described below, there are cultures which are not clearly either one or the other, and the sensible name of 'epi-palaeolithic' is sometimes given to them.[4]

Among such 'epi-palaeolithic' cultures may be included the Ahrensburgian, which is a reindeer-hunter culture in several ways similar to the Hamburgian, and in much the same area, using its own types of harpoons and tanged points, but substantially later than the Hamburgian in date. At the important site of Stellmoor,

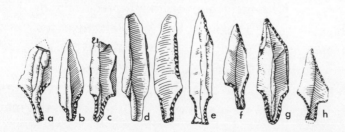

35 Ahrensburgian tanged points from north German sites: *a, d, h*, Negernbötel; *b*, Ketzendorf II; *c, g*, Kl. Vollbüttel; *e*, Stellmoor; *f*, Lavenstedt. Scale: × *c.* ½.

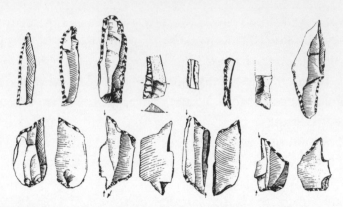

36 *'Federmesser-gruppen'* flints from Rissen, Site 3, near Hamburg,
including *'federmesser'* blades (top row, first two from left),
other backed-blade types, a tanged point (top row, extreme right),
various burins, etc. Scale: × *c.* ½.

very near Meiendorf, levels of both Hamburgian and Ahrensburgian occupation were found, and between them was a deposit
attributable to the Allerød warm oscillation (see Table 4). The
Ahrensburgian at Stellmoor thus belongs to the very last cold
phase of all, the Younger Dryas.

The Allerød period itself has produced traces of an industry at
Bromme in Zealand which has heavy tanged points accompanied
by scrapers and burins—the latter, noted above as being found in
all cultures of the Upper Palaeolithic, are also found at most stages
of the Mesolithic (and, indeed, sometimes in even later periods of
prehistory).

There are other epi-palaeolithic cultures or groups too, in
which the tanged point is important. The Swiderian culture of
Poland and the Ukraine is one, although precise dating is lacking
for it. Further west, a group of closely related industries at the
western end of the north European plain has been given the
collective name of Federmesser-Gruppen. Federmesser is the
German for penknife, and small backed blade tools very much of
penknife blade shape are a tool type common to all the members

92

of the group. Tanged points are also often a constitutent of the industries.[5] One of the clearest of the various industries is that discovered at, and called after, Rissen near Hamburg. It was here found to underlie an Ahrensburgian level, and the Federmesser industries thus seem likely to date in general from the latter part

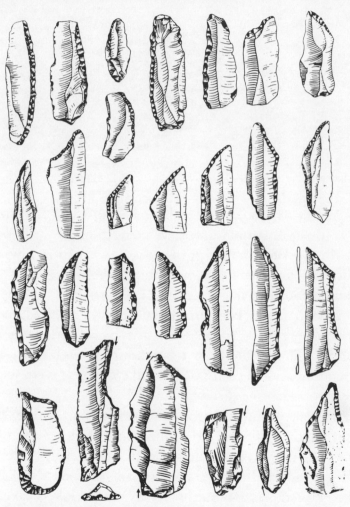

37 Creswellian flints from Gough's Cave, Cheddar, Somerset, including various backed and/or truncated blades, some trapeze-like forms, several burins, etc. Scale: × ½.

38 Star Carr, Seamer, Yorkshire : part of the site during excavation, showing the archaeological layer and part of the birch-wood platform

of the Allerød warm period, and the beginning of the Younger Dryas cold phase. An industry that seems to have much in common with this Federmesser group was discovered in England at Hengistbury Head, near Bournemouth.[6]

It is unfortunate that none of the Federmesser sites, nor those of the Swiderian, nor Bromme, nor Hengistbury Head, has produced any bonework to help fill in the picture of these epipalaeolithic cultures and their relationships to each other and to earlier cultures, but in each case the soil conditions were such that the bonework did not survive.

Also epi-palaeolithic is the British Creswellian Culture, known from several cave sites in Derbyshire, south Wales, Somerset and **37** Devon.[7] The dominant features are various backed blade types, including points and trapeze shapes made on sections of blades, and also end-scrapers and burins. At Aveline's Hole, a cave in the Mendips, a harpoon of Magdalenian style was found with a Creswellian industry; more harpoons came from Kent's Cavern,

Torquay, where the Creswellian is also represented, while a fine bone needle, again like those of the Magdalenian, was found in a Creswellian level at the Cathole cave in the Gower peninsula, south Wales. The Creswellian Culture is usually associated with cold fauna in the British caves, and is thought likely to date mainly from the pre-Allerød part of late Würm, although a late variant appears from carbon dates to have lasted right down to the seventh millennium B.C. at a cave called Mother Grundy's Parlour in Derbyshire.

The various epi-palaeolithic cultures may be regarded as ending with the close of Late Glacial conditions and the beginning of the Pre-Boreal phase. To say that they ended merely means that they became merged into their more fully Mesolithic successors; the real change that takes place is climatic and environmental, not cultural, and it is characterised by the growth of forests in response to the warmer postglacial climate. This forest development gives the name to the Pre-Boreal and Boreal phases, and is the underlying cause of most of the changes in tool types to be seen in the accompanying Mesolithic industries. The most obvious example is the appearance of the first true axe tools, as a response to the increasingly urgent need for tree-felling and woodworking.

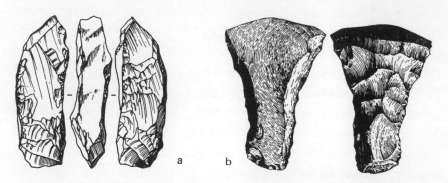

39   Mesolithic axes: a, Proto-Maglemosian core axe from Star Carr, length 9·9 cm.; b, flake axe, later Maglemosian or Ertebølle Culture, Denmark, length 10·7 cm. Scale: × ¼.

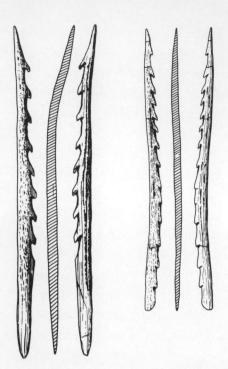

40
Harpoons or barbed projectile
heads made from splinters
of red deer antler,
Star Carr, Seamer, Yorkshire.
Scale: × $\frac{1}{4}$.

The first main axe–using culture is the Maglemosian. This
culture combined the use of flint axes with that of microliths.
The latter are diminutive flint tools made on portions of small
blades or flakes, which are divided up into sections by a characteristic and recognisable process of notching and snapping them.[8]
Microliths make their first appearance in later Upper Palaeolithic times, but are more typical of the Mesolithic cultures;
they are mostly arrow or projectile points, and several would
42 have been mounted together in the same shaft. Burins for engraving and working bone and antler are also present, and the
Maglemosians made much use of barbed harpoon heads made of
these materials in their fishing and hunting weapons. Flint awls
and scrapers are also common, especially the latter. Wooden bows
and arrows are known; wooden arrow–shafts, incidentally, were
abundantly represented in the Ahrensburgian levels at Stellmoor.[9]

The earliest stages of the Maglemosian Culture are well seen at such sites as Klosterlund in Jutland and Star Carr in Yorkshire, during Pre-Boreal times. At Star Carr there were prolific finds of typical flints and bonework where the hunter-fishers had lived 38 on an artificial platform of birchwood at the marshy edge of a lake.[10] The axe marks on the felled birch trees could be clearly seen. Waterlogged conditions preserved admirably objects of an organic nature, so that such details were recovered as small rolls of the birch bark from which resin was obtained to fix arrow points to their shafts. The bone and antler industry contained quantities of harpoon heads, but also heavier elements like picks 40 or mattocks of elk antler. There were also masks adapted from the front part of deer skulls, with antlers left in position; these 41 can be interpreted as ceremonial masks for ritual use, or alternatively as devices of disguise to be worn by deer-hunters. A wooden paddle was another significant find, though no actual boat came to light.[11] A radiocarbon date near to 7500 B.C. was obtained for the Star Carr settlement.

From such finds a vivid picture can be reconstructed of the life of the early Maglemosians, while the faunal remains give an account of the game, fish and fowl on which they lived, and pollen analysis enables their landscape and environment to be imagined with fair accuracy. The Maglemosian Culture in its 42 later stages extended from western Russia to Britain, and northwards well into Norway and Sweden. The evidence suggests that

41
Perforated stag frontlet,
Star Carr, Seamer, Yorkshire.
52 cm. wide overall.

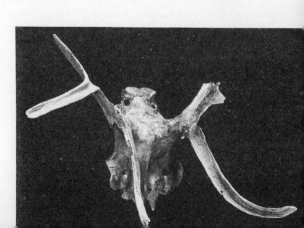

it persisted until the end of Boreal times, while its influence lasts well into the Atlantic period. The late Mesolithic Coastal Culture of the west Baltic and Scandinavia, which must have developed at least in part from the Maglemosian, lasts right down until the coming of the first farmers. Two features, traditional hall-marks, as it were, of the Neolithic spread, pottery and axes with a cutting edge sharpened by grinding instead of chipping, gradually make their appearance in these Coastal industries, without otherwise disrupting the strongly Mesolithic background. This phase of the late Mesolithic Coastal Culture is called after a site at Ertebølle, and it is the later Ertebølle stages which absorb the first clear Neolithic influences to reach this part of the world.

All the epi-palaeolithic and Mesolithic cultures so far mentioned have belonged to northern Europe, sometimes as far west as Britain or as far east as the borders of Russia. It should be realised that the English Channel of today did not come into existence in

42 Maglemosian artifacts from Denmark:
From the top Model of bear carved in amber, Resen, Jutland; harpoon or projectile head made by setting flints into a slotted bone point, with the aid of resin, Trørød, near Copenhagen; barbed bone harpoon or projectile head, Slangerup, near Copenhagen; carved and perforated amber model of elk head, Ege-marke, Zealand; aurochs bone decorated with incised anthropomorphic decoration, Ryemarkgård, Zealand. Scale: × *c.* $\frac{1}{3}$.

43

Azilian harpoon head with perforated base, Longueroche, Dordogne, France. Length 12·5 cm. from base to the break at the tip. Scale × $\frac{2}{5}$.

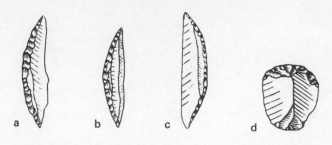

44 Azilian flints from Longueroche, Dordogne, France : *a–c*, crescent-shaped 'Azilian points' ; *d*, 'thumb-nail scraper'. Scale × $\frac{1}{2}$.

Post-Glacial times before about 6000 B.C., and the present bed of the North Sea was for a long while therefore a land area which must have been much frequented by the Maglemosians and some of their predecessors.[12] But further south, rather different Mesolithic cultures were to be found.

In the classic cave area of south France, and in parts of north Spain, the immediate successor of the Magdalenian culture was that of the Azilians. Links in both bonework and flintwork, and the closeness with which Azilian levels appear to follow Magdalenian ones in several caves, make it reasonable to see in the Azilian culture a direct but sadly impoverished survival of the Magdalenian population into conditions with which the culture was ill equipped to cope. The Azilian harpoons,[13] for example, uniserially or biserially barbed, and made of stag-antler, are a clear Magdalenian contribution. The flintwork develops towards geometric shapes in some respects, notably in the 'Azilian points', which are rather crescent-shaped backed blade types, pointed at each end and having an arched back. Burins are rather rare, and true microliths absent. Of the glorious flowering of late Magdalenian art, almost the only echo is numerous small pebbles which bear roughly painted geometric designs of a few strokes. Some of these patterns may represent very stylised human figures. Art

43

44

45

99

45
Azilian painted pebbles,
Mas d'Azil, Ariège, France.
The designs are painted
in red. Scale: × ½.

and ornament of any kind are in fact rather rare in the European Mesolithic, but in the Maglemosian Culture in its developed form, linear and geometric designs sometimes occur, scratched or incised or roughly drilled on bone, antler and even amber objects; animal and anthropomorphic representations are sometimes found, including a few charming and elegant little sculptured animals (see Fig. 42).

In French caves a little south of the Dordogne, in Guyenne, there are also Azilian levels, which are then followed by traces of two further Mesolithic cultures, the Sauveterrian and the Tardenoisian. Although there are important differences between these two cultures, they have a strongly microlithic nature in common, and neither of them makes regular use of axes. They have markedly geometric tool forms, notably tiny crescent and triangle shapes in the Sauveterrian, and trapezes and allied forms in the Tardenoisian.[14] The Sauveterrian is the earlier of the two, and its influence clearly extends northwards to Britain, where there are abundant Mesolithic sites belonging to this microlithic, non-axe-using tradition. The Pennines have produced numerous sites, and so has East Anglia, and the distribution extends as far as south-west England and Wales.[15] This spread to Britain had certainly taken place before the end of the Boreal Period, so that it would be contemporary with the later part of the Maglemosian Culture there. The Tardenoisian however does not seem to reach Britain in its typical form, and the most likely reason for this would be the barrier provided by the newly formed English Channel, which came into being after the Sauveterrians had passed over the land bridge.

The British Mesolithic sequence produces its own peculiarities. In the south, there are variants mainly of Late Boreal or Atlantic age which combine a microlithic element and such forms as small hollow-based arrow-points, with heavy axe tools.[16] In the

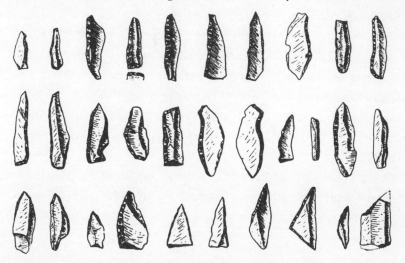

46 Sauveterrian microlithic flints, Le Cuzoul de Gramat, level 1, Lot, France. Scale: × $\frac{2}{3}$.

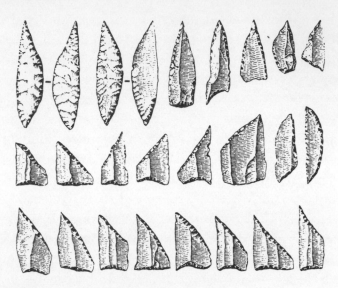

47 Tardenoisian microlithic flints, including trapezes and other geometric forms, Fère-en-Tardenois, Aisne, France. Scale: × ⅔.

north-west, in northern Ireland and south-west Scotland, astride the North Channel, coastal hunter-fisher groups called Larnian and Obanian existed, and their industries on the Scottish side produced yet another set of harpoons. The style of these used to make it customary for them to be linked with the Azilian, but the wide geographical gap between western Scotland and southern France, not to mention a considerable gap in time, makes this idea hard to support. The industries are now known to be of Atlantic age, and may have developed as a direct response to local conditions, while the formative influences probably included elements from the Baltic Coastal cultures which followed the Maglemosian.

Of the remainder of Europe in general, south of the Maglemosian territory, cultures not basically dissimilar to the Sauveterrian and Tardenoisian occupy the greater part of the Mesolithic Period, from Portugal in the west to Russia in the east. The local variants can as yet add little helpful knowledge, and it is only rarely that any light can be cast at all on the more informative aspects of the cultures. An exception is to be seen in the few but remarkable Mesolithic cemeteries, belonging to settlements of broadly Tardenoisian affinities. Numerous burials were found in Mesolithic midden sites in the Tagus valley in Portugal, but the details have been better observed and recorded on the small islands of Téviec and Hoëdic off the coast of Brittany.[17] At Téviec a total of ten graves produced burials of twenty-three individuals—one grave contained as many as six. The burials contained such traces **48** of ceremonial as scattered red ochre, the remains of shell necklaces and armlets, and sometimes the ritual covering of the interments with piles of stag antlers. Ritual hearths were also associated with the burials. The Hoëdic evidence was generally comparable, while in Bavaria, at the cave of Ofnet, two remarkable 'nests' **49** containing thirty-three human skulls in all were found. It is worth mentioning by way of contrast that the entire Mesolithic occupation of Britain has not yet produced a single burial.

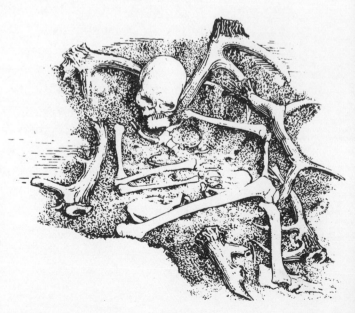

48
Mesolithic burial,
accompanied by
red deer antlers,
island of Hoëdic,
Morbihan, France

49 Mesolithic 'nests of skulls', Grosse Ofnethöhle, Bavaria

The Tardenoisian people, although they are generally classified as Mesolithic, are now known to have been acquainted, at least in the later stages of the culture, with what is properly a Neolithic trait, the domestication of animals. This is revealed by the character of the animal bones found in some Tardenoisian occupation levels: the structure and dimensions of the bones of 'domesticated' animals come with time to differ considerably from those of wild examples of the same species, for reasons connected with diet and the different pattern of the animals' existence. It follows that the animal bones recovered from archaeological levels can often be identified as belonging to 'wild' or 'domestic' forms. The Maglemosians, even at the early stage of their culture represented at Star Carr, in Pre-Boreal times, had domesticated the dog, but they never established this relationship with sheep or goats or cattle, as the Tardenoisians seem to have done—domestication of quite a different order. It may be, of course, that the Tardenoisians merely had access to domesticated animals belonging to early Neolithic immigrants into Europe, but it can in any case be said that this culture heralds the Neolithic Period in western Europe, and that it must have received the impact of the first farming settlers, with whom the next chapter will deal.

This west European picture of the status of the Tardenoisian receives support from as far east as the Crimea, where at two caves, Shan Koba and Tash Aïr, a generally similar picture is presented. A Mesolithic industry characterised by the usual microlithic trapeze-shaped tools is closely followed by one with basically similar flintwork, but with the addition of clear Neolithic elements such as pottery and domestic animal bones. The early Neolithic influences seem once again to have been absorbed by the existing Mesolithic population.

It remains only to describe the nature of the Mesolithic Period in the vital area of south-west Asia, mentioned at the beginning of the chapter. A number of late-Pleistocene or immediately post-Pleistocene microlith-using cultures are known here, generally similar in type, and the best studied of these is the Natufian.[18] The Natufians are first seen as cave-dwelling hunters, in the area of the Levant coast, in the tenth millennium B.C.; their industries are found for example in the famous caves of Mount Carmel.

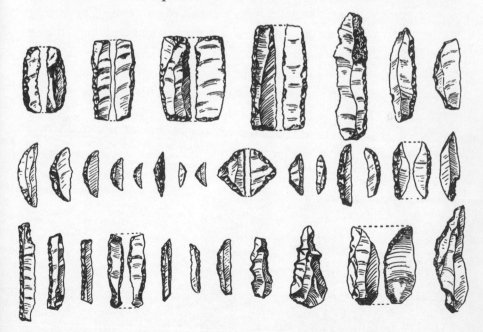

50 Natufian flint artifacts, including sickle flints (top row), narrow-backed blades, geometric microliths and notched blades, Mugharet El-Wad, level B2, Mount Carmel. Scale: × *c.* ½.

Their flint tool types included crescent-shaped microliths and narrow backed blades, and they also made bone tools of some elaboration, including points, barbed spearheads and fish-hooks. But perhaps the most significant of their tools are flint blades which can fairly be regarded as sickles, because they show the readily identifiable peculiar lustrous polish and wear produced by use in cutting the stalks of cereal plants. These reaping tools, and the presence of pestles and mortars for the grinding of grain, make it clear that the Natufians were accustomed to harvest cereals, though it cannot yet be said with certainty whether they sowed them for themselves, or merely made use of the colonies of wild grain-bearing cereal grasses, the ancestors of modern wheat, which are known to have existed in their territory. Hunting, in any case, remained their main method of obtaining food.

The vigorous and advanced nature of the Natufian Culture is to be seen in two further important ways. First, there are large and elaborate cemeteries, in which some of the tombs represent quite a feat of building, especially a round paved and walled one containing a ceremonial burial of seven people, found at Eynan, a Natufian open site in north Palestine. Such sophistication would surely be beyond the scope of simple bands of hunters merely struggling to exist.

But it is not only in such lavish treatment of the dead that Natufian achievements give cause for surprise. One of the most

51
Natufian stone-built tomb,
Eynan, Ain Mallaha,
Jordan Valley

52
Traces of structure belonging to the Natufian settlement at the base of the Jericho mound, including a clay platform surrounded by a stone wall with settings for wooden posts

unexpected archaeological discoveries of recent years was the revelation that the Natufians, recognised by perfectly typical artifacts, were the earliest settled occupants of what was later to become the site of the city of Jericho.[19] The surprising thing was not that they merely occupied the site, but that they apparently established a permanent village and perhaps a shrine there, well back in the tenth millennium B.C. To anticipate the next chapter slightly, their descendants, who can still not be called fully Neolithic, were to show themselves capable of erecting a remarkable and massive stone-built defensive wall around the settlement, with towers some thirty feet high. The contrast of human **54** achievement is enormous between this admittedly favoured area and north-west Europe, where the Proto-Maglemosian site at Star Carr is an approximate contemporary of this ten-acre walled town, as it may reasonably be called, at Jericho.

Further north and east of the Natufian area, there is comparable evidence to show that industries which can fairly be called Mesolithic were succeeded by others which, with no marked break in their traditions of flint and bone tools, began to show Neolithic influences such as animal domestication. A succession of this sort in the Crimea has already been mentioned, and another can be seen at the Belt Cave, which is situated near the south-eastern corner of the Caspian Sea, where the Mesolithic levels go back towards 10,000 B.C.

The so-called 'Neolithic Revolution' in this important area was not a sudden or simple event. The next chapter must consider how, when, where and even why it took place, and what was its effect on the course of prehistory.

NOTES

1. It is extremely difficult to discern a pattern of evolution in the many Gravettian and epi-Gravettian industries of central and eastern Europe and the U.S.S.R. There are several reasons for this. First, comparatively little of the material has yet been fully published, and much of the publication is of course in Russian, which few western archaeologists yet speak. Secondly, as a glance at a physical map will show, the area available for settlement is almost un-believably vast, even when allowance is made for the ice-sheets at their fullest extent, while the area which has been archaeologically explored is infinitesimal. Thirdly, we have far too little idea yet of the chronology of those sites which are known. The best studied sequence of industries in the U.S.S.R. occurs in the Don valley, in the Kostenki area, where a classic East Gravettian industry of perhaps late Paudorf date is represented at Kostenki Site 1 layer 1. (An interesting recent reference here is Grigor'ev, 1967.) There are numerous other industries stratigraphically older than this, and others nearby which are certainly younger. Many other important sites lie farther west, for example in the Ukraine and in the Crimean peninsula. A useful published source in English is Golomshtok, 1938, but this work is of course by no means up to date. Few readily accessible sources can be suggested for the central and east European sites either, most being published in the local or national journals; see however Klíma, 1954 and 1962 and Müller-Karpe, 1966. Another paper of interest is Okladnikov, 1962, though it does not deal exclusively with the Upper Palaeolithic material. A very brief general account of the Moravian sites, with a few illustrations, will be found in the early chapters of *Czechoslovakia before the Slavs* (Neustupný and Neustupný, 1961).

2. For an analysis of the impact of radiocarbon dating on the study of Upper Paleolithic and Late Glacial cultures, see Movius, 1960; while several

more dates have been obtained since 1960, this paper contains much valuable basic information.

3. For details of the Hamburgian and Ahrensburgian cultures (the latter is referred to later in the chapter), see Rust, 1937 and 1943. For those who do not read German, the most important facts are of course mentioned, if not treated in detail, in the appropriate main source works mentioned in n. 4 below. A lively and informative account of Rust's work at Meiendorf, Stellmoor and elsewhere is given by G. Bibby (Bibby, 1957, Ch. 10).

4. For background reading on the more general aspects of the Epi-Palaeolithic and Mesolithic cultures, the reader should consult the appropriate chapters in various works by Professor J. G. D. Clark, especially Clark, J. G. D., 1936, 1950, 1952, 1962 and 1967, and also Clark J. G. D., and Piggott, 1965.

5. See Schwabedissen, 1954.

6. See Mace, 1959.

7. The standard work on the British Upper Palaeolithic is still that by Professor Dorothy Garrod (Garrod, 1926), but this is now considerably out of date. Recent field work on British cave sites has been carried out by Dr C. B. M. McBurney, but is mostly not yet published. See, however, McBurney, 1959, and the relevant parts of McBurney, 1964; see also Manby, 1966.

8. This is rather misleadingly called the 'microburin technique', from the superficial resemblance of the waste-product to a tiny burin.

9. For the evidence for archery in prehistoric times, see Clark, J. G. D., 1963; for the prehistory of fishing, see Clark, J. G. D., 1948.

10. Fully described by Professor J. G. D. Clark and others in Clark, 1954.

11. An actual Maglemosian dug-out canoe, of slightly later date, is known from Pesse in Holland.

12. If ever major archaeological investigations could be carried out on the southern part of the present North Sea bed, much light would be forthcoming

53
Maglemosian barbed bone point or harpoon head, dredged up by a fishing trawler from the North Sea bed near the Leman and Ower banks. Length 22 cm.

on the period covered by this chapter. The find of a Maglemosian harpoon head between the Leman and Ower Banks some twenty-five miles off the Norfolk coast bears witness to this: it was brought up in the net of a fishing trawler in 1931, from a depth of some twenty fathoms.

13. Described in Thompson, 1954.

14. A readily accessible reference for the industries of Sauveterrian and Tardenoisian type in France, and indeed throughout Europe, is Clark, 1958, in which many other sources are quoted, though naturally few are in English. The latest substantial reference to the Tagus Valley Mesolithic is Roche, 1960.

15. The basic work on the British Mesolithic material is Clark, 1932, though it can no longer be considered an up-to-date account. An important later paper by the same author is Clark, 1955. Several papers by various authors, incorporating a number of excavation reports, are spread over the most recent dozen or so volumes of the *Proceedings of the Prehistoric Society*.

16. A somewhat nebulous 'Horsham Culture' has been distinguished amongst industries of this kind, and the name 'Horsham point' has been given to the hollow-based arrowhead type. Probably the various industries are too scattered and inconsistent to warrant the title of a culture. The most likely explanation of them is that they are the outcome of interaction between the Sauveterrians and the indigenous Maglemosian or epi-Maglemosian population they encountered. The name 'Wealden Culture' has sometimes been applied to them.

17. See Péquart and Péquart, 1937 and 1954.

18. Described by Professor Dorothy Garrod in Garrod, 1957. Another useful source of information is the chapter 'The Mesolithic Cultures of the Near East, *c.* 10,000–9000 B.C.' in Mellaart, 1965.

19. See Kenyon, 1965, Ch. 2.

4 The New Stone Age

The Neolithic Period laid the first essential foundations for the complicated human groups which go by the name of 'civilisations'. Civilisation implies such things as highly organised society, settlements on the scale of cities, government, class-structure, extensive organised trade, and usually the achievement of literacy, which by definition takes most developed civilisations out of the province of prehistory.[1] It is easy enough to see that the very basis of civilisation is a settled existence, and this was something the Palaeolithic and Mesolithic hunting bands could not have, since their means of livelihood, the game herds, forced them to be nomadic. The development of the Neolithic arts of crop-growing and animal husbandry changed this, and made possible the life of permanent villages. Much more was needed before the villages could become cities. The Neolithic Period did not itself achieve civilisation, but it certainly established the firm economic basis upon which the early civilisations could quite rapidly grow up.

Man could not enter a Neolithic phase at will; the necessary raw material of Neolithic status had to exist, and the stimulus to make use of it had to be provided. By 'raw material' here is meant the wild prototypes of both the animals and the cereal grasses which were first domesticated. The wild ancestors of the first domestic sheep and goats existed in Asia Minor and south-west Asia from the Mediterranean coasts eastwards about half way across the continent. The wild ancestors of the domestic cattle were much more widely distributed, in a broad belt across most of Europe and Asia except the far north, and they also occurred in north Africa. Wild pigs also had a very wide distribution. As regards the cereal grasses, the prototypes of the early Emmer and Einkorn wheats, and of different types of barley, were to be found in different parts of the Near and Middle East, especially in Asia Minor, Palestine, and as far east as the southern end of the Caspian Sea.[2]

The raw material was thus ready to hand, and only the stimulus was required to turn the inventive attention of man to it. It seems clear that this stimulus was provided by the altered post-Pleistocene climate, though it is less easy to see exactly what were the mechanisms which operated to get the processes of domestication started; these may never be known in detail. The area in question seems to have been Palestine and Iraq or the immediately surrounding lands, and the animal and plant proto-types were certainly present here to provide the opportunity. As regards the climatic change, there is evidence that in some parts of this area at least it took the form of increasing dryness; such changes would be likely to have an adverse effect on the customary food supplies of both animals and men.

This factor especially may have turned man's attention to the cereal grasses, and the possibilities of sowing their seed in appro-priate conditions to ensure a regular and easily accessible supply of them; gathering of vegetable and plant food and fruit was presumably a general habit even as early as Lower Palaeolithic times, and certainly in the Mesolithic Period. As regards animal domestication, the hunter's driving of game towards traps was a process not so very different from rounding up animals in the herding sense, and the first notion of herding was probably to ensure a future food supply, bearing in mind the new (climatic) pressure on food sources, whereas hunting is essentially concerned with immediate hand-to-mouth living. From the animals' point of view, and for the same ultimately climatic reasons, a closer relationship with man probably became essential to survival, because man could favourably affect their food supply. His newly found grain crops would soon become a powerful attraction. But it is worth mentioning that, according to present knowledge, the first herding may well have preceded the first crop growing, and there is no doubt that the whole initiative came from man. Herding is recorded as early as about 9000 B.C. at Shanidar in northern Iraq.

Both crop-growing and animal herding would be processes bound to grow and develop once the first step had been successfully taken. In crop-growing, there was the chance to improve seed by selection, to discover new crops, and to learn such essential processes as crop rotation and the fertilisation of ground. In herding, there would be the realisation that the animals were not merely a ready-to-hand supply of present and future meat and skins, but a source of milk, and that their grazing and manure were of value to the land which grew the crops. With careful breeding, and this is, of course, a process extending far beyond the Neolithic Period, many aspects of their usefulness could be improved—the wool of sheep and the milk and beef of cattle for example. It was comparatively late in prehistoric times, though essentially a part of the same process, that animals became used for riding and for traction.

Two other features have always been held by archaeologists to be highly characteristic of the Neolithic Period, namely the first making of pottery, and the first making of stone axes not by chipping and flaking, but by grinding and polishing. Such axes, made of flint or other kinds of stone, are extremely efficient, sharp and durable tools.

78, 79

Pottery and polished stone axes are certainly typical Neolithic features. However, over the past ten years or so, it has come to be realised that the earliest communities to practise farming had not yet learnt the art of pottery making, and to these the term Pre-pottery Neolithic is sometimes applied. Such an idea would once have been regarded as a contradiction in terms, and ridiculous, but it was shown in the last chapter that the first food-producing communities, especially those of the Natufian culture, were of a remarkably high antiquity, while the first reapers of grain were frankly Mesolithic, with hunting still a far stronger feature of their economy. It might not be quite correct to describe the earliest Natufians as 'food-producing', since they may never have been actual sowers of crops. But the Natufian first settlers of Jericho were not much later in time, and they could hardly have managed to live in a permanent village without some fair command of agriculture. The widely distributed European blade-and-trapeze groups like the Tardenoisians also seem to have been at least in contact with animal herders even if they were not herders themselves; they too certainly knew nothing of pottery making at first.

At Jericho[3] the levels which follow the first occupation by a Natufian community can be ascribed to Pre-pottery Neolithic people, who were, however, apparently close descendants of the Natufians; their settlement of mud-brick houses amounted to eight or ten acres in all, and, as mentioned in the last chapter, was surrounded by unexpectedly elaborate and massive walls.

54

This phase must begin in the eighth millennium B.C., but the succeeding one, in which pottery first makes an appearance at Jericho, does not seem to start much before about 5000 B.C. Pre-pottery Neolithic (or aceramic) occupations have been discovered at several other sites besides Jericho; Jarmo, in northern Iraq, is another important one, and so are Hacilar in southern Anatolia, and Khirokitia in Cyprus. Recently, several Pre-pottery Neolithic settlements have been found south of Jericho—in Jordan, at Beidha and other places nearby. It is also important to note that a number of Pre-pottery Neolithic sites, presumably of comparable date (probably seventh millennium B.C.) existed in south-east Europe—a good example is one at Argissa in Thessaly.[4]

For all the impoverished sound of the cumbersome phrase 'Pre-pottery Neolithic', the cultures so described were vigorous and sometimes surprisingly sophisticated. The monumental walls of Jericho have already been mentioned, and at the same site a

54
Stone tower of defensive
wall at Jericho,
Pre-pottery Neolithic

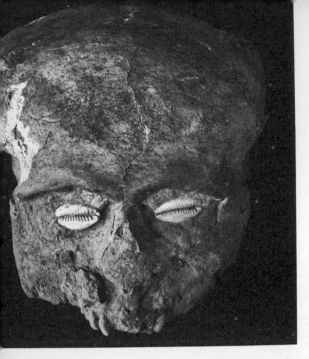

55
Skull from Pre-pottery
Neolithic levels at Jericho,
with cowrie-shell eyes and
remains of plaster features.
Breadth 14·5 cm.

remarkable ritual practice involved the modelling and painting of
55 clay features on human skulls, with carefully made eyes formed
of shells.

Another highly important Anatolian site with early Neolithic
levels is Çatal Hüyük.[5] Here pottery is present, but in extremely
small quantities. Excavation has not yet reached the base of the
settlement mound, so it may well be that future digging will
reveal aceramic levels here too.

At Çatal Hüyük, the excavations revealed even more remarkable ritual details, belonging on the latest interpretation to early
Neolithic cultures with pottery of the later seventh millennium
56, 57 and earlier sixth millennium B.C. Shrines or cult-centres were
found, consisting of rooms decorated with mural paintings on
plaster, and the horns and plaster-modelled heads of bulls. Bulls
also feature prominently in the wall-paintings, along with other
animals, including leopards, and various scenes are depicted, one
of the most striking of which shows vultures hovering above

116

56a

56b

Two views of parts of early Neolithic shrine at Çatal Hüyük, Anatolia, with arrangements of horn cores of wild bull *(Bos primigenius)*, as excavated; for reconstruction drawing, see Fig. 57

headless human victims. Some lively hunting scenes also occur. Even if at Çatal Hüyük these finds relate to a Neolithic people who used pottery, such vigorous artistic and ritual expressions must surely have a long tradition behind them at least locally. **58, 59**

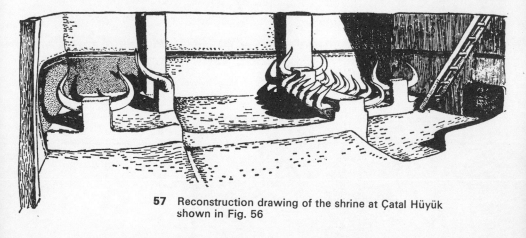

57 Reconstruction drawing of the shrine at Çatal Hüyük shown in Fig. 56

58 Part of Early Neolithic mural painting at Çatal Hüyük, Anatolia, as excavated, showing vultures hovering over headless human victims; for reconstruction drawing, see Fig. 59

The Neolithic cultures with pottery succeed those which lacked it at rather different dates according to area, but often before the end of the seventh millennium B.C.[6] The aceramic cultures had vessels and containers of stone, basketwork and wood. At Jericho there is something of a break in the sequence before the arrival of the pottery-makers, by which time more than forty feet of deposit belonging to the aceramic occupation had already accumulated. There seem to be two waves of pre-pottery occupation at Jericho in these earlier levels, characterised by such things as different shaped houses, with round plans for the earlier

59
Reconstruction of the vulture painting shown in Fig. 58

(post-Natufian) phase, and rectangular for the later one. Jericho is a good example of a tell mound: the houses were built of mud-brick, and lasted only a few decades; when they collapsed, new ones were built on top of the fallen material. Hence the growth of a considerable mound on the settlement site, consisting entirely of occupation material and mud-brick building debris; 'tell' is the name given to a settlement mound of this nature. The whole mound at Jericho today is something like a hundred feet high.

The earliest pottery in the Near East and in Europe contains both plain and decorated wares. According to the styles of pottery decoration, the spreads of the various cultures can be determined, and their origins to some extent fixed. Early Neolithic levels with pottery are well seen at Jarmo and Hassuna in Mesopotamia, and Hacilar and Mersin in Anatolia, as well as at Jericho and Çatal Hüyük.[7]

In and around Mesopotamia a great cultural sequence can be traced from the earliest levels of village settlements like Ali Kosh and Hassuna, through evolving cultural stages called after the sites of Halaf, Ubaid, Uruk and Jemdet Nasr, through the introduction of metal working and the building of cities, right up to the beginnings of history and the literate civilisation of the Sumerians around 3000 B.C. A comparable sequence is known in Egypt, though completely different in detail; here the earliest known settlements of pottery-using people apparently date from as late as the second half of the fifth millennium B.C., though earlier material may well lie under the Nile silt. The final break-through to civilisation in Egypt seems to owe much to influence from Mesopotamia and the early Sumerian civilisation, and takes place very soon after 3000 B.C.

In India too, a fully developed civilisation appears in the third millennium B.C.; it is called after the Indus valley and is mainly known from the two city sites of Harappa and Mohenjo-daro. The very existence of this early Indian civilisation more or less demands an extensive sequence of earlier settlement and a Neolithic period of the same kind as existed in the areas mentioned above, but traces of this are still very scarce in the archaeological record.

In Asia Minor, literate civilisation becomes established early in the second millennium B.C., substantially later than in Mesopotamia, Egypt or India, and from not long afterwards the Hittite documents provide a more or less continuous record. But from as early as the middle of the third millennium, there are already clear signs of the concentration of power and wealth. In northwest Anatolia, Troy was already a strongly fortified citadel (the 'Second City' phase); from the excavation of its ruins came rich treasures hastily buried before its destruction, including fine vessels and other objects of precious metals, and much jewellery. At Alaca Hüyük in central Anatolia, 'royal graves' were discovered, evidently belonging to a local dynasty of the late third millennium: the dead were buried with an impressive array of rich treasures, including gold and silver vessels, personal ornaments and ceremonial weapons. There were also animal figures, which have sometimes been described as 'standards', of cast copper with gold and silver inlay and mounts.

Palestine, too, was an area late in achieving actual literacy, although so important in the vital early period as a contributor to the 'Neolithic Revolution'. But all these facts really lie far beyond the scope of the present chapter, and are only included for the sake of completeness, since the fascinating story of emergent civilisation in the Near East is outside the range of an introductory book of this kind.[8] Meanwhile it is time to turn to the spread of the early Neolithic communities through Europe[9] and their eventual extension to distant Britain.[9]

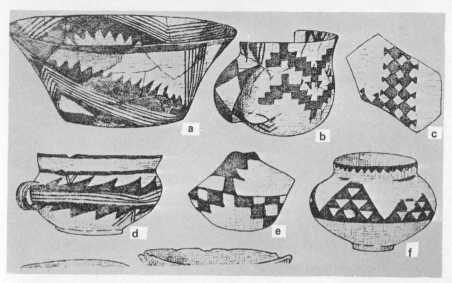

60 Painted pottery of the Sesklo Culture:
a, d, Tsangli, Central Thessaly; *b, c, e*, Tsani, Western
Thessaly; *f*, Chaeronea, Boeotia

It was mentioned earlier that Pre-pottery Neolithic sites are known in south-east Europe. The Balkans and Greece are so placed geographically as to receive the earliest Neolithic impact upon Europe and several early Neolithic sites are now known in this area, with painted and unpainted pottery, some of the latter being decorated with impressed patterns. The culture names of Sesklo and Starčevo-Körös, after local sites, have been given to some of these earliest pottery-using farming settlers of south-eastern Europe, and a recent dig at the tell mound of Nea Nikomedeia in Macedonia has revealed one of their settlements. At another one, Elateia, also in Greece, there are dates from about 5750 B.C. onwards. In Crete, an early Neolithic settlement was found at Knossos, and was dated to about 6000 B.C.—something like four thousand years older than the famous palace of the Minoan civilisation which was afterwards to flourish on the same site.

61
Early Neolithic figurines from
Nea Nikomedeia, Greek Macedonia;
two female human figures and
a goat head. The figurine on
the right is seven inches high.
Scale: × ⅔.

These early cultures in south-east Europe are in many respects comparable with the contemporary ones in south-west Asia, except that the villages of the European tell settlements consist of separate individual houses, rather than the dense clusters of interconnected rectangular rooms and courtyards which are typical of the Near East in general. The European cultures share with the south-west Asian ones such traits as the making of little **61** figurines, animal and human; some of the latter have often been interpreted as Mother-Goddess representations, probably for ritual use of some kind, and if this is so it would be perfectly well in keeping, one would think, with the religious ideas of a people vitally interested in the fertility of the land and the animals.

The main Neolithic spread west and north from the Balkan area follows the loess soils of the Danube region at first, and has accordingly sometimes been called 'Danubian'. There are no tells here; the settlements consist of villages of large rectangular houses sometimes well over a hundred feet long, whose plans are known from the surviving pattern of post-holes and bedding trenches for the heavy timbers of their framework. Such houses may have been shared by several related families, in the manner of certain primitive peoples of more recent date, or they may have been divided between men and animals. The origins of this Danubian culture are very poorly known, and it certainly does not seem to derive directly from the Starčevo or Sesklo cultures. The pottery is very different, with a highly typical decoration of incised ribbon-like motifs defined by parallel lines; from this style, the names *Linearbandkeramik* or Linear Pottery Culture are often used instead of the name Danubian. Elements of this culture in a typical form had penetrated as far west as Holland soon after 4500 B.C.

62, 63

64

Another typical item of Danubian material culture is polished stone adze blades of a characteristic shape. Such equipment is to be expected in a culture which was carrying the new farming economy into a more forested environment, very different from the lands where the Neolithic Revolution had taken place. Figurines in the south-east European or south-west Asian tradition are extremely rare in the Danubian culture. The grain crops, emmer, einkorn and barley, and the livestock, sheep, goats, cattle

62 Ground plan of a long-house (Building W.4) at the Linearbandkeramik settlement at Geleen, Netherlands, revealed by excavation, with pegs marking the post holes. The dimensions of the building are: length, 28·9 metres; breadth at widest point, 6·6 metres.

and pigs, do not differ from those found in south-west Asia, from where they no doubt ultimately derived, though not necessarily directly.

The Early Danubian Culture lasts until about 3800 B.C. in Austria, Hungary, Czechoslovakia and adjacent areas; thereafter, certain changes in the house plans can be seen, and 'stroke-ornamented' pottery replaces the earlier style. After about 3500 B.C., there are further developments, whose origins lie in the settlement-mound cultures of the north Balkans. Smaller houses become fashionable, shorter in length and sometimes with one apsidal end. They still form villages, and no tells occur, but some of the settlements have defensive features. There are many new pottery types, some decorated with coloured washes: there are vessels in the form of animals, and pottery models of men and women are also found. Quite by the beginning of the third millennium, the first signs of metal working reached central Europe, and copper shaft-hole axes appear in the archaeological record.

There is another spread of early Neolithic influence westward, quite separate from the inland continental spread of the Danubians. It follows the islands and coastline of the Mediterranean, evidently passing by sea routes, and is characterised by pottery with impressed decoration, the patterns often consisting of groups of wavy lines made by pressing the edge of a Cardium shell into the wet clay. The name Cardial Culture has sometimes been given to the settlements concerned. The latter are found in Italy and Sicily, southern France and Spain, and north Africa, and the origins of the spread may lie in the early Neolithic cultures of Syria and the east Mediterranean littoral.

But in western Europe, these coastal settlers seem to turn inland, and their influence contributes to the earliest Neolithic of France and Switzerland, and thus to the whole complex of local

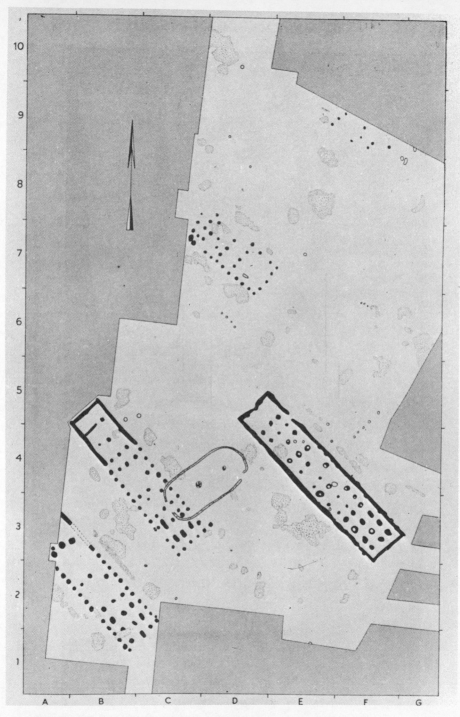

63 Plan of part of a Linearbandkeramik settlement at Sittard, Netherlands, as revealed by excavation, showing typical large rectangular house plans. Scale: 1/625.

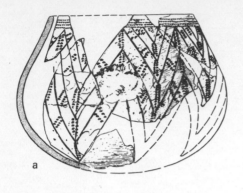
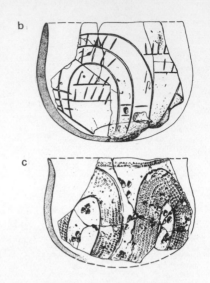
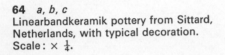

64 *a, b, c*
Linearbandkeramik pottery from Sittard,
Netherlands, with typical decoration.
Scale: × ¼.

cultures known as the Western Neolithic, comprising the first
farming settlements of Atlantic Europe, including Britain. This
Western Neolithic begins late by comparison with the Near East
and south-eastern Europe; for example, the earliest Neolithic
dates so far obtained from Britain suggest a first arrival of the
farming settlers not much earlier than 3500 B.C.—by which time
the Sumerian civilisation was about to begin in Mesopotamia,
and at least two thousand five hundred years had passed since
the first pottery using cultures had reached Greece.[10]

No remains are known of the ships or boats used by the
settlers who reached western Europe by way of the Mediterranean,
or crossed the Channel to Britain, bringing livestock with them.
But the craft can hardly have been other than flimsy, and the
voyages accomplished in them were therefore considerable feats
of navigation.

Another area in which the Neolithic period has a late beginning
is northern Europe—that is, the European plain north of the
Danubian province, and Scandinavia. The influences here are

126

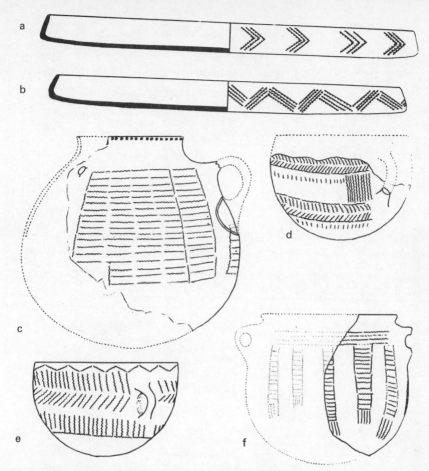

65 Neolithic pottery with decoration made of *cardium* shell impressions from southern France: *a, b*, Grotte de la Montade, Bouches-du-Rhône; *c, f*, Grotte Saint-Vérédème, Vallée du Gardon; *d*, Grotte de Courtiou, Marseille; *e*, Abri de Châteauneuf-de-Martigues, Bouches-du-Rhône

most likely to have come from central Europe, though the way also lies open from south Russia. In any case, local features soon develop, including the type of pots known from their shape as 'funnel-beakers', which are quite different from those of the Linear Pottery culture. The thriving Mesolithic cultures of this part of Europe, notably that of Ertebølle, retain a strong influence,

66

absorbing the new Neolithic techniques of pottery making, agriculture and the domestication of animals, and the grinding of stone axes, without however suffering any immediate profound change of their own culture and way of life. On present dating their contact with Neolithic cultures and the initial spread of Neolithic influence in northern Europe may not have begun much before 3000 B.C.

In the Western Neolithic, various local cultures can be detected, for example those called after Chassey and Cortaillod, with centres respectively in France and Switzerland, and the Windmill Hill Culture of southern Britain. The greatest detail of the material culture is to be seen in the Cortaillod lakeside settlements of Switzerland, where waterlogging of the archaeological levels has had the effect of preserving organic materials so that even linen

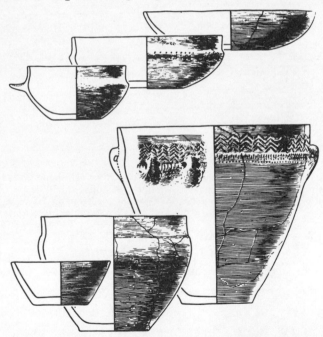

66 Pottery of the 'Funnel-Beaker' Culture, Angelslo, Drenthe, Netherlands. Scale: × $\frac{1}{5}$.

68

67

Well-preserved objects from the
Swiss Neolithic lake-side settlement of Egolzwil, Lucerne:

67 Wooden axe haft of ash, with
original stone axe blade still
in place. Scale: × $\frac{1}{3}$.

68 Small wooden cup, height about
5·5 cm., greatest diameter
about 10 cm.

69 Remains of basket-like or bag-
like container, the woven part
of twisted flaxen threads,
length (as shown) 28 cm.

Schweizerisches Landesmuseum,
Berne, Switzerland

69

textiles survive, and so do fragments of fishing nets, baskets,
wooden objects and the 'sleeves' made of antler which were used
for hafting small polished stone axes—some of them with the
axes still in position. Even the pips and stones of soft fruit were
found.

The pottery of the Western Neolithic cultures is often plain,
with a burnished surface, but incised and impressed decoration

also occurs. Polished axes of flint and other kinds of stone are a regular feature, and both crop growing and animal herding are included in the economy. The nature of the settlements and actual dwellings is for the most part very poorly known, but certainly there is no sign of the substantially built villages of central European style.

71 In Britain, the Windmill Hill Culture is called after a type-site in north Wiltshire, though it is now known that the main occupation there does not belong to the very earliest period of British Neolithic settlement.[11] The culture is well within the Western Neolithic traditions, and apart from pottery of the usual rather clumsy kind, with plain or sparsely decorated round-bottomed bowls, there are other features for which continental parallels can be found, though the question of origins is not a simple one;

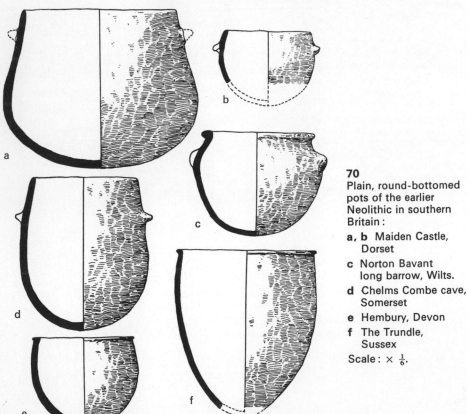

70
Plain, round-bottomed pots of the earlier Neolithic in southern Britain:

a, b Maiden Castle, Dorset

c Norton Bavant long barrow, Wilts.

d Chelms Combe cave, Somerset

e Hembury, Devon

f The Trundle, Sussex

Scale: × $\frac{1}{6}$.

Britain is after all well placed to receive a number of different influences across the Channel and the North Sea. One well marked feature is the kind of earthwork structure known as a 'causewayed camp', of which the Windmill Hill site itself is an example—a large enclosure surrounded by interrupted ditches which do not seem to be of a defensive character. Causewayed camps were possibly tribal gathering places of some sort, though it has also been suggested that they were cattle corrals. Over a dozen of them are now known in Britain, and one, Hembury in Devon, has produced one of the earliest British Neolithic carbon dates so far (see note 10 to this chapter).

There are two other important classes of monument in Britain which have been attributed to the Windmill Hill Culture: flint **72** mines, and the large burial mounds known as long barrows. **73** The flint mines consist of shafts dug deep down into the chalk to reach the pure flint which occurs naturally in it; sometimes the shafts have galleries radiating out from them to follow the seams of the precious raw material. The digging of such mines

71
Aerial photograph of the Neolithic 'causewayed camp' at Windmill Hill, Wilts., taken in 1948

72
Neolithic flint mine at Grimes Graves, Weeting, Norfolk, showing galleries leading off from the base of the main shaft. Nodules of dark flint can be seen *in situ* in the chalk walls of the main shaft itself.

with tools only of bone, antler and perhaps wood was a remarkable achievement. The most famous British flint-mining site is Grimes Graves in Norfolk, where some hundreds of these mining shafts exist; excavated examples can be visited and explored in detail by torchlight.[12] The Grimes Graves mines themselves, however, were perhaps not used until rather later in the Neolithic Period, and at the moment it is uncertain whether as much flint mining was carried out by the Windmill Hill people as has been suggested in the past.

The long barrows were large mounds, erected (again by a considerable feat of primitive labour) to cover burials, several people being interred together. The burials are not usually accompanied by many grave goods, though occasionally traces have been found of a funeral feast held at the raising of the mound. Sometimes there are also signs that temporary mortuary structures were erected to contain the collected dead of a community, or perhaps of a particular family, before the building of the barrow took place. These long barrows are a fairly common sight on the chalk lands of southern Britain, though much less frequent than the round barrows of the Bronze Age. The mounds are mainly constructed of chalk, and although now turf-covered, they must have remained pure white for at least a while after they were first raised, and would have been impressive monuments. Wor Barrow, on Cranborne Chase, Dorset, is a well-known example of a long barrow, and an instructive one, because excavation showed that it had been built over the site of a mortuary house of the kind mentioned above.[13]

Among small objects which are typical finds at Windmill Hill **74** sites may be included sickle flints, finely made 'combs' of antler, perhaps used for the cleaning of skins, and well-made small flint arrowheads of a pointed, leaf-shaped outline. Picks for use in digging were also made of antler, many broken examples having been recovered from earthwork sites of all kinds. Shovels made from the shoulder-blades of cattle or deer are sometimes encountered.

The Windmill Hill Culture is not the only culture of the British Neolithic. There is also a group of cultures characterised by their use of decorated pottery in contrast to the usually plainer **75** Windmill Hill wares; to these the name Secondary Neolithic has been given, on the theory that they developed out of the exchange of influence between the native Mesolithic population and the incoming Primary Neolithic Windmill Hill settlers. This theory has required a certain amount of modification, as the decorated pottery has on several occasions turned up in rather early contexts alongside the plain wares. The decoration is mainly achieved by impressing different objects into the clay while wet—anything from a finger to a piece of cord or the end of a

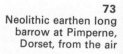

73
Neolithic earthen long barrow at Pimperne, Dorset, from the air

bird bone. Another feature of the Secondary Neolithic cultures is a form of arrowhead different from that used by the Windmill Hill people, not leaf-shaped, but trapezoidal, with a sharp, **76** squared, transverse cutting edge ('chisel-ended') instead of a point. This type has been regarded as a development from the native Mesolithic flint-work. The difference in arrowhead types between Primary and Secondary Neolithic is perhaps not quite as exclusive as was once supposed, but as a general rule it seems to hold good.

The general name given to the decorated pottery of the main British Secondary Neolithic culture is Peterborough ware, and there are subdivisions of it known as the Ebbsfleet, Mortlake and

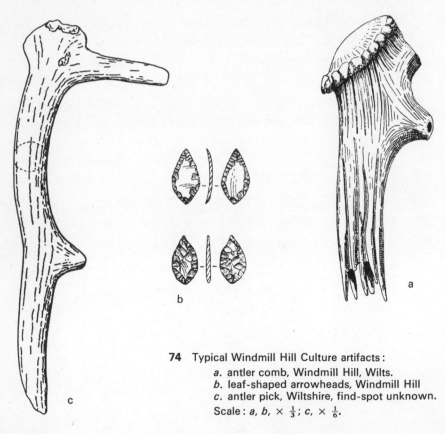

74 Typical Windmill Hill Culture artifacts:
 a. antler comb, Windmill Hill, Wilts.
 b. leaf-shaped arrowheads, Windmill Hill
 c. antler pick, Wiltshire, find-spot unknown.
 Scale: *a, b,* $\times \frac{1}{3}$; *c,* $\times \frac{1}{6}$.

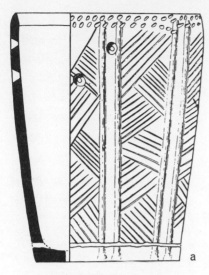

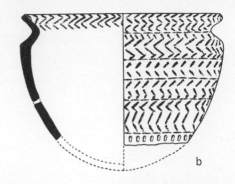

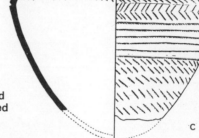

75 Decorated pottery of the British Neolithic. Scale: × $\frac{1}{4}$.

a. 'Rinyo-Clacton' pot with impressed and grooved decoration and applied vertical cordons, Wilsford, Barrow G.51, Wilts.

b. 'Peterborough' bowl with cord impressions and, below, probable bird-bone impressions, same source as last

c. 'Peterborough' bowl with cord impressions, West Kennet long barrow, Avebury, Wilts.

Devizes Museum, Wilts.

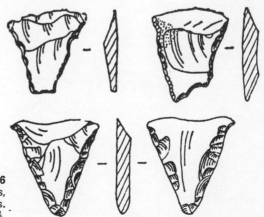

76
Chisel-ended arrowheads, Windmill Hill, Wilts.
Scale: × $\frac{2}{3}$.

Fengate styles, distinguished by variations of decoration and shape. Another Secondary Neolithic group of Rinyo-Clacton pottery has been recognised, but the scattered nature of its distribution makes it doubtful whether a true and distinct culture is represented by it. The most notable site falling within the Rinyo-Clacton series is the Neolithic village settlement of Skara Brae, Orkney, with stone-built partly subterranean houses, well preserved under wind-blown sand. Some unusual details of interior furnishing survive, all in stone, including bed-places, hearths, cupboard-like recesses, and what can only be described as built-in dressers.[14]

A flourishing trade in ground and polished axes, made of particularly suitable kinds of rock at special 'factory' sites, is well represented in Secondary Neolithic contexts, though it begins much earlier in the British Neolithic sequence. From the archaeologist's point of view, a major item of importance with these axes is that the rocks of which they are made can quite often be

77 Interior of Neolithic house at Skara Brae, Orkney, showing stone furnishings

78

Polished stone axes of the British Neolithic:

78 Graig Lwyd axe, found at Ravencliffe
Cave, Bakewell, Derbyshire.
Length 12 cm. British Museum

79 Axe of Cumbrian type, probably from the
Langdale factory, found near Bampton,
Oxon. Length 22·4 cm.
Pitt Rivers Museum, Oxford.

79

identified and traced to their sources;[15] some actual axe-factory
sites have been discovered in this way, revealed by roughouts
and the debris of quarrying and axe manufacture scattered widely
over areas of the hillside. More significantly, the finding in different parts of the country of identifiable stone axes gives a clear
indication of trade-routes and lines of communication within
Britain. The axe-factories at Great Langdale in the Lake District,
Westmorland, and at Graig Lwyd in Caernarvonshire, north
Wales, are two of the best-known ones, and in several other cases
the rock sources used have been identified by petrology at least
in terms of their general area. Such rock sources existed in various
parts of Britain including Cornwall, Shropshire, south Wales and
northern Ireland, though not all of them had come into use before

80
Chambered
megalithic tomb,
simply constructed
of orthostats
and a capstone:
the gallery grave of
La Pierre Couverte,
Duneau, Sarthe,
France

the end of the Neolithic Period; some began to be exploited during the earlier part of the Bronze Age for the making of maceheads, axe-hammers and battleaxes, all with shaft-holes.

Upon the general picture of Neolithic settlement in Europe, especially in western and northern Europe, there is superimposed another great spread, of a rather more subtle nature than the movements of the primary settlers. This is the diffusion of the practice of building megalithic monuments, especially tombs for collective burial. As the name suggests, megalithic monuments are structures built from large stones, in the case of the tombs typically with upright slabs (orthostats) forming the side walls, and capstones for roofing, though in certain cases a more sophisticated roofing technique is used, in the placing of smaller overlapping slabs to form a corbelled vault. The megalithic tombs were originally most often contained in an earth mound or a cairn, though in many cases this has since vanished. Apart from the megalithic tombs, there are single standing stones, and stone circles or grouped settings of standing stones, which in their most complicated forms can properly be regarded as temples: these, however, in western Europe, are by no means confined to the Neolithic Period, and it would of course be quite wrong to think of 'megaliths' as a single unified phenomenon. Earthwork monuments, too, sometimes incorporate megalithic structures of one kind or another, as in the case of the great site at Avebury, Wiltshire.[16] 90

If the temple structures are mainly later, the megalithic tombs of western Europe certainly begin well back in the Neolithic period. The simplest essential typological division of them is into 'passage' and 'gallery' graves; in the former case, a passage of megalithic construction leads to a burial chamber often deep 82 in the mound, while a gallery grave in its classic form consists of an elongated chamber which may be divided by transverse slabs into several burial compartments. Another form of gallery grave, which is closer in some respects to the passage graves, has burial chambers opening laterally off a passage, rather as transepts open off the nave of a cruciform church—this type (the 'transepted gallery grave') is well represented in Britain and

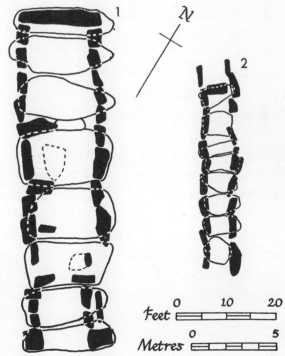

81
Megalithic gallery
grave plans:
1, Essé; 2, Tressé,
both in Ille-et-Vilaine,
Brittany

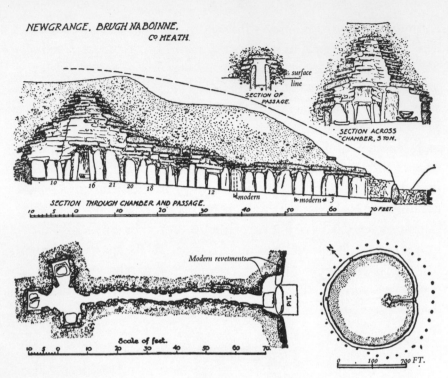

NEWGRANGE, BRUGH NA BOINNE.
C.º MEATH.

SECTION OF PASSAGE.

SECTION ACROSS CHAMBER, 5 TON.

SECTION THROUGH CHAMBER AND PASSAGE.

Modern revetments

Scale of feet.

82 Megalithic passage grave, plans and sections: New Grange, Co. Meath, Eire

France. There are, of course, many other sub-types of megalithic tomb.

As a generalisation, the tombs, which are used for collective burial, can best be regarded as family monuments, used and reused over a long period of time. It has often been suggested that their origin may lie in the east Mediterranean, where the practice of collective burial goes back far enough, although the tombs there are not properly megalithic, being built of dry stone walling, or else cut out of solid rock. If this were indeed the area of origin,[17] then the translation of the idea into megalithic terms should have taken place during the movement westwards through the Mediterranean of settlers, to whom the religion involved was a powerful enough impulse for the expenditure of vast amounts of labour and time in the erection of monuments whose stone elements on occasion have a total weight of some thousands of tons. Suitable prototypes for the European megalithic tombs are however hard to find anywhere, and the widespread distribution of megalithic monuments from the south of Spain to the Northern Isles of Scotland, and over parts of northern and much of north-western Europe, may owe much more to the spread of ideas, especially religious ideas, than to any large-scale movement of one particular people. The bare idea of incorporating large stones in the construction of tombs was probably invented more than once—certainly in northern Europe its first appearance may be a local invention rather than the result of intrusive influence.

Although this brief account of megalithic monuments appears in a chapter devoted to the Neolithic, it does so only because they first appear against a Neolithic background in north-western Europe. Their use and building continues much later, and indeed it has sometimes been argued that the spread of megalithic ideas owes much to the movements of prospectors searching for new sources of metal in the barbarian west—prospectors who had therefore themselves progressed beyond a Neolithic technological stage.

Many notable local concentrations of megalithic monuments exist, especially in western Europe, which there is no room to describe in detail, and their dating is of course not wholly within the Neolithic period. Three famous examples from Spain and Portugal are the cemeteries of megalithic tombs at Los Millares and Almizaraque in Almeria, and Alcalá in Algarve, at the first two of which contemporary town settlements are also known. In France there is a splendid concentration in the Morbihan area of Brittany, especially around Carnac. Other cemetery groups of

83 Decorated capstone in the north side-chamber at New Grange, Co. Meath, Eire, showing spirals, chevrons, 'oculi' and other typical motifs of megalithic art

different megalithic types exist in Ireland, the most famous being the group of fine passage graves in the Boyne river valley a little way north of Dublin, with the famous New Grange and Knowth tombs at its heart. In Britain, a rather more widely scattered group of gallery graves in south Wales and the English south-west Midlands has been given the name Severn–Cotswold Group; as in other cases, there is sub-grouping within this parent group. The Severn–Cotswold tombs quite often occur locally in pairs—

142

for example, the East and West Kennet chambered tombs near Marlborough in Wiltshire, or the Tinkinswood and St Lythans examples near Cardiff.

There are many other British groups, some of them smaller; another well defined large one is the Clyde–Carlingford series of south-west Scotland and the north of Ireland, probably closely related to the Severn–Cotswold Group. Much farther north, and omitting monuments of the intervening area, elaborate chambered tombs of different types are concentrated in the Scottish islands and northern mainland. This distribution makes it clear that some extraordinary sea voyages in light craft must have taken place.

Associated with the megalithic spread in the Mediterranean and western Europe, notably with the finest and largest passage graves, there is a characteristic tradition of art. Representations of a supposed Funerary Goddess or Mother Goddess, motifs including stylised eyes and eyebrows (*oculi* or 'Eye Goddess' motifs), and geometric patterns consisting of triangles, lozenges, chevrons and spirals, all occur, and are variously found both on portable objects like the decorated plaques of schist well known in Portugal and southern Spain, and also carved on the walls of the tombs themselves. Statue-stones with representatives of the 'goddess' figure also occur, notably in France, and motifs from megalithic art including *oculi* also find their way into pottery decoration in Spain, France and even northern Europe. There is one British example from a non-megalithic burial, in the well-known decorated drum-shaped objects from Folkton, Yorkshire. But in the British Isles the art is seen at its best in the Boyne passage graves in Ireland, especially at New Grange and Knowth. It normally takes the form of carvings on stones directly associated with the **83** structure of the tomb itself, or its immediately associated features —for example, the decorated kerb stones of some of the mounds in the Boyne Group.

While megalithic monuments are among the most striking Neolithic structures which can be inspected today in Britain, there are monuments of a ritual or sacred nature which are often no longer visible on the ground, but which were evidently of considerable importance to their makers, who invested much labour in their construction. Among these, the two classes of widest occurrence are the 'cursus' and 'henge' monuments,[18] which are best known from aerial photography and reconnaissance: in their original form, they were monuments dug into the ground, and in the course of time their pits and ditches have usually filled up, and any small banks that belonged to them have become levelled.

A cursus is a structure consisting of two parallel ditches, which may run for as much as several miles across country, usually quite straight. Cursus monuments are sometimes clearly associated with long barrows, and their purpose is assumed to be religious, but it is in fact utterly unknown.

84 Air photograph of crop-marks near Crowmarsh, Oxon., including a Neolithic 'cursus' monument (bottom, centre). Various ring-ditch monuments also appear in the photograph. The cursus is some 800 feet long and 36 feet broad.

Henge monuments have a considerable variety of forms, among which the essential features include a circular bank and a ditch (usually internal), with one or more entrances, and circles of pits or settings of timber posts or stones. This class of monument most often belongs to the later Neolithic Period, frequently as a feature of the Secondary Neolithic cultures, while the more complex examples may be of later date, including the developed phases of Stonehenge itself.[19] Stonehenge is a multi-period monument, and the earliest version of it was very different from the final temple which survives, though much damaged, today; the first Stonehenge had no stones at all, and was a simple Neolithic henge monument with bank and ditch and a circle of pits, many of which contained cremated human bones—a feature known from a few other Neolithic henges, though by no means a common occurrence at such sites. Other important Neolithic henge monuments have been excavated near Dorchester-on-Thames, Oxfordshire, and, more recently, in the Welland valley near Maxey (Northants), at Llandegai (Caernarvonshire) and at Durrington Walls (Wiltshire).[20]

It is not possible to bring this chapter on the Neolithic Period to a close by drawing a sharp dividing line, and saying that here metal was introduced and the Stone Age finally ended. That such rigid divisions exist between successive periods is the very last impression it was intended to convey by the adoption of such conventional and generalised chapter-headings. The use of metal, like the techniques of farming and pottery making, spread erratically to many different areas at many different dates, and, as will be seen in the next chapter, it was not bronze but copper which was the first metal to be used, although in the old expanded Three Age System, the Bronze Age is supposed directly to succeed the Neolithic or New Stone Age. The above outline sketch of the Neolithic Period is aimed only at describing some of the main features which fit into that general stage of the prehistoric sequence which is associated with the emergence of the new, settled, food-producing way of life. If chronology and the order of events are often provisional, and the picture is sometimes blurred, it is because this account is written too soon after the invigorating impact of the recently discovered scientific techniques of calculating dates,[21] and of studying environmental archaeology and related fields in several new ways. New information is still pouring in, and many long-established notions are in process of being replaced. The archaeology of the Neolithic Period in the late 1960s is in a state of healthy and dynamic development.

NOTES

1. The traits which can properly be held to constitute 'civilisation' were an important theme in the writings of the late Professor V. G. Childe: cf. for example Childe, 1951a.

2. Useful distribution maps to illustrate these animal and cereal distributions will be found in Piggott, 1965, Figs 8–9, or in Cole, 1961, Figs 3–4. The former work, especially, quotes further references. For animal domestication, see also Zeuner, 1963.

3. A major work on the Jericho excavations, consisting of several volumes, is in preparation, but so much specialist study of the enormous quantity of finds remains to be done that it will be some while before the earlier levels of the site are fully published. See, however, Dr Kathleen Kenyon's various reports in the journal, *Palestine Exploration Quarterly*, 1952–8, and her books (Kenyon, 1957 and 1965).

4. An excellent fairly recent source book for the general period covered in this chapter is Piggott, 1965, already referred to in n. 2 to this chapter; see especially his Ch. 2. While Piggott's text is comparatively short, and to some extent selective, he also gives extremely valuable notes and up-to-date references which will provide further reading on most of the sites mentioned here when no more specific sources are indicated. See also the relevant chapters of Clark, J. G. D. and Piggott, 1965, and for certain aspects, Clark, J. G. D., 1952.

5. The excavator of Çatal Hüyük, James Mellaart, has produced several interim reports on the site in the journal *Anatolian Studies*, from 1962 (vol. XII) onwards. See also Mellaart, 1967.

6. An interesting analysis of the spread of the early Neolithic peoples, with radiocarbon dates, is contained in a paper by Professor J. G. D. Clark, which is recent enough to remain very useful (Clark, J. G. D., 1965).

7. Apart from other sources already quoted, or mentioned later, an important work of reference for Jarmo and other early sites is Braidwood, Howe *et al.*, 1960. For Hacilar, see especially the four annual interim reports on the excavations, by James Mellaart, published in *Anatolian Studies*, vols VIII–XI (1958–61). A book of wider scope by the same author (Mellaart, 1965) is also a useful source for further reading on much of the ground covered in the first part of this chapter.

8. See, for example, Professor V. G. Childe's *New Light on the Most Ancient East*; the edition with the latest corrections is Childe, 1952, but it should be remembered that this book was written before the full impact of radiocarbon dating. Much information can also be gained from the appropriate parts of Braidwood and Willey, eds, 1962, and from Piggott, ed, 1961, a large and well-illustrated volume. For India, an inexpensive source is Piggott, 1961; for the Hittites, see Gurney, 1952.

9. Apart from the sources already recommended for this chapter, the reader should consult three books by Professor V. G. Childe (Childe, 1929, 1957 and 1958), and also Hawkes, 1940, but in matters of interpretation and especially of absolute chronology, the works of more recent date than these should usually be followed. Numerous individual volumes in the Thames & Hudson series *Ancient Peoples and Places* (general editor, Dr Glyn Daniel) are also excellent sources of further information about individual areas within Europe (and, indeed, farther afield), e.g. those on Denmark, Finland, Norway, Sweden, Poland, Czechoslovakia, Romania, the Low Countries, etc. Naturally, very many of the most important accounts of specific sites and subjects on the Continent are published in foreign monographs or journals—e.g. the important description of Linearbandkeramik settlements in the Netherlands, in German, in vols 6–7 (1958–9) of *Palaeohistoria* published by the Biologisch-Archaeologisch Instituut der Rijksuniversiteit, Groningen. Such references are given here only in exceptional cases, but can usually be obtained from the bibliographies in the works in English quoted, like Piggott, 1965.

10. Among the earliest British radiocarbon dates are three readings obtained from charcoal from the 'causewayed camp' site at Hembury, Devon: the latest values for these are 3303 B.C. ±150 years, 3395 B.C. ±150 years and 3488 B.C.

±150 years. A sample from the Fussell's Lodge long barrow gave 3230 B.C. ±180 years, but this is subject to a certain revision upwards following recent work on the radiocarbon dating method in general. There are several dates well into the mid-fourth millennium B.C: for traces of Neolithic activity in Ireland. See also Clark, J. G. D., and Godwin, 1962.

11. Major excavations were carried out at Windmill Hill by Alexander Keiller, up to the beginning of the Second World War, but he died without publishing the results. A full report on the excavations and finds has now been produced (Smith, I. F., ed., 1965). The main source book for the British Neolithic Period in general has long been Piggott, 1954, but some of the chronological interpretations in this work have been shown by radiocarbon dating to be seriously wrong, and a new up-to-date textbook is a pressing need.

12. A readily accessible brief account occurs in Clarke, R. R., 1960; see pp. 51–4, etc., and plates 6–9. Much of the early literature on Grimes Graves is out of date and misleading in many respects.

13. Almost any local archaeological handbook covering an area of lowland Britain will give other examples; see also Grinsell, 1953. For recent excavation reports on long barrows see, for example, Manby, 1963, Morgan, 1959, Ashbee, 1958 and 1966.

14. Fully described by Professor V. G. Childe, in an admittedly somewhat out-of-date work (Childe, 1931). Most of the important details will also be found in Piggott, 1954, Ch. 10.

15. See Evens *et al.*, 1962 and references quoted there. For a report on the discovery of one of the axe factory sites, that at Great Langdale, see Bunch and Fell, 1949.

16. The most readily accessible special reference for the megaliths in general, as referred to in this and subsequent paragraphs, is Daniel, 1958. See also Ó Ríordáin and Daniel, 1964, Ch. 5; cf. also more recent relevant comments by Dr Daniel in Daniel, 1967b. For the French megalithic tombs, see Daniel, 1960. For the British material, see Daniel, 1950b and Henshall, 1963. For Avebury, see Smith, I. F., ed., 1965.

The New Grange tomb itself (referred to later in this chapter), is of course fully described by Ó Ríordáin and Daniel in the first part of their book, with excellent illustrations, though further work has been carried out at the site since their account was written, and important new finds, not yet fully published, have also been made at another of the Boyne tombs, Knowth. (See Eogan, 1967, a note with some fine illustrations, and 1968, also well illustrated.) Ó Ríordáin and Daniel also include a useful study of megalithic art, with particular reference to the Irish examples. For a recent excavation report on an important megalithic tomb of the Severn–Cotswold Group (referred to later in the chapter) see Piggott, 1962.

17. In particular, the idea that the Iberian megalithic tombs and accompanying settlements were the work of 'colonists' from the east Mediterranean has been critically examined by Dr A. C. Renfrew (1967). Many useful references are quoted. Dr Renfrew suggests the alternative possibility 'that the Chalcolithic of Iberia developed locally, with the local invention of metallurgy and a minimum of outside influence'.

18. Both are discussed in Atkinson et al., 1951.

19. For an easily accessible account of Stonehenge, the reader cannot do better than refer to Atkinson, 1960. For the current controversy over the interpretation of the monument and its purpose, in which Professors Atkinson, Hawkins and Hoyle have joined, see various numbers of the quarterly journal *Antiquity* for 1966–7, vols XL–XLI, and also Hawkins, 1965.

20. For the Dorchester henge monuments, see Atkinson et al., 1951; the other three excavations are not yet fully published, and at Llandegai and Durrington Walls the digging was carried out only in 1967; see, however, Wainwright, 1968.

21. Not to mention the secondary disturbance caused by a recent wave of refinements to the radiocarbon dating method itself, and the discovery of certain inconsistencies in its results, which mean that many published dates need correction, while others are less reliable or less accurate than had been hoped (cf. pp. 234, 257 below).

5 The Bronze Age

Of all the period names in the expanded Three Age System, 'Bronze Age' may well be the one which retains least value for modern prehistorians, especially when it is a question of describing the very beginning or the very end of the period thus designated. The importance of this phase of prehistory is that it sees the spread of the techniques of early metallurgy, and subsequently of somewhat improved metallurgical processes, and the consequent flowering of richer prehistoric cultures than in any of the earlier periods.

This book is not closely concerned with those cultures and societies which, as briefly shown in the last chapter, were on the verge of attaining to literate civilisation even before the first farming influences had reached the western and northern extremes of Europe—or not, at any rate, with the later stages of their story. But their presence beyond the southern and eastern boundaries of prehistoric, barbarian Europe is extremely important as an ultimate source of inventions and technology whose spread provides the essence of the Bronze Age. The other way in which they are important is in the matter of trade and prospecting: a demand for bronze implements involves a demand at the very least for sources of two metallic ores, those of copper and tin. Certain areas of Europe were richly endowed with .such natural resources, as indeed also with supplies of gold and amber, two other materials particularly attractive to the civilised societies.

Possession of the eagerly sought raw materials had two effects for barbarian Europe. First, it attracted from outside prospectors who were themselves familiar with more advanced techniques or cultural traits, some of which they passed on to prehistoric communities in Europe, along with actual exotic traded objects. Secondly, it set up subsidiary trading movements within Europe, as a result of which vigorous prehistoric cultures flourished in their own right by acting as 'middlemen' in the trade to the civilised societies. Such a culture was the Wessex Culture[1] of the earlier British Bronze Age, dominated by warrior-chiefs who organised to their own benefit the working of tin and copper and gold, much of which they passed on to be traded as far afield as central Europe and even Mycenaean Greece. It is possible that the chieftains of this Wessex Culture themselves moved into Britain from continental Europe specifically to organise this exploitation of British mineral resources. Their presence affects the whole nature of the British Bronze Age.

The Bronze Age in general is thus a period which sees a continual circulation of ideas and a certain amount of movement of peoples. The interplay between the civilised powers and their barbarian neighbours is fascinating and important, but so far as the remoter parts of Europe are concerned, and this would include Britain, the relationship is generally very indirect.[2]

The actual nature of copper and bronze as raw materials is important, as well as the question of who were the first users of them, and how the knowledge of early metallurgy came to

Europe.[3] It was mentioned at the close of the last chapter that, in spite of the name 'Bronze Age', the first metal to be used was copper.

Copper can occur naturally, in the form known as 'native copper', in a state permitting cold hammering into shape to make rough tools or such objects as beads for a necklace, although this does not really constitute metallurgy. Examples of such a use of native copper are sometimes of considerable antiquity—for instance, it has been noted in the Early Neolithic levels of Çatal Hüyük (see page 117), dating from perhaps even the late seventh millennium B.C.

Later, it was found that native copper could be melted and poured into a mould to achieve a wide range of shapes. But for copper to be produced from the ores in which it usually occurs, for casting into tools, requires a more intimate knowledge of its properties, and at least a simple process of smelting—that is, of extracting the metal from the ore by heating it under the right conditions. The actual casting of implements from the molten metal also naturally presents its own technical problems.

Now when pure copper is used for the manufacture of implements, the result is a metal not particularly easy to cast, especially in a closed mould; it was the presence of low percentages of other elements such as arsenic in the copper produced by prehistoric man which gave a more satisfactory product. These other elements can occur naturally in the ores as impurities, and the control of them in the smelting process, or the subsequent addition of them, was also something that had to be learnt.

Bronze, on the other hand, is a deliberate mixture of metals. In general terms, it is produced by the addition to copper of a quantity of tin, which for the best results should be of the order of ten per cent, though there is a considerable variation in the tin content of such prehistoric bronze artifacts as have been analysed. The result of the copper–tin alloy was a fine, tough metal, well able to hold a hard, sharp cutting edge, and easy to cast. From this point of view, the introduction of bronze-working is certainly a step forward from the making of copper implements only.

The techniques of metallurgy, as opposed to the simple use of native copper, are seen in Mesopotamia at the Ubaid stage of the sequence of cultures developing towards the Sumerian civilisation (see page 119)—that is to say, copper was being properly smelted in Mesopotamia at least from the earlier part of the fourth millennium B.C. while to the west, in Anatolia, evidence of copper smelting has been found at Çatal Hüyük dating even from the beginning of the sixth millennium.

It is thus from the eastern end of the Mediterranean that the first metal-seeking prospectors and traders eventually entered Europe, reaching the copper-bearing areas of the Balkan, Carpathian and Slovakian mountains probably about 3000 B.C. It has also been maintained, as noted in the last chapter, that others passed by sea routes along the Mediterranean to southern Iberia at about the same time, or perhaps a few centuries later—the supposed colonist builders of the settlements and passage grave cemeteries such as Los Millares. That these people really were direct colonists from the east Mediterranean seems hard to prove, however (cf. pages 140–1 and note 17 on page 149).

Such, then, were the earliest intrusions into Europe of metal-workers or metal-seekers from the east, during what from the point of view of the receiving areas was still a Neolithic phase. But there are other incursions of slightly later date, which were also to contribute notably to various aspects of the European Bronze Age. Immigrants can be detected from the middle centuries of the third millennium B.C. onwards, who come from a different source: southern Russia.

85 Shaft hole axes of the Battle Axe or Corded Ware Culture from Denmark (exact find-spots not recorded). Length of axe farthest from camera, 18·4 cm. Pitt Rivers Museum, Oxford.

Space does not permit any discussion of the preceding archaeological sequence in that area, but the peoples who now began to make their way into Europe seem to have been warriors rather than traders and prospectors. The archaeological record suggests that there were various different but related arrivals, and in all cases some acquaintance with metal work seems already present. To eastern Europe came people who buried their dead singly under barrows or tumulus mounds, of which one at Hamangia in Romania dates from rather before 2500 B.C.[4] In central Europe and over almost all the north European plain, as far west as the Netherlands and as far north as Denmark and southern Scandinavia, there are found traces of other immigrants who have become known as the Battle-Axe or Corded Ware folk. They too buried their dead in single graves, often under barrows, and the most typical objects of their material culture are their pottery vessels with decoration made by impressing lengths of twisted cord into the clay before firing, and also their finely made ground or polished stone battle-axes, which were perforated by drilling **85** to take a wooden handle. It was customary for these axes to be buried with the dead, presumably as weapons befitting warriors on their arrival in the next world. These Corded Ware or Battle-Axe people seem to assume dominance over a large area, which they would have found occupied by the descendants of various different early Neolithic farming settlers.

Yet more intrusive peoples of a broadly similar date can be recognised, in east central Europe: the bearers of the Baden Culture of Austria, Hungary and Czechoslovakia. While their culture has at least some local roots, various features of their pottery and their implements and ornaments of copper show signs of a south-easterly origin, perhaps in part from Anatolia. In the Baden Culture, four-wheeled waggons appear for the first time in Europe; some attractive pottery models of them have **87** been found. Two-wheeled vehicles, probably ox-drawn carts, were also in use further north at about the same date, and several

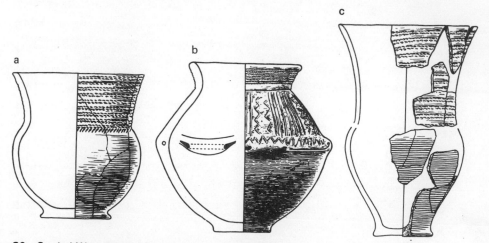

86 Corded Ware pottery from Drenthe, Netherlands:
a, Hankenberg, near Emmen; *b*, Schipborg; *c*, Hees, near Ruinen. Scale: × *c.* ¼

87
Pottery model of a
four-wheeled waggon,
Budakalàsz, Kom. Pest,
Hungary (Baden Culture).
Height 8·1 cm. Scale: $\times \frac{7}{10}$.
Szentendre Museum.

examples of their solid, disc-like timber wheels have come from
north Holland, being dated to around 2000 B.C. These two-
wheeled carts may well be associated with the Corded Ware
peoples. The invention of the wheel itself may have taken place
in Mesopotamia during the fourth millennium B.C.[5]

These then are some of the main primary movements of
people during the third millennium B.C. which between them
were to help initiate the Bronze Age of prehistoric Europe, with
a preceding copper-using phase in many areas. But the picture is
more complicated than this brief enumeration of a number of
primary migrations may suggest, and there are secondary currents
of movement to consider, whose practical effect was undoubtedly
greater.

The most striking of these is the phenomenon of the Beaker
Culture, though 'culture' is perhaps too simple a name for the
sum total of several related wide-ranging movements and a
variety of local developments. The Beaker folk stand at the very
threshold of the Bronze Age in western Europe, or some would
place them at the very close of the Neolithic Period; and they
were among the first bringers of metal-working to the British

Isles, among other parts of Atlantic Europe. They take their name from the standardised class of attractively decorated and usually well-fired pottery drinking vessels which are everywhere associated with their burials, and it is also clear from their other 88, 89 artifacts that they were bowmen, and workers of some skill in copper and even gold. Their flint-work too, with arrow-heads and flat knives and daggers, was of high quality, and so was their working of pieces of bone or jet into such objects as buttons or beads, the latter being occasionally made up into necklaces.

Apart from the evidence of the arrow-heads, their use of archery is attested by the presence in Beaker graves of perforated stone wrist-guards of the kind a bowman straps to his wrist to protect it against the recoil of the bow-string. The distribution of Beaker finds also makes it clear that the Beaker people were adventurous navigators, as well as travellers overland; they crossed the Bay of Biscay, the North Sea, the Irish Sea and the English Channel, and sailed between Sicily and Sardinia as well as making various coastal voyages.

88 Three Beaker grave groups, left to right:
  Radley, Berks., beaker with three barbed and tanged arrowheads of flint and a pair of gold basket-shaped ear-rings;
  Dorchester, Oxon., beaker with archer's wrist-guard of slate, tanged copper knife and riveted knife;
  Stanton Harcourt, Oxon., beaker with flint flake and bone 'polisher'.
  Height of the Dorchester beaker, 8·6 inches. Ashmolean Museum, Oxford.

89
Beaker burial at
Crichel Down, Dorset
(Barrow 14), as excavated.
The skeleton is crouched,
and the damaged beaker is
seen below the flexed legs.

Although the origins of the Beaker folk are not fully understood, the most frequently found explanation is that they first
emerged from a local Neolithic population in Spain, gaining
some knowledge of copper-working from the metal-seeking
colonists there of ultimately east Mediterranean origin.[6] From
Spain, they spread widely and rapidly in a series of primary and
secondary movements which eventually covered much of Europe
—as far east as Poland, as far south as Sicily, and as far north and
west as Scotland and Ireland. They came into contact with the
Battle-Axe cultures just described, and the decorative styles of
Beaker pottery accordingly became influenced by Corded Ware
traditions; so too battle axes occasionally accompany Beaker
burials, which also sometimes follow the Battle-Axe people's

tradition of single graves under large and prominent round barrows.

The Beaker penetration of Britain seems to be relatively late;[7] the Beaker phenomenon as a whole may begin in Spain scarcely earlier than 2300 B.C., and it is doubtful whether it lasted anywhere for long after 1700 B.C. British Beakers were originally grouped into three main types named A, B and C, according to differences mainly of shape and decoration, and these classes had further subdivisions. In the most general terms, it is now realised that contrary to earlier ideas type B is the first to arrive—the classic, bell-shaped Beaker of flowing, curved outline, with decoration in horizontal bands. The short-necked Beakers of class C clearly represent a penetration of north Britain, especially eastern Scotland, from the Netherlands, and the long-necked Beakers of class A may well be a purely British local development from class C.

In Britain it is clear that Beaker pottery is often contemporary with that belonging to the Secondary Neolithic cultures, and it is sometimes found in association with the henge monuments briefly mentioned at the close of the last chapter. The first phase of stone-erection at Stonehenge is also attributed to the Beaker folk, and this involved the famous transporting of the bluestones, which are of considerable size, from the Preseli mountains in south Wales to Wiltshire. Other British henges and stone circles are attributable to the Beaker people, including **90** the huge ceremonial monument at Avebury.

The Beaker folk in Britain are known to have made copper daggers and a small number of gold objects, including on occasion **88** earrings of basket-like shape. They were perhaps the first users of the rich metal resources of Ireland. Their contact with the Secondary Neolithic peoples seems to provide an influence on some subsequent pottery styles of the British Bronze Age; an example of this is to be seen in the so-called 'food vessels', which appear at the close of Beaker times. These are widely distributed over Britain and often accompany single-grave burials in the Beaker or Battle Axe manner, though the 'food vessel' pottery seems to continue after the close of the Beaker period in Britain. It is also not.hard to pick out details in the succeeding Bronze Age pottery which can reasonably be traced back to a Secondary Neolithic and Beaker ancestry.[8]

But before any description of the post-Beaker period sequence in Britain or continental Europe, it is necessary to return to the far south-east. Here is to be seen perhaps the most powerful source of all, so far as north-west Europe was concerned, of prospectors and traders and the ideas they brought. This source is the first development of literate civilisation in Europe itself, namely the Minoan civilisation of the island of Crete,[9] and also the Mycenaean civilisation of mainland Greece.[10]

Crete, like the adjacent islands of the Aegean Sea, was geographically extremely well placed to receive vigorous Neolithic

90 Aerial photograph of the great henge monument at Avebury, Wilts.

and later influences originating in a number of areas on or beyond the east Mediterranean coast. Mention was made in the last chapter, for example, of the early Neolithic level dating from about 6000 B.C. at the base of the sequence at Knossos itself (see page 121). There is also clear evidence for Cretan trade with another important area to the south, namely Egypt.

The stages grouped under the name of Early Minoan belong to the third millennium B.C., and by the end of Middle Minoan and during Late Minoan times, a distinctive civilisation emerged, fully cognisant of the techniques of metal-working, and using the script known as Linear A (still untranslated). The rulers dwelt in such palaces as the famous one at Knossos, and their craftsmen drew upon a lively tradition of naturalistic art to decorate the many fine objects they made. Minoan power was at its height in the sixteenth and fifteenth centuries B.C., but in the fourteenth century it declined, while Mycenaean power flourished, and the Minoan civilisation became absorbed into the Mycenaean dominance of the Aegean.

This Mycenaean civilisation, based at first on the Greek mainland, has much in common with that of the Minoans, and must have received much influence from them; its geographical position must again have been a primary cause of the underlying rapid cultural growth. Literacy, however, was not achieved so early as in Crete, and the Mycenaean Linear B script seems in fact to be derived from the Cretan one.[11] But the make-up of Mycenaean civilisation also appears to contain a foreign contribution of rather uncertain origin: some have suggested influences ultimately from south Russia, via Anatolia, and have quoted as an example one of the best-known features of Mycenae itself—the royal shaft graves, with their rich yield of gold and silver treasures. Structurally, these certainly seem to require origins somewhere other than in Crete, but prototypes of a suitable age are hard to find.

91

92

91 Clay tablets with Linear B writing from Knossos, Crete, early 14th century B.C. Scale: about × ⅓. Ashmolean Museum, Oxford.

In Greece, the Mycenaean civilisation began to reach its height in the sixteenth century B.C., and outlasted that of the Minoans, down to a little after 1200 B.C. Any examination of these two civilisations in detail would pass beyond the limits of prehistory, and it is their presence in an otherwise barbarian Europe that is the important thing in the present context, because their trade and their demand for raw materials—copper, tin, gold, silver and amber—had repercussions as far away as distant Britain. Mycenaean trading posts and small colonies were set up, not only in the east Mediterranean but also in the central Mediterranean, in southern Italy and Sicily, and actual traded objects, or signs of Mycenaean influence in decoration or the manufacture of weapons or ornaments, occur in north-west Europe, notably the British Isles, and also in central and eastern Europe. The commonest of the traded objects of east Mediterranean origin are beads of faience (an artificial glass-like substance), but occasionally metalwork, including rapiers or double axes, and also bone objects, of Mycenaean type occur.

162

At various points on these Mycenaean trade-routes, rich local Bronze Age cultures developed, and local metal-working flourished. In central Europe, a vigorous Bronze Age had already begun a few centuries before Mycenaean times, based on the rich metalliferous deposits of the Carpathians, central Germany, and to some extent the Alps. There are numerous regional cultures, the most notable being that called after Únětice, a cemetery site near Prague. Tumulus burial is a recurrent feature, with a number of rich and elaborate barrow-burials evidently of members of the local aristocracy. These cultures came to have trading relations of their own with north-west Europe, notably Denmark and Britain, in respect of the trade both in metals and also in amber. The amber trade is especially complex, since it seems that amber of Danish origin sometimes passed first to Britain, where it was manufactured into beads, some of which **93**

92 Mycenae, Greece, showing grave circle with shaft graves in the foreground. The double circle of upright slabs enclosed a roughly circular area, diameter about 27·5 metres, in which the shaft graves were dug.

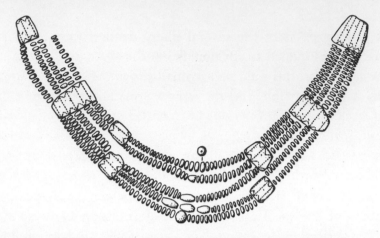

93 Amber necklace of beads and spacer plates, from barrow at Upton Lovell, Wilts. Scale: × ¼. Devizes Museum, Wilts.

reached Mycenae either via the Mediterranean trading posts, or else via central Europe—probably both routes were in use.

In Denmark, too, a thriving local Bronze Age sprang up, initially based on imported metal objects, but afterwards certainly on fine local craftsmanship. Many superb objects of bronze and gold distinguish all phases of the Danish and Scandinavian Bronze Age, while numerous rich barrow burials again suggest the presence of a ruling aristocracy.[12]

The Wessex Culture of southern Britain, also of this date, has already been referred to. It existed at the British end of the long trade routes, and therefore has contacts with Denmark and central Europe, and with the Mycenaean trading outposts, even if not directly with Mycenae itself. The culture is known from the rich round-barrow burials of warrior-chieftains, mainly on the Wessex chalk-land, notably in Wiltshire, but with some outlying examples. The grave-goods usually found include elegantly shaped stone battle-axes, metal daggers whose wooden handles sometimes had decorative motifs executed in gold, and precious ornamental objects often of gold or amber.

96

164

As just two out of the several likely examples of ultimately Mycenaean influence in Britain from the Wessex graves, one may cite the famous gold cup from Rillaton, Cornwall, with its corrugated decoration, and the almost equally well-known supposed ceremonial staff with ornamental bone mounts from the Bush Barrow grave-group in Wiltshire.[13] To the Wessex Culture is also attributed the final and most elaborate arrangement of the sarsen stones and bluestones at Stonehenge—that version of the monument's long history, in fact, which survives in fragmentary form today. Here too, Mycenaean influence has been claimed, both in a carved representation of a dagger thought to be of Mycenaean type, which appears on one of the huge sarsen orthostats, and also in a certain sophistication of technique in the actual shaping of the stones, not to mention the whole architecture of the temple, which is felt to be beyond the scope of the local barbarian Bronze Age population, whereas parallels for some of the technical devices can be found in actual Mycenaean buildings. The transporting from perhaps as far away as thirty miles of the huge Stonehenge sarsens, and their erection, incidentally imply the existence of large organised labour forces, and this casts an interesting light on the status and power of the Wessex chieftains.

96

95

94
Gold cup with corrugated decoration, Rillaton, Cornwall. Height about 3¼ inches. British Museum.

The Wessex Culture must have lasted for about two centuries, and probably dates from about 1600 to 1400 B.C., during which time two phases are recognisable archaeologically. The barrows of the earlier phase usually contain inhumation burials, and those of the later one cremations, the cremated bones often being deposited in an urn, and being generally speaking accompanied by less rich grave goods than those of the first phase. The Wessex metal dagger types can also be used to distinguish the two phases;[14] in the typology of these daggers, and also of the ornamental metal pins which are sometimes found, it is the Wessex contacts with Únětice and other central European cultures that seem to be important, and it is probably from somewhere within that area,

95 Objects from the famous Wessex grave group from Bush Barrow, Wilsford, Wilts.: copper dagger (top right), bronze dagger (next to it), both with traces of scabbards adhering; polished perforated macehead of limestone, and bone ferrules and mounts, shown as a 'sceptre' on a modern wooden shaft made to fit them; flanged axe; large lozenge-shaped plate of sheet gold (bottom left), small lozenge-shaped plate of sheet gold, and belt-hook of hammered gold. All three gold objects have incised decoration. The bronze dagger is 32·7 cm. long. Devizes Museum, Wilts., and British Museum.

96 Stonehenge, Wilts., from the air—a photograph taken before
the restoration work of 1958. A fine round barrow can be seen
close to the road in the middle distance.

but perhaps also from Brittany, that some of the warrior chieftains themselves came to southern England. However, some of
the pottery of the Wessex Culture, including the 'collared'
burial urns (so called from their heavy overhanging rims), clearly
has its ancestry in the native Secondary Neolithic wares of Britain,
with a certain amount of Beaker influence. Apart from the urns,
attractive miniature pottery vessels sometimes accompany Wessex
burials, usually those of women.

The Wessex Culture is the most spectacular element of the
British Early Bronze Age proper, if the Beaker phase is regarded
as final Neolithic and transitional. The succeeding Middle Bronze

167

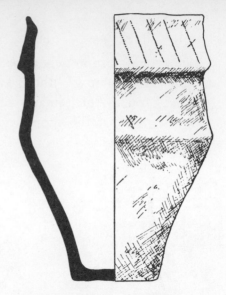

97 Middle Bronze Age urn, inverted over cremated bones of a child, shown *in situ* during excavation of a barrow near Llandow, Glamorgan; see also Fig. 98

98 The urn from Llandow shown in Fig. 97. Height 25·8 cm. National Museum of Wales, Cardiff.

Age in Britain is rather harder to describe, because although a mass of material has been collected, especially metalwork, there is a scarcity of burials with grave-goods other than pottery, and of close dating evidence for those domestic sites which have been found. It is clear that the long-range trade declined, and the effective influences seem now to come from north-west Europe mainly, while there is some movement of ideas from Britain across the English Channel and North Sea in return. The most commonly found pottery types are the large urns frequently used to contain cremated bones. These continue the collared series already encountered in the Wessex Culture, but with certain differences of shape and decoration, and now with some evidence for regional styles.[15]

The Middle Bronze Age in southern Britain includes a number of local traditions, to several of which the collective culture name of Deverel-Rimbury (after two Dorset sites, a barrow and a cemetery) has been loosely applied. A number of earthworks and settlements are known, though their precise dating within the Middle Bronze Age remains rather obscure. The general impression given of the economy suggests farming, both stock-raising and agriculture, on a somewhat larger scale than before. Such farming settlements occur for example at Itford Hill (Sussex), Thorny Down (Wiltshire) and Gwithian (Cornwall).[16] Field systems can be traced, suggesting the use of some light form of plough or ard, and earthworks forming cattle pounds and droveways have been claimed. Traces of light cross-ploughing can in fact be seen rather earlier also at Gwithian, dating from perhaps even the very beginning of the Bronze Age: actual plough marks were found here, and they have been recognised on a number of occasions elsewhere, preserved on old land-surfaces over which barrows have been raised.

Further light can be cast on the Middle Bronze Age in Britain by a study of the bronze implements. Several tool classes fortunately offer quite a helpful series: the typology of the axes is an example. The earliest metal axes in Britain were flat ones of copper;[17] an advance made during Wessex times was the production by hammering or casting of flanges along the sides of the tools, which were now of bronze, to assist hafting. The Middle Bronze Age, however, sees the introduction of various bronze axe types, notably a further improved form, the palstave. Palstaves are of rather narrower shape than the flat axes which preceded them, and the developments designed to facilitate hafting include the enlargement of the side flanges, the provision of a transverse stop-ridge, and sometimes the addition of a cast loop to which a thong could be attached, perhaps further to anchor the axe to its wooden handle. Another Middle Bronze Age axe type is the 'wing-flanged' axe, in which the side-flanges are exaggerated and bent round to overlap the haft.

99

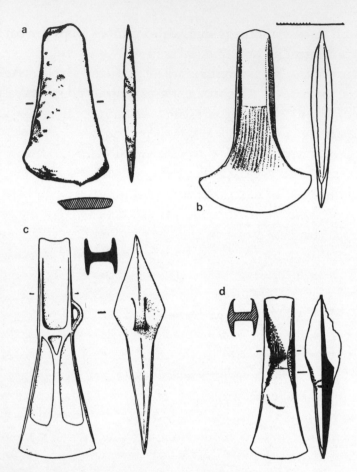

99 Metal axe types, final Neolithic, Early and Middle Bronze Age.
All those figured are of bronze. Scale: × ⅓.

a. flat axe, Migdale, Sutherland
b. axe with stop ridge and raised side flanges,
   Westbury-on-Trym, Glos.
c. palstave, with loop for thong attachment,
   Wilton, Wilts.
d. wing-flanged axe, Trillick, Co. Tyrone.

100 Other Middle Bronze Age metal types include rapiers, which, as thrusting weapons, were a considerable improvement on the Wessex daggers, the first slashing swords with long cutting edges at the sides of the blade, and spearheads, hafted by means of a socket and usually also provided with a pair of loops for cord or thong attachment as well.

For the key to an understanding of the Late Bronze Age in Britain, it is necessary to return again to central and south-eastern Europe. At a date not far removed from 1200 B.C., the great Mycenaean civilisation seems to have met a violent end at the hands of barbarian people; these may have been in part, if not all, recruited from the European barbarian Bronze Age cultures, although it is not clear who their leaders were. The cessation of Mycenaean demand released all the metal supplies of central Europe for local and north-west European use.

In central Europe, bronze working had been thriving for several centuries, but a period of innovation now ensues. Certain advanced metallurgical techniques are introduced, and this may imply the arrival of new peoples. The immigrants might have

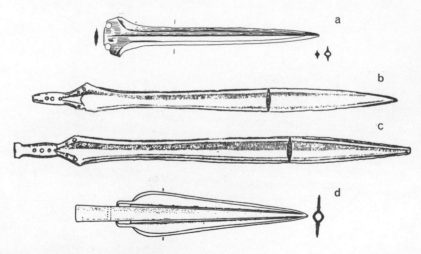

100 Middle Bronze Age weapons. Scale: × $\frac{1}{7}$.
    a. rapier, Wilsford Down, Wilts.
    b. sword, Cwm-du, Brecon
    c. sword, Penrhyndeudraeth, Merioneth
    d. spearhead with basal loops, Tempo, Co. Fermanagh.

171

a

101 Late Urnfield settlement at Biskupin, Poland:
  a. General view of part of the timber-built settlement, showing streets and buildings, taken from a captive balloon during the excavations of 1934–8
  b. Detail of a street and the lower parts of adjacent buildings, from ground level
  c. Visitors admire a reconstructed part of the site, 1966.

b

amounted to no more than a few craftsmen, displaced in what was a period of general disturbance, and the destruction of higher civilised cultures. Apart from the Mycenaean empire, the civilisation of the Hittites in Anatolia had also been overthrown by barbarian invaders at about this time. Or the new knowledge could have been acquired by mercenary soldiers from central Europe, who were now returning to their homeland.

It is interesting, however, to see also at this time a general change of the burial rite in the central European Bronze Age. The rite of inhumation burial in tumulus mounds, first brought to this area by the Battle-Axe people, had become the general rule during Middle Bronze Age times, and indeed gave the name to the Tumulus Culture of this period. Now, however, there is a rather sudden spread of the use of flat cemeteries known as urnfields, for the burial in urns of the ashes from cremations which had taken place elsewhere. Outside western Hungary, where it had started considerably earlier, this practice is something fundamentally new in central Europe, and does not even compare with the kind of cremation when a barrow is raised actually over the site of a funeral pyre, which had been introduced in certain regions shortly before the spread of the Urnfield rite began. It is not clear how far the widespread adoption of the new rite is merely a change in fashion, and how far it may again suggest the arrival of new peoples.

An Urnfield Culture soon began to expand from central Europe, from towards the close of the second millennium B.C. onwards, and it is these movements which precipitated the final stages of the European Bronze Age. Apart from the cemeteries, various Urnfield settlement sites are known, often in the form of defended villages, like an island site called the Wasserburg, in the Federsee lake in south Germany. Biskupin, in Poland, which dates from the very end of Urnfield times, is another settlement

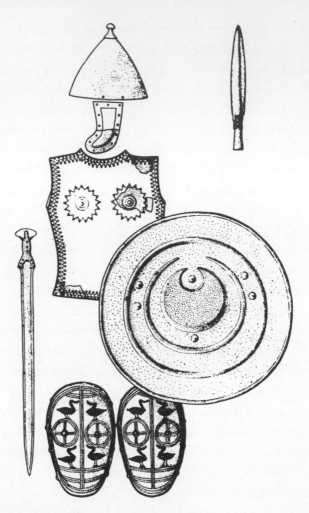

102 Late Bronze Age armour and weapons, central Europe. These pieces were not found together, but have been assembled from different graves and hoards to give an impression of what the full equipment of a warrior of the period must have been like. Some of the items are reconstructions, based on fragments found, e.g. the corselet; the greaves are shown as a pair, although only one was found. The objects are: bronze helmet, Gusterita, near Sibiu, Romania; bronze cheek-piece, Wöllersdorf, Lower Austria; bronze corselet, Čaka, Czechoslovakia; bronze spearhead, Gau-Algesheim, Bingen, Rheinland-Pfalz; bronze sword, Stätzling, Friedberg, Bavaria; greaves, Rinyaszentkirály, Kom. Somogny, Hungary; bronze shield, Pilsen (Plzn). Bohemia. Scale: × $\frac{1}{12}$.

174

with a lake to assist its defences; this time it is on a promontory, and the natural and artificial defences enclose a village or small town, carefully laid out in a most orderly manner.[18] **101**

Urnfield settlers leave clear traces in countries as far west as Spain, France and the Netherlands. How far the actual migration of Urnfield peoples affected Britain, if at all, is not clear, but something of their metal-working styles and techniques certainly reached the British Isles. Among these was a special skill in making thin sheets of bronze, by beating out the metal with periodic reheating. Such sheet bronze could be used for the manufacture of vessels or other objects like helmets and shields, which were **102** not so effectively made by a mere process of casting.

In Britain there are few actual sites or structures that can clearly be assigned to the Late Bronze Age, but there are very many **103** finds of bronze implements of late types, either singly or in hoards. Many British Bronze Age hoards are known: a number of them are of Middle Bronze Age date, but most are later. They are of various kinds: a votive hoard consists of a small quantity of fine bronze objects ritually or sacrificially deposited; a personal hoard involves the personal weapons, lost or hidden together, of a single individual; a merchant's hoard represents the abandoned stock-in-trade of a travelling seller of new, finished bronze implements; a founder's hoard, finally, represents a collection of scrap metal, usually with many worn-out and broken implements, gathered up evidently for melting down and recasting into new tools. There are British examples of all these types, with the last-named perhaps the most prolific. A comparatively recent find of a founder's hoard at Isleham in Cambridgeshire, for example, contained the best part of seven thousand broken implements or other fragments of bronze.[19]

There are many new types among the Late Bronze Age metal objects of Britain. Socketed axes are the commonest objects in **104a**

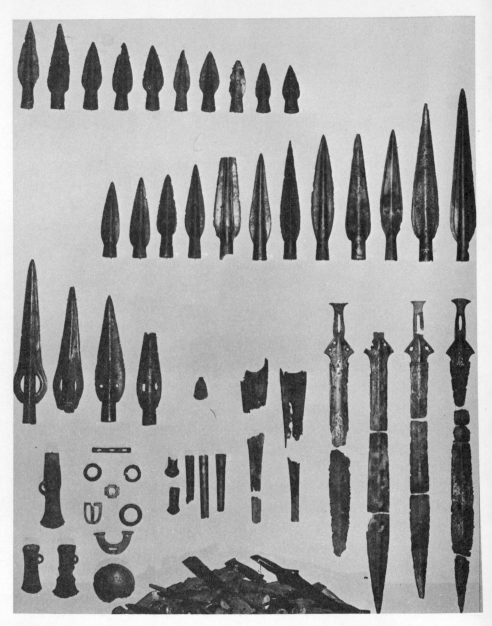

103 Bronze Age hoard from Wilburton, Cambs., consisting mainly of weapons, many of them worn or broken. University Museum of Archaeology and Ethnology, Cambridge.

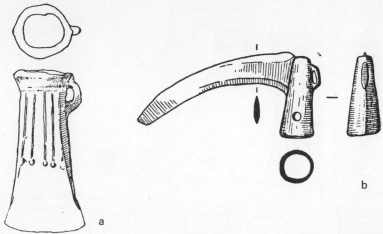

104 *a.* bronze socketed axe, Llynfawr, Glamorgan. National Museum of Wales, Cardiff.
b. bronze socketed sickle, Winterbourne Monkton, Wilts. Devizes Museum. Scale: × ⅓.

hoards of this date; this type, which was actually introduced before the end of the Middle Bronze Age, constitutes the final development after the earlier attempts to find the best method of hafting an axe. The hollow socket designed to receive the haft was achieved by casting the axe in a two-piece mould which contained a core, and a loop was still usually provided for the addition of a thong or cord attachment. Swords with broad cutting blades now come into widespread use, to the final exclusion of the Middle Bronze Age narrow, pointed thrusting rapiers, and this is a classic Late Bronze Age weapon type far beyond Britain. Light and heavy spearheads are found, while socketed gouges and chisels, and socketed reaping sickles, were also in use. There are items of horse harness, and belt-fastenings of various kinds.

The rarer and most costly objects, represented both in Britain and on the Continent, include bronze shields, large cauldrons made from riveted bronze sheets, and even a number of musical

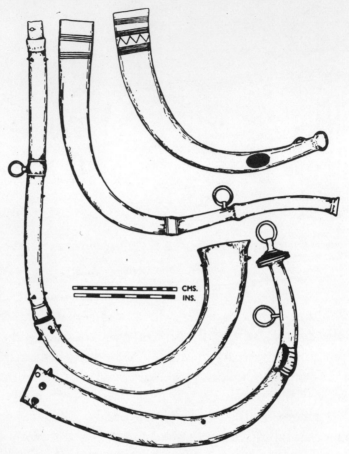

105 Horns of the later Bronze Age from Ireland:
1. Find-spot not known
2. Drumbest, Co. Antrim
3. Chute Hall. Co. Kerry
4. Derrynane, Co. Kerry
National Museum of Ireland, Dublin

instruments of horn type. About a hundred of the latter are known from Ireland, but they are simpler instruments than the beautiful and famous *lur* horns of Denmark, of which about fifty have been found.[20]

Apart from the bronze work, there is the gold. Especially in Ireland, the craft of the Bronze Age goldsmith flourished, and

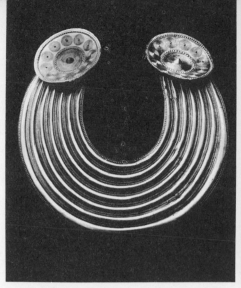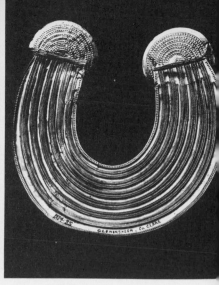

106 Irish Bronze Age gold work: both sides of gold gorget, Gleninsheen, Co. Clare. Width 30·5 cm. National Museum of Ireland, Dublin.

that country has produced a dazzling quantity of gold torcs, bracelets, crescent-shaped gorgets, and other personal jewellery, often finely decorated,[21] some of which can safely be given a Middle Bronze Age date, but much of which dates from the Late Bronze Age, a long-lasting period in Ireland. Similar objects have come from other parts of Britain, including a number from the East Anglian fens, but many must be imports of Irish manufacture. In Denmark, too, abundant finds of superb objects of gold have been made.

Yet for all the fine metal objects known, many aspects of the British Late Bronze Age remain obscure, with a sad lack of sites and even of burials, though for this latter deficiency some particular cremation rite might be partly to blame.

Long before the end of the Bronze Age in Britain, iron-working, occasionally used in the Near East even as early as the third millennium B.C., had spread to central Europe. In due course it would reach Britain, too; but the introduction of iron-working does not come as a great cultural break, or bring the beginning of a new epoch in anything but name. Yet its coming brings conveniently to a close this particular chapter of prehistory, the so-called Bronze Age, which has covered the turbulent period of the spread of the new techniques of early metallurgy, against a background of the rise and fall of the first European civilisations. The narrative has a continuous thread of far-flung trade, and wide-ranging movement of peoples. Nowhere was the sequence of events wholly peaceful; this asymmetrical pattern of strife, movement and conquest, but also of higher and higher technological and artistic achievement, was to endure for the remainder of prehistoric times, and indeed well into the historic period.

NOTES

1. The term 'Wessex Culture' will suffice for the present introductory account, but it is coming to be increasingly criticised by prehistorians, mainly on the grounds that the surviving material does not constitute a proper culture. After all, there is little evidence except a number of rich burials: domestic sites are lacking, and there is no proper typical range of pottery and artifacts, other than those of a ceremonial or funerary nature. Culture or no culture, however, the presence of a certain rich aristocratic element in southern Britain at this time can hardly be denied, and that is what is important in the present context. Further reference to the Wessex culture is made later in the chapter.

2. The general source books for the period covered by this chapter are much the same as those quoted for the last one (see notes 4, 8 and 9 to Ch. 4), including the appropriate chapters of Piggott, 1965, Clark, J. G. D. and Piggott, 1965, Childe, 1957 and 1958, Hawkes, 1940, Clark, J. G. D., 1952, and Piggott, ed., 1961, and appropriate volumes in the Thames & Hudson *Ancient Peoples and Places* series. To these may be added Fox, 1959.

It is worth stressing at the outset of this chapter that there are differing views on the precise nature of the main cultural events referred to in its first few pages —events which influenced the whole character of the European Bronze Age. Current views seem to regard the theories which involve actual invasions and migrations with much less favour than they enjoyed only a few years ago. No doubt in my present brief account I have allowed for too many arrivals of new peoples to satisfy many of the scholars of this period of prehistory, but it is a matter on which there is still no general agreement, and some movements of population must certainly have taken place. But the reader must always beware of the idea that changes, even major changes, in material culture in any archaeological sequence, at any period of prehistory, *necessarily* imply the arrival of new people in quantity: ideas can travel, and new artifacts and techniques can be introduced, by other media than invasions or mass migrations (cf. Clark, J. G. D., 1966). The trouble is that the identification of those media is often quite beyond the limits of inference from the available archaeological evidence: naturally, conflicting interpretations are put forward.

3. A useful book for further reading on this subject is Tylecote, 1962.

4. A monumental source book in English (Gimbutas, 1965) now exists for the central and east European sites and finds, of which the various previously published accounts had been mainly buried in what to British archaeologists are rather obscure and inaccessible foreign periodicals.

5. The prehistory of wheeled vehicles has been described by Professor V. G. Childe in Childe, 1951*b*; see also van der Waals, 1964.

6. Cf. for example Piggott, 1965, pp. 98–102. Useful references for further study are quoted here, but not all of them are in English or readily obtainable outside a specialist library.

7. See Piggott, 1963, and Clarke, D. L., 1962. A forthcoming book by Dr Clarke, based on his Cambridge University Ph.D. thesis, will no doubt become a standard work on British Beakers, and should also be consulted when available for information on the Beaker people in general, and their origins.

8. See Longworth, 1961.

9. An excellent and inexpensive book for further study is Hutchinson, 1962, and it has a very useful bibliography. See also Marinatos, 1960, with very fine photographs by M. Hirmer. The relevant parts of the *Cambridge Ancient History* should also be consulted, and certain sections have now been issued with recent revision as separate and inexpensive fascicles.

10. A readily accessible source book is Taylour, 1964, while a larger recent account is Mylonas, 1966. Marinatos, 1960, and the *Cambridge Ancient History*, as referred to in the last note, should also be consulted.

11. See Chadwick, 1961.

12. Some good illustrations and much information will be found in Klindt-Jensen, 1957.

13. The Rillaton cup is now in the British Museum. The various components of the supposed ceremonial staff from Bush Barrow are in Devizes Museum (Wiltshire); some doubt may be felt as to whether they really do belong together, and whether the staff interpretation is correct. Further illustrations of

the Rillaton cup and the Bush Barrow grave group will be found in Piggott, 1965, plate xviib and Fig. 68.

14. See ApSimon, 1954. More information on the Wessex Culture, and a collected bibliography for it, will be found in Paul Ashbee's *The Bronze Age Round Barrow in Britain* (Ashbee, 1960); this book is more wide ranging than its title might suggest, and includes a brief study of the British Bronze Age cultures with reference to their continental context.

15. See Longworth, 1961.

16. The main references to these three important British sites are as follows: Itford Hill: Burstow and Holleyman, 1957; Thorny Down: Stone, 1941; Gwithian: Thomas, 1958.

An account of the traces of early agriculture at Gwithian will be found in Megaw *et al.*, 1961.

17. The earliest metal work in Britain can be followed up in two important papers which themselves both contain further references: see Coghlan and Case, 1957, and Britton, 1963.

18. An account of Biskupin in English will be found in Kostrewski, 1938. The original account of the Wasserburg site is in German, and difficult to obtain, but various more general works offer a brief account and a plan of the site, e.g. Piggott, 1965, p. 147 and Figs 82–3, and Clark, 1952, p. 156 and Figs 83–4.

19. See Britton, 1960. The hoard is now in the Moyse's Hall Museum, Bury St Edmunds, Suffolk. Many museums have Bronze Age hoards on display— good examples of several kinds can be seen for example at the Cambridge University Museum of Archaeology and Ethnology.

20. See Coles, 1963.

21. A particularly fine collection of Irish Bronze Age gold-work is in the National Museum of Ireland at Dublin. A useful source of information on the later Bronze Age in Ireland is Eogan, 1964.

6 The Iron Age

By Iron Age here is meant the Pre-Roman Iron Age of Europe, since it is the spread of the Roman Empire which brings this short account of prehistory to a close, however incomplete it must thereby remain. The literate civilisation of Rome, for all its stranglehold on the ancient world, did not penetrate to every corner of even Europe: the legions never reached Scandinavia, or central Germany, or even the far west and north of the British Isles, although Britain was a Roman province. Thus certain areas even within Europe remained in a prehistoric phase right up to what was elsewhere the Medieval Period, and certain areas also reverted to a barbarian state when the collapse of the Roman Empire took place.

Nor does space permit any account of the later prehistoric sequence in the vast territories to the south and east of Europe— of those parts of Africa and Asia, for example, which remained quite unaffected by literate civilisation until very recent times indeed. Farther away still lie Australia and New Zealand and the whole of the New World, of whose prehistory no account can be given here, although a whole book of this length devoted to each of them would be quite insufficient.[1]

Within these limitations, therefore, an account of 'The Iron Age' has to deal with a smaller area than that covered in previous chapters, and an area which dwindles as the period progresses, more and more territory being absorbed by the expanding power of Rome. The first step is to sketch in the containing outline of this area, and the framework of the period, taking up the threads of the story in central Europe where they were left in the previous chapter, that is, with the expansion of the Late Bronze Age Urnfield Culture.[2] This of course began long before the Roman Republic, let alone the Roman Empire, had come into being. The point must here be stressed again, which was made at the close of the last chapter, that the advent of iron-working does not create a sharp cultural break, in most places, when it first reaches them; quite often, so far as can be told, the populations remained basically the same, and it was the new items of technological knowledge which moved from place to place.

The development and expansion of the Urnfield peoples, it will be remembered, took place soon after the time of the disturbances and movements of barbarian peoples, which had around 1200 B.C. led to the overthrow of the Mycenaean and Hittite civilisations, and which, moreover, had threatened the powers farther to the south and south-east, including Egypt. In Greece, a 'Dark Age' period ensued, but out of it after a few centuries arose the civilisation of Classical Greece, composed of a number of separate city-states, whose lack of unity was in fact eventually to be a cause of their downfall. This emergence becomes clear in the archaeological record by the eighth century B.C., although the highest achievements of Classical Greece belong to the sixth and fifth centuries. Greek trading colonies were established both eastwards and westwards, one of the more important ones from the point of view of European prehistory being at Massilia, near the mouth of the river Rhone, founded about the close of the seventh century.

Farther south, the development of the maritime civilisation of the Phoenicians coincided with that of Greece. It was based on the Levantine coast and Cyprus, but the Phoenicians too established trading colonies and outposts in the west Mediterranean, the best known being Carthage on the coast of Tunisia. Apart from their own trading contacts with barbarian Europe in the Late Bronze Age and Early Iron Age, the Phoenicians are of importance because of the effect their activities had on the policies of Greece and Rome, but this is a matter which need not be described in detail here. The Phoenician alphabet had already in the eighth century been adopted, and indeed adapted, by the Greeks.

In northern and western Italy, the contemporary of Classical Greece was the Etruscan civilisation. Etruscan origins are not by any means fully understood, and it has often been suggested that direct colonisation from Asia Minor played a part. In the archaeological record, the local early Iron Age culture, known as the Villanovan, is seen to enjoy a period of thriving expansion, assisted by trading contacts with the Greek colonies in south Italy, perhaps also with the Phoenicians, and certainly with the rich Late Bronze Age cultures of central Europe. The Villanovan Culture emerged from the rather vague Urnfield background in north Italy in the ninth century B.C., poor at first but already with a knowledge of iron working. Throughout the eighth century, its graves get steadily richer, with fine bronze work and imported Greek pots, and in the seventh century the culture turns into the literate Etruscan civilisation. The Etruscan inscriptions are written in Greek letters, and can therefore be read, but the language is not understood.

Like Classical Greece, the Etruscan civilisation was made up of city-states, and once more the lack of unity between them was a contributory cause of downfall. The city of Rome was originally an Etruscan foundation (though earlier settlement existed on the site), but in 509 B.C. Rome successfully became a republic, following the expulsion of Etruscan rulers, the house of Tarquin. Thereafter, during the first half of the fourth century, the Etruscan cities came under heavy attack, not only from the Greek cities in the south, but also from barbarian Celtic invaders from the north, and although the barbarians penetrated far to the south, and Rome itself was sacked in the process, the Roman Republic profited by the Etruscans' weakened state, and emerged gradually as the supreme power in central Italy.

Thereafter, Roman arms were turned first against southern Italy and Sicily, and then against Carthage and Spain; eventually afterwards almost all the countries with a Mediterranean coastline, including even Egypt, were conquered. By early in the second century B.C. the Romans had also finally subdued the Celtic invaders who had remained south of the Alps, following their attacks on the Etruscans, and who constituted what was known to the Romans as Cisalpine Gaul, but it was considerably later that the whole of Transalpine Gaul (France) was conquered under Julius Caesar, and later still (A.D. 43) that Britain was the object of full-scale invasion, excluding Caesar's own exploratory and punitive expeditions of the mid-first century B.C.

Eventually the limits of the Roman inroads upon barbarian Europe came more or less to be defined by the line of the rivers Rhine and Danube; the greatest extension northward was not reached until the beginning of the second century A.D. Beyond this frontier, the barbarians—that is, the various remaining Celtic and Germanic cultures of the north European Iron Age—were left unconquered even if they were from time to time affected.

This digression beyond the limits of prehistory should give

some idea of the background to the European Iron Age sequence, and the gradual contraction of the prehistoric world. It also goes without saying that there were constant trade relations between the barbarian and civilised cultures, just as there had been in Bronze Age times. The most consistent and widespread example is the demand of the Celtic world, or at least the chieftains of it, for wine, in quantity, from Greek and Etruscan and afterwards Roman sources. Jugs, strainers and mixing-bowls of bronze, occasionally with pottery cups and the proper *amphorae* wine containers and other items connected with wine drinking, all of Mediterranean origin, turn up from time to time in quite remote Celtic contexts: a good example is provided by certain graves of Belgic chieftains as far afield as southern Britain.[3]

But if conviviality, trade and conquest were the mixed offering of the South to Iron Age Europe, the way also lay open from the East, as indeed it had done since Palaeolithic times, from the

107 Roman wine amphorae in a sunken merchant ship, photographed on the sea bed off Spargi, Sardinia

stecpe-lands of Eurasia, southern and central Russia and beyond. Here no civilised power blocked the European frontier, and that people and influences did come from this direction, too, will be evident from a consideration of the European Iron Age sequence, to which, after one further preliminary, it is time to turn.

The final preliminary point is merely to consider the nature of the metal iron itself.[4] Its major advantage was the wide and therefore inexpensive availability of the ores from which the metal could be obtained; there was no question of alloying, and iron was also an admirable raw material for the manufacture of weapons and such woodworking tools as saws, axes and adzes; iron nails, too, were made in enormous numbers in Iron Age as well as in Roman times. But iron was a good deal harder to process than copper and bronze, and was never in prehistoric times able to be heated to a high enough temperature for casting in a mould. The metal had first to be obtained by reduction of the ore in a smelting furnace under the right conditions, and then the pieces of iron thus acquired had to be picked out from the slag and reheated in what is called a smithing hearth, to bring them together into a single lump; the latter could then be forged by hammering into whatever shape was required. In addition, tempering processes were necessary to produce iron tools with the best possible cutting edge. Since the whole process is so different from the making of copper or bronze implements, it is not surprising that it was never a natural independent 'follow-up' invention by the European bronze smiths.

Iron appears to have been first extensively used in Anatolia by the Hittites, and it seems that the diffusion of iron-working techniques to Europe must have come about as a result of the break-up of the Hittite civilisation. Its earliest appearance in Europe on any scale is in Macedonia and Greece, after the fall of Mycenae and during the formative period before Classical times, while its arrival in the pre-Etruscan Villanovan culture, mentioned above, is somewhat later. Iron objects even appear sporadically at later Urnfield Culture sites in central Europe, but iron-working did not take place on a wide scale there until the earliest stages of the succeeding culture, that called after a site at Hallstatt. There is no reason however to suppose any major lack of continuity between the late Urnfield and earliest Hallstatt phases as regards the actual population, although certain intrusive cultural elements can be seen. The Hallstatt peoples can properly be called Celtic. The origins of the Celts themselves must, of course, go much further back than this, but they are not easy to discern in the European archaeological sequence.

The Hallstatt Culture emerges from the late Urnfield background in the seventh and sixth centuries B.C., and is found widely over central and western Europe, notably in south Germany, Switzerland and eastern France, but also as far east down the Danube as Czechoslovakia, Yugoslavia and Austria. Apart from the rich trading possibilities southwards implied by this area geographically, the territory itself was rich in its own right, well endowed with metal resources, especially copper, and also with supplies of another substance which now began to be prized: salt, which in Hallstatt times became the object of organised mining. Its chief use was in the preservation of foods rather than the mere flavouring of them.

In the archaeological record, the appearance of the Hallstatt Culture brings long iron swords as the most striking objects made **108** of the new metal. But perhaps the most remarkable feature of the new culture is its rich chieftain burials. In these, the rite is inhumation with costly grave-goods and the accompaniment of a cart or waggon, usually of four-wheeled type; often there is a containing timber structure, and the whole grave is covered by **111** a substantial barrow mound. This type of burial, although reserved

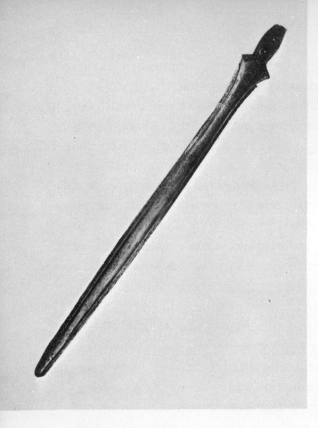

108
Bronze sword of central European
Hallstatt type (find-spot uncertain).
Length 66 cm. (Extreme top of hilt
missing.) Pitt Rivers Museum, Oxford.

for the Hallstatt aristocracy, is so different from the typical
Urnfield rite that its introduction almost demands exotic
influences.

In brief, the source of these influences is to be sought in the
south Russian steppe country, where there are good parallels for
burials in timber structures contained in barrows, and for the
occurrence of whole carts, or their wheels, in graves, reaching
back even to the third millennium B.C. A little farther south, in
the Caucasus and Armenia, waggon burials of the later second
millennium are known. The domestication of the horse as a
riding and traction animal in the south Russian steppe-lands took
place during the early second millennium if not before, and
horses were certainly used in Europe during Urnfield times. In

the Urnfield phases which precede Hallstatt, and also in earliest
Hallstatt times, there is evidence for a considerable influx of
horse-bits and harness attachments of specifically Eastern type,
and the actual bones of horses dating from this period can be
shown to belong to steppe-land breeds. All this evidence adds
up to at least definite contact between central Europe and the
south Russian and Caucasian area in the centuries leading up to
the appearance of the Hallstatt waggon graves, and it is not to
be forgotten that the technique of iron-working itself came from
very much the same part of the world at about the same time,
though perhaps by a different route.

There seems little doubt that the contacts in question, or at
least some of them, arose out of population movements associated
with a known barbarian event referred to by early writers,
namely the expansion of the people known as the Scyths or
Scythians from their south Russian territory; they both drove
out their neighbours, the Cimmerians, and also spread westwards,
probably in at least two waves, into eastern Europe.

The Hallstatt people too evidently moved westwards, up the
Danube valley, whether as part of a chain reaction caused by
the Scythian movements, or for other reasons. The dating of
Hallstatt cemeteries and settlements is clearly earliest in the east,
in Czechoslovakia, Austria, Switzerland and south-west Germany,
and somewhat later in France and Belgium, the movement
finally influencing, even if it did not actually reach, southern and
eastern Britain, where the first Iron Age settlements probably date
from the beginning of the sixth century B.C., although traded
Hallstatt objects may well have begun to arrive a little earlier.

There are many important Hallstatt settlements and cemeteries
scattered along this spread.[5] The type site itself, Hallstatt near
Salzburg, has a cemetery of about 2000 graves—ordinary burials,
not waggon graves—and there are also important and extensive

109 The Heuneburg hill-fort, Saulgau, Württemberg

salt mines. In south Germany, in Württemberg, there is the Heuneburg hill-fort, a defended settlement with three main phases of building, in the second of which bastioned mud-brick walls were in places built instead of the customary timber-faced ramparts—a technique suggesting East Mediterranean influence. The third phase has some imported Greek pottery and amphorae, the latter doubtless obtained full of wine by way of the Greek trading-post at Massilia away to the south-west.

Adjacent to the Heuneburg fort is the large and important Hohmichele Hallstatt waggon grave, where, apart from a four-

110 Artist's impression of the bastioned defences at the Heuneberg (see Fig. 109)

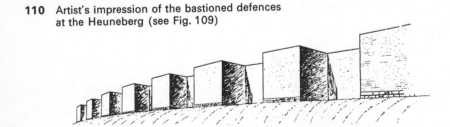

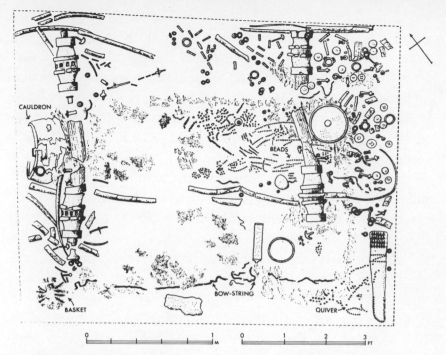

111 Plan of the Hohmichele Hallstatt waggon grave near the Heuneburg, as excavated

wheeled waggon, the rich grave-goods included a large cauldron and the remains of a quiver full of iron-tipped arrows; the grave had a containing wooden chamber, under an enormous tumulus. Another outstanding tomb, again with a timber-built chamber, is that of Vix in the Côte d'Or area of eastern France, where a female burial was accompanied by a carefully dismantled four-wheeled waggon. The grave-goods included more imports from the civilised world, with a really huge bronze crater (or wine-mixing bowl) of Greek manufacture. A major Hallstatt settlement with a hill-fort and more graves is nearby. Etruscan objects also appear occasionally in Hallstatt graves.

The richness of the culture is attested by the wealth of the grave-goods in these admittedly exceptional tombs. A considerable amount of goldwork is found, especially in south Germany and eastern France, including such pieces as annular head or neck ornaments made from sheet gold. The Hallstatt craftsmen were of high technical ability, as the construction of the waggons shows, as well as the frequent fine metalwork of all kinds. Bronze was still very much used alongside iron, and weapons, harness attachments and domestic objects were all often made of it. Many of the metal objects, and no doubt also many of the more perishable things which have not survived, were decorated with attractively executed mainly geometric patterns.[6] Animal motifs also often occur.

The Hallstatt penetration of Britain will be discussed later, along with the rest of the British Iron Age sequence, and meanwhile the next stage in the continental part of the story is the development out of the Hallstatt Culture, in the course of the fifth century, of the succeeding one, which takes the name La Tène.

There is much to link the two, and once more no reason for supposing that any major incursion of new peoples was the cause of the cultural change. The eventual La Tène area covers the

112 Bronze bowl from grave at Hallstatt, ornamented with figures of cow and calf, and with geometric decoration around the rim and upper part. The cow figure is 14·4 cm. long. Scale: × ¼.

whole of the Hallstatt territory, and extends beyond it in most directions, including that of Britain. In fact Celtic bands of La Tène date penetrated on occasion far beyond the bounds of the area indicated above as that of the European Iron Age, and sometimes drove deep into the civilised world. The sack of Rome, already referred to, was the work of La Tène elements; so too was a great raid into Greece aimed at Delphi, in the earlier half of the third century B.C., and an even more remarkable expedition shortly afterwards which took Celtic warriors into Asia Minor, where they established and indeed maintained their colony of Galatia.[7] La Tène Celts also returned with interest the pressure which the Scythians had put upon their Hallstatt predecessors, and objects in the La Tène style have been found in Poland and even Russia. The La Tène culture, incorporating a number of local variants, in fact comprises the remainder of the Celtic Iron Age, and in parts of barbarian Europe its influence was destined long to outlast the expansion of Rome, even if the actual name La Tène passes away.

The most striking feature of the La Tène material culture is certainly the decorative art. This is something far more impressive than the simple, if attractive, mainly geometric style of Hallstatt, in which unsophisticated animal or bird figures also appeared. La Tène art combines these Hallstatt motifs with a contribution from the Classical world, whose use of conventionalised foliage and tendrils and flowing curvilinear patterns seems to have had a **113, 114** special appeal for the Celtic mind, although there is no influence from Classical sculpture of the human form, and only rarely is any attempt made to copy the idea of depicting narrative scenes in which human figures participate. The art of the Scyths, in which fantastic and eclectic animal representations are a recurrent theme, is also thought by some to be a formative source of the La Tène art style.

114
La Tène ornamented gold work:
torc and bracelets of gold from
the Waldalgesheim chariot grave,
Kreuznach. The diameter of
the twisted ring-bracelet is
$3\frac{1}{4}$ inches (internal).
Rheinisches Landesmuseum, Bonn.

113   La Tène bronze mirror from Old Warden, Bedfordshire, the back with
typical incised and chased decoration. Length 11 inches.

Decoration in the La Tène style is applied to metalwork of all
kinds, particularly shields, helmets, scabbards, harness attachments,
brooches and personal ornaments, vessels such as bowls, cauldrons
and even flagons, and domestic objects such as iron firedogs or
the famous La Tène hand mirrors, whose reflecting surface was
of polished bronze. Many of the best objects are of bronze, and
sometimes the decoration incorporates studs of coral or of
coloured enamel. Gold, too, was most skilfully used. Apart from
124   the metalwork, pottery is often decorated in a similar tradition,
notably with curvilinear patterns, incised, or, more rarely, painted.
The best La Tène pottery is made with the use of a potter's
wheel, rather than being built up by hand as it had been since
Neolithic times in Europe.

The continuity and the development from Hallstatt to La Tène are both exemplified by the La Tène chariot burials. The four-wheeled waggon most typical of Hallstatt aristocratic graves is now replaced by a light two-wheeled chariot, in whose manufacture certain remarkably advanced techniques are to be noted: for example, the spoked wheels had iron hoop tyres fixed on to the circular wooden frame by a process of shrinking—in other words, the iron hoop was applied while red hot and allowed to tighten itself into position by the natural process of contraction on cooling. La Tène chariot graves are seen at their best in the middle Rhineland and the valley of the Marne, and it is here that the culture and its art style really have their birth.[8] Chariot graves also occur in Britain, and some examples will be given later on. It is of course well known from Roman and other early authors that the Celtic peoples made much use of chariots in battle.

La Tène settlements include many large hill forts, defended in depth with multiple stone and earth ramparts, strengthened by interlaced timbers, and later by timbers nailed together. Not all attempts to use timber strengthening for ramparts proved as successful as the defenders hoped. Such defences proved vulnerable to attack by fire, and sometimes the blaze was so fierce that the stone parts of the ramparts became vitrified with the heat. The Highland Zone of Britain has quite a number of small 'vitrified forts' which were violently destroyed in this way. Many later hill-fort defences in Britain were built without timber reinforcements.

The large La Tène defended settlements developed into fortified tribal capitals on the scale of towns;[9] these are the *oppida* of the enemy mentioned in Caesar's campaign accounts. La Tène settlements occasionally incorporate ritual or 'cult' sites, hardly describable as temples, though 'shrines' would perhaps be an acceptable term. These can often reasonably be attributed to the

115 La Tène chariot burial, La Gorge-Meillet, Marne, France. Two warriors were buried, one directly above the other, with rich grave goods. The whole burial is now exhibited at the Musée des Antiquités Nationales, Saint-Germain-en-Laye.

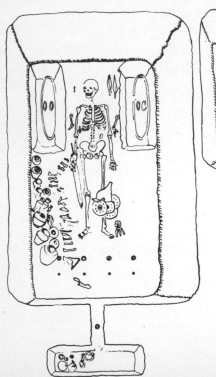

116 Plan of La Tène chariot burial with rich grave goods, Châlons-sur-Marne, Marne, France. The small adjacent grave contains a wild boar skeleton. Scale: × $\frac{1}{50}$.

Druids, the Celtic priesthood; the Druids are known from the literary rather than the archaeological sources, and it is not clear whether their religion goes back beyond La Tène times. Much that has been written about them is pure fantasy, not least the idea that they were closely connected with Stonehenge: there is no archaeological evidence to suggest that they ever took over that far more ancient monument.[10]

One further striking innovation is to be found in the La Tène phase of European prehistory, namely the first use of a coinage. This practice was of course derived from neighbouring civilised powers, and the first Celtic coins were copied from Macedonian silver ones, perhaps even before the end of the third century B.C. Gold coins were being struck by the middle of the second century by the Western Celts in France. How far the early Celtic coins really had the function of currency for their users is not clear, but it appears that the idea of money was at least partly understood by the later La Tène peoples. Some of the later coins are even inscribed with a tribe's or ruler's name in copied Roman letters.[11]

This general survey of some of the main aspects of the Hallstatt and La Tène cultures of the Continent provides the background for a brief account of the Iron Age sequence in Britain. The

117 Ground-plan of Iron Age shrine or small temple at Heath Row, Middlesex, as revealed by excavated post holes and beam slots

118 Belgic gold coins from Britain, inscribed CAMV for Camulodunum
(Colchester) and CVN or CVNO for Cunobelin. Scale: × ³⁄₂.
Colchester and Essex Museum.

general nature of the British sequence is not hard to guess, in
view of the geographical position of Britain and the examples
already noted of European tribes or peoples being forced to move
by pressure coming from outside their own borders; Britain was
perfectly placed to receive the tail end of any movement westwards across the European plain, or northwards away from the
encroaching Roman armies.

Yet the evidence is that actual immigrants from the Continent
came more as an intermittent gentle flow than in sudden torrents;
thus Britain was not taken by storm culturally in this period,
and the gentler infusion of new elements allowed the British Iron
Age to develop a certain insular character, even though British
examples can be found of most of the items of Iron Age material
culture so far mentioned.

The classic interpretation of the British Iron Age has divided
it into A, B and C groups, which are themselves much subdivided,

200

and also affected by overlapping and regional variation.[12] Iron Age A is characterised by the arrival of the first new influences, ultimately of late Hallstatt and earliest La Tène origin, but doubtless with a contribution from the late surviving Urnfield communities of the west; Iron Age B incorporates the arrival of Middle La Tène elements; Iron Age C comprises the specifically Belgic Late La Tène incursions into Britain, the earliest of which are actually mentioned by Caesar. These primary divisions were not intended to be rigid, nor supposed to have the same meaning or chronology all over the country: not everywhere had a C phase, for example, and in some parts the A phase must have lingered on for a long while undisturbed, or merged indistinguishably into B.

And apart from any incoming people, there remained the older populations, which need nowhere have vanished or died out. Just as in the Early Bronze Age, new arrivals had absorbed the Late Neolithic population, or vice versa, so would Early Iron Age settlers have merged with the existing inhabitants. And in southeast Britain anyhow, there must have been settlers who had come within the Late Bronze Age itself, from the fringes of the Urnfield Culture before the Hallstatt phase replaced it. The Iron Age settlers were simply continuing the movement already then begun, though now of course they had taken to Hallstatt ways, and could work the new metal, iron. Warlike leaders from among them, too, with swords in the Hallstatt style (whether made of iron or even still of bronze) could strike out beyond the south-eastern settlements, and go further afield, setting themselves up over wholly indigenous communities in the north and west, and in Ireland. It would be wrong to think of the coming of the Iron Age as a total take-over by quite new peoples. In interpreting the British Iron Age sequence, some prehistorians have laid more stress on the invading or immigrant elements, and others on those surviving from earlier times: it is not necessary to choose between these views as though they were in conflict, since each has its share of the truth, and between them they offer an understanding of at least the general outline of events in this final phase of British prehistory.

Two intrusions of people from the Continent are very clearly seen: the first is represented by chariot burials in the La Tène tradition, mainly confined to Yorkshire.[13] To the sites involved, the name of Arras Culture has been given, after the cemetery at Arras near Beverley. The second and much later incursion is that of Caesar's Belgae, and it is well proved by the presence of settlements, cemeteries and isolated finds over much of southern and eastern Britain, and by the evidence of Belgic coins. The Belgic people, as already mentioned, belong to a late phase of the Continental La Tène Culture. How early they began to arrive in England from their homeland in the Low Countries and northern France is not precisely known, but they must certainly have been arriving during the first half of the first century B.C., and perhaps even earlier, and they continued to come during the post-Caesarian period.

To return to the beginning of the sequence, however, there are British sites which are certainly earlier than those of the Arras group: they have a southern and eastern distribution, not penetrating far inland, and as examples may be quoted settlements at Scarborough and Staple Howe in Yorkshire, All Cannings Cross and Longbridge Deverell Cow Down in Wiltshire, and Park Brow in Sussex, among several others.[14] These are farming settlements, sometimes defended at least by a simple timber palisade. They show little change from the farming settlements of the Middle Bronze Age, and were evidently based on mixed farming; even the house-plans remain circular, in the long-established British tradition, as opposed to rectangular plans at

Continental Hallstatt sites. Yet certain artifacts are of ultimately Continental type—for example, bronze razors of Hallstatt type at Staple Howe—and iron objects are present, in admittedly small numbers, the commonest being simple pins with the head formed by a ring (ring-headed) or an S-shape (swan-necked), though even these are sometimes made of bronze. The pottery

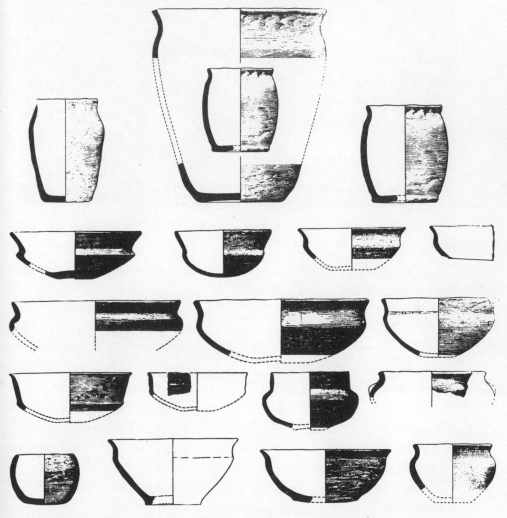

119 Pottery of the earlier Iron Age, Maiden Castle, Dorset. Scale: × $\frac{1}{6}$.

120 A British Iron Age hill-fort: St Catherine's Hill, Winchester, Hants

associated with these settlements also has some features which can be paralleled on the Continent and are new to Britain, though in part it still continues older native traditions. The earlier of the sites in question date from the beginning of the sixth century B.C., or perhaps even the end of the seventh. No doubt occupation at them goes back into the Late Bronze Age.

Over much of southern England, this settlement pattern survives right down to Belgic times, with the obvious proviso that any later incoming people must be of La Tène rather than Hallstatt origin. Indeed, considerable La Tène invasions have sometimes been claimed for the period before about 250 B.C., but at present the evidence of the sites gives no clear picture of the actual amount of immigration that took place.

To the period between the earliest Iron Age settlements and those of the Belgic invaders, most of the visible and excavated Iron Age sites of southern Britain belong. The most spectacular monuments are the great hill-forts, some of the best examples of **120, 121** which dominate the highest points of the blocks of chalk downland in Sussex, Hampshire, Wiltshire or Dorset.[15] The idea of a hill-fort itself came to Britain as a continental influence. In Britain, hill-forts are probably best regarded as tribal centres and occasional refuges in times of disturbance for the scattered communities of a whole area, and their large size suggests the provision of accommodation too for flocks and herds. Some were begun quite early on in the Iron Age, with a simple rampart and ditch following

121　A British Iron Age hill-fort from the air:
Herefordshire Beacon, Malvern, from the north

the contours around the crown of a hill, but they became more complicated, with multi-vallate defences, and were also sometimes enlarged, as time passed. One reason for the addition of new ramparts and ditches alongside the old was the introduction of the sling as a weapon; it became necessary for the defenders to put a greater distance between themselves and the attackers, to keep out of the slingers' range.

Some hill-forts may have been first erected, or else may have had existing defences strengthened, against La Tène invaders, while much of the later elaboration of defences must surely have been a response to the coming of the Belgae first and of the Romans not long afterwards. Nor is evidence lacking for the violent capture of British hill-forts by these peoples: Belgic raiders may have been responsible for a massacre at Bredon Hill in Gloucestershire,[16] for instance, and the Roman forces under the future emperor Vespasian, in the opening campaigns of the Roman Conquest sacked many hill-forts, of which Hod Hill and Maiden Castle in Dorset are the most famous and best excavated examples.

Other Iron Age sites of this period include many farming settlements, of which a well-known example has been partly
122 examined in detail at Little Woodbury, Wiltshire.[17] This, like many others, was not a village but a large single farmstead of circular plan, defended by a palisade. Structural features of such settlements included additional huts or barns, underground grain-storage pits, and raised timber granaries and corn-drying racks, whose post-hole settings survive. Sites of Little Woodbury type leave few visible traces on the ground, although they can be recognised by archaeological observation and photography from the air. 'Celtic Fields', however, are readily identifiable from the ground: these are simple cultivation systems, often defined by
123 terraces and banks on a smooth hillside. These traces were left by the redisposition of the soil loosened by continual light

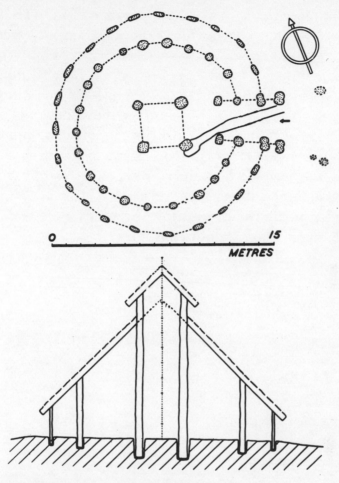

122 Plan and suggested elevation of Iron Age farmstead, Little Woodbury, Wilts.

ploughing: it slipped down the slope and piled up against the now vanished fences or hedges marking the field boundaries.

There are certainly regional variations within this middle period of Iron Age settlement in southern England, but these cannot be followed up in detail here. However, mention must be made of the far south-west, where Cornish tin still proved a strong attraction; it was sought by, amongst others, the La Tène population of Brittany, known from historical sources to have been led by the tribe of the Veneti. Their direct relations across the Channel with the extreme south-west of Britain brought in various continental influences; for example, the Iron Age inhabitants of Cornwall began to construct the 'cliff-castle' type of hill-fort, closely paralleled in Brittany, in which a promontory, naturally defended for most of its perimeter by steep cliffs and the sea, was fortified by artificial defences across the landward approach. Some still remoter influences, attributable to direct connections across the sea with north Spain, may also be discerned in the extreme south-west of England.

123 'Celtic fields', seen from the air:
Windover Hill, near Alfriston, Sussex

124 Decorated Iron Age pottery from Glastonbury, Somerset. The larger pot is 8¼ inches high.

Under the invigorating stimulus of these direct La Tène contacts, and no doubt also a certain amount of immigration, a thriving South-Western Iron Age culture developed, extending at least as far east as the so-called 'lake-village' sites of Meare and Glastonbury[18] in Somerset. Attractive pottery with curvilinear decoration is found here; many organic remains are preserved by waterlogging, and there is also evidence for a fine tradition of metalwork. No doubt the south-western approaches to Britain were one route of entry for the influences, and perhaps for the actual craftsmen, instrumental in the development of the particular British version of La Tène art seen at its best on sword-scabbards and shields, and on the backs of the bronze mirrors like the famous **113** Desborough and Birdlip examples.

It was also no doubt by sea-routes from the Atlantic coasts of Europe that Iron Age influences reached Ireland. Ireland of course remained untouched by the Roman Conquest of Britain, and the fusion of Late Bronze Age traditions with those of Hallstatt and La Tène newcomers lasted a very long time. It was still a prehistoric Celtic Ireland to which the early Christian missionaries came in the fifth century A.D.[19] Some of the circular 'rath' farmsteads whose earth banks are such a common sight in parts of Ireland may be of Early Iron Age origin, but in many cases their occupation certainly lasted through the first several centuries A.D.

The most clearly seen pre-Belgic La Tène encroachment on Britain, as opposed to steady casual immigration, was that of the Arras Culture already mentioned. The leading cemetery sites with chariot burials in Yorkshire are those of Arras itself, Cowlam and the misleadingly named Danes Graves near Driffield, with several isolated outlying graves, and even some rather uncertain evidence for a few similar burials as far south as East Anglia. The dating is not well known in all cases, though the earlier graves go back to the fifth century B.C.

Away from lowland Britain and into the highland zone, notably in Scotland, the Iron Age structures and settlements take on a very different aspect, and are not easy to connect directly with southern cultures or groups. Small units of settlement are most often found, as appropriate to a harsher terrain, and the lowland timber buildings with earthen rampart defences are largely replaced by structures with walls of stone. Small, circular, tower-like stone forts, known as brochs, with hollow galleried walls surrounding the living area, occur over wide areas of the northern and western Scottish Highlands and islands, and these are only one aspect of a whole class of related structures. Another version of the same theme is the 'wheelhouse', which takes its name from the radial piers inside the circular stone wall, probably designed to support the roof structure. Wheelhouses, however, are lower and much less massive structures than brochs, and are

125

126

125 The broch of Mousa, Shetland

126 A wheelhouse, as excavated: À Cheardach Mhor, North Uist

clearly farmhouses or dwellings.[20] The material culture associated with the brochs and wheelhouses has local elements as well as those derived ultimately from southern Britain. Like Ireland, the north of Scotland lay beyond the frontier of Roman Britain, and the local Iron Age substantially outlasted the Roman occupation of Britain. For the present brief account, the Scottish and Irish Iron Ages must be regarded as loose and rather remote variants of that combination of native and intrusive elements which is the backbone of the whole British Iron Age sequence. Even the term 'Pre-Roman Iron Age' loses its meaning in these areas.

It remains only to consider the final pre-Roman event, the coming of the Belgae. The main groups who invaded eastern Britain were induced to move from their homeland, if not actually driven out, by the combination of the Roman campaigns against Gaul, and invasions from Germanic tribes across their own eastern borders, which they seem to have repulsed with some difficulty. They came as tribes or major parts of tribes—no mere trickle of traders, settlers or helpless refugees, and generally they came with violence, though this may not have been true of the earliest Belgic arrivals which were taking place long before Caesar's Gallic campaigns, and possibly even some way back into the second century B.C.

Belgic technology was considerably superior to that of the Britain the invaders found; their weapons, their metalwork, their advanced agriculture with heavy ploughs, and their wheel-made pottery, all underline this. Their social organisation too was superior, as is seen from their system of coinage, the power of their chiefs and kings, and the scale of the *oppida* they soon began to establish—sites such as those at Colchester (Essex), Prae Wood, St Albans (Hertfordshire), or Bagendon (Gloucestershire).[21] They maintained trade relationships across the Channel, as the presence of much imported pottery shows, including such pieces

128

as the wine amphorae from a few chieftains' graves like one at
Snailwell near Newmarket, Cambridgeshire. One of the items
they exported in return was British slaves, and several examples
of grim-looking gang-chains have been found.[22] Apart from
trading across the Channel, they were even able to send military
aid to the foes of Caesar—one reason for the first Roman invasions
in 55–4 B.C.

127 Belgic slave chain, with six collars, Lords Bridge, Barton, Cambs.
Length of chain: 12 feet. The collars are about 5 inches in diameter.
University Museum of Archaeology and Ethnology, Cambridge.

213

The Belgic burial rite was cremation, the ashes often being placed in an urn of pedestal-based shape, of the new wheel-turned pottery. Good examples of the typical Belgic flat cemeteries of cremation burials exist at Aylesford and Swarling in Kent, although these are now known to date mostly from after the time of Caesar.[23] Grave-goods are frequent, although there are certainly poor as well as rich burials. The articles buried with the dead

128 Belgic grave-group at Aylesford, Kent—a reconstruction of the objects *in situ* rather than an accurate representation of the find, which was made in 1886. The grave goods included a fine bronze-mounted bucket, a bronze jug or flagon and a bronze skillet or ladle, the last two objects being of exotic origin. (Not precisely to scale, but the bucket is about 26 cm. high.)

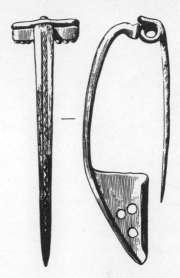

129
Brooch of Belgic type
Maiden Castle, Dorset.
Length 9 cm.

include brooches of iron, bronze or even silver, various other metal objects and some fine examples of wooden buckets with **128** ornamental bronze mounts, besides more exceptional offerings like cauldrons, iron fire-dogs, generous provision of food for the journey to the after-world, the amphorae already mentioned (probably filled with wine), quantities of other pottery, and vases made not of pottery, but of shale, turned on a lathe.

Apart from the objects buried as grave-goods, there are other fine examples of Celtic decorated metalwork which date from this final phase of the British Pre-Roman Iron Age, though these are not all attributable exclusively to Belgic craftsmen. The most spectacular find is the series of hoards making up the treasure from Snettisham, Norfolk, in the territory of the Iceni, including over fifty torcs, several made of gold or of gold alloys.[24] Many **130** late Iron Age gold and silver coins found in Britain are also of **118** attractive workmanship in the fine Late La Tène tradition.

Belgic arrivals continued probably all through the second half of the first century B.C., and sporadically later still. The area of Britain occupied or at least influenced by the various Belgic

215

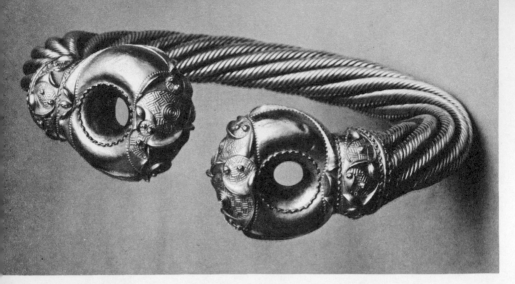

130 Ring-terminal torc of gold alloy, diameter 8 inches, the finest of the torcs from the treasure found at Snettisham, Norfolk. British Museum.

tribes grew to include most of southern and eastern England as far north as the Humber. Gradually names of tribes and their rulers become known, through the evidence of Roman authors, helped too by the evidence of inscribed coins. Even details of the frequent inter-tribal wars and intrigues of the period are preserved. Of these much has been written, but they are not within the scope of this book.

When it becomes possible to replace the prehistorian's stock phrases like 'local culture' and 'members of a ruling aristocracy' with actual names like 'Atrebates' or 'Catuvellauni' and 'Tasciovanus', 'Commius' or 'Cunobelinus', then prehistory is giving way to history; thus the end has been reached, from the British point of view, of a phase of the human story begun locally perhaps half a million years ago. To revert to the pile of pennies of the introductory chapter of this book: a mere one and sevenpence stands between the Belgae and mid-twentieth century Britain.

216

NOTES

1. For guidance in the study of such other areas, the reader might start with Clark, J. G. D., 1962 and Clark, J. G. D. and Piggott, 1965. Individual volumes in the wide-ranging Thames & Hudson *Ancient Peoples and Places* series will as usual be found helpful for particular areas. In the case of African prehistory, some of the wide gaps left in the present account can also be filled by reference to Cole, 1964 and Clark, J. D., 1959 and Bishop and Clark, J. D., ed., 1968. All the works mentioned in this note contain helpful bibliographies to guide further reading.

2. The general source books for the period covered by this chapter include the relevant chapters of those books quoted for the last two chapters, and by now, it is hoped, thoroughly familiar to the reader—notably Piggott, 1965 and Clark, J. G. D. and Piggott, 1965. The former, especially, contains many valuable references. Clark, J. G. D., 1952 and several of the other works quoted in the notes to Chs 4 and 5 above also remain highly relevant. To this list may be added Powell, 1958, and useful accounts of specific areas (cf. Ch. 4, n. 9 above) and specific peoples (e.g. Scythians, Etruscans, Phoenicians, etc.) will be found in other volumes of the same excellent series (Thames & Hudson, *Ancient Peoples and Places*). For the British Iron Age, see n. 12 to this chapter. No attempt can be made here to provide a bibliography for Classical Greece or Rome or other early civilisations mentioned.

3. For example, one at Snailwell, not far from Cambridge, which included amphorae. The finds from this grave are now admirably displayed at the Cambridge University Museum of Archaeology and Ethnology. See Lethbridge, 1953. Cf. also p. 214, fig. 128, above.

4. See Tylecote, 1962.

5. As is only natural, the most important detailed site reports are in French or German, or other continental languages, although Piggott, 1965, and the other general source books are helpful. The following references, however, would be a minimum essential to any proper study of the sites mentioned in the next few paragraphs:—

For Hallstatt itself, see Kromer, 1963; a huge work by the same author deals specifically with the cemetery there (Kromer, 1959).

For the Heuneburg: a brief summary of the site and its literature up to 1956, in English, is contained in a review by Professor C. F. C. Hawkes in the *Antiquaries Journal*, xxxvi (1956) 91–2. Another brief note in English, entitled 'A Prehistoric Wall of Sun-dried Brick' occurs in the quarterly periodical *Antiquity*, xxvii (1953) 164–5 (with plate v). An important article of greater length is Dehn, 1958, and the latest substantial article is Kimmig and Gersbach, 1966.

For the Hohmichele grave, see Riek, 1962. For Vix, see Joffroy, 1954. Joffroy, 1958, is of interest for other Hallstatt waggon graves. It must be borne in mind that only a very small selection of the leading Hallstatt Culture sites has been mentioned, and there are plenty more each with its own literature.

6. Celtic art, first appearing in Hallstatt times and reaching its finest development in the succeeding La Tène period (described later in the chapter), has been studied in various works, most of them liberally illustrated. See, for example, Jacobsthal, 1944, Fox, 1958, and the appropriate parts of Powell, 1966.

7. The full Celtic distribution in La Tène times is well described in the first chapter of Powell, 1958. The Celtic raids are also mentioned here.

8. See, for example, Joffroy and Bretz-Mahler, 1959.

9. The famous site of Manching, Bavaria, is a fine example, and it has been well and recently examined and published, including a readily accessible short account translated into English (Krämer, 1960); fuller accounts, in German, will be found in Krämer, 1958, and the same author's two reports in the periodical *Germania*, xxxix (1961) and xl (1962).

10. For authoritative accounts of the Druids, see Kendrick, 1928, and Powell, 1958, in ch. III especially. For the lengths to which 'Druidomania' has sometimes been taken, see Piggott, 1950, describing some aspects of the life of William Stukeley (1687–1765), especially chs 4 and 5. A new book on the Druids by Professor Piggott is due to be published in 1968 in Thames & Hudson's *Ancient Peoples and Places* series.

11. The Celtic coinage of Britain is only one aspect of the general La Tène system of currency, but it is the easiest to follow up in the literature. A number of papers on the subject have been published by Derek Allen; see for example Allen, 1961.

12. It may be some while before any wide-ranging account of the British Iron Age is available which takes into consideration all the new finds of the last decade or so. As indicated later in this chapter, there is a lack of general agreement on interpretation of the wider cultural context of the British finds— what is the extent of direct immigration and actual 'invasions' of Britain during the period, and how far the changes in material culture were due to indigenous development stimulated by the mere acquisition of ideas from outside, through, for example, trading contacts. A considerable amount of excavation and field work takes place every year on British Iron Age sites, and it seems reasonable to hope that the examination and comparison of properly sealed and well dated sites will before too long permit a fresh synthesis, but many of the more

218

impoverished Iron Age sites produce sparse finds and are notoriously hard to date in precise terms. Meanwhile the following source works for further study should prove useful, and between them they contain a wealth of further references: Frere, 1961 (among the many important papers which make up this volume is Professor C. F. C. Hawkes's classic article 'The ABC of the British Iron Age', pp. 1–16); Rivet, ed., 1966; Hodson, 1964; Birchall, 1965. See also Clark, J. G. D., 1966.

For those who wish to visit British Iron Age sites, the *Ordnance Survey Map of Southern Britain in the Iron Age* (published by the Director-General of the Ordnance Survey, Chessington, Surrey, 1962) will be found invaluable, and there is also much to be learnt from it, and its accompanying text, by those who do not propose to use it primarily as a field guide.

13. See Stead, 1965.

14. The best of these sites is Staple Howe: see Brewster, 1963. For Park Brow, see Wolseley and Smith, 1924, and also Wolseley *et al.*, 1927. For Scarborough, see Rowntree, ed., 1931, Ch. 1, 'Prehistoric Scarborough' by R. E. M. Wheeler, especially pp. 19–33. For All Cannings Cross, see Cunnington, 1923. Longbridge Deverell Cow Down is not yet published, apart from a brief description by Sonia Chadwick in 'Some Smaller Settlements: A Symposium' by Professor W. F. Grimes in Frere, ed., 1961.

A useful reference to another excavated British Iron Age settlement site of early date, at West Harling, Norfolk, is Clark, J. G. D., and Fell, 1953.

15. For British hill-forts in general, see various articles in Frere, ed., 1961, and also Hawkes, 1931. The most famous British hill-fort is undoubtedly Maiden Castle in Dorset, the subject of a classic excavation and a massive monograph: see Wheeler, 1943. The site, just outside Dorchester, is large and impressive, and well worth a visit. Other major hill-forts can readily be located with the help of the Ordnance Survey's Iron Age Map (see n. 12 to this chapter). Many of the leading national and local archaeological periodicals will be found to contain recent excavation reports on British hill-forts.

16. See Hencken, 1938, especially pp. 54–8.

17. See Bersu, 1940, Brailsford and Jackson, 1948, and Brailsford, 1949.

18. The reports on the original excavations (Bulleid and Gray, 1911–17 and 1948–53) contain a mass of information, though naturally they do not constitute a fully up-to-date account of the general context of the sites. Recently excavation has been recommenced at Meare, but the results are not yet published. Various more general works offer at least a brief passing account of the lake villages, e.g. Fox, Lady A., 1964, 126–7.

19. Two more volumes of the *Ancient Peoples and Places* series will be found useful here: de Paor and de Paor, 1958, and a forthcoming volume by

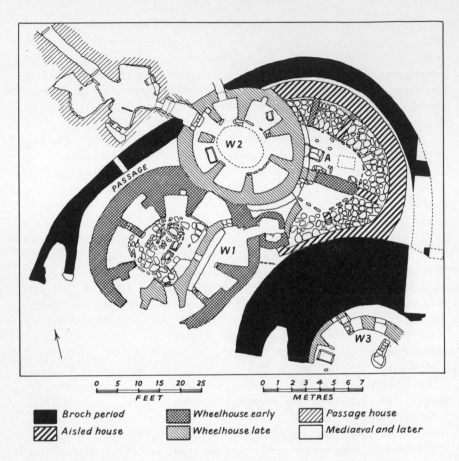

W 2

PASSAGE

A

W 1

W 3

| 0 | 5 | 10 | 15 | 20 | 25 |
| FEET | | | | | |

| 0 | 1 | 2 | 3 | 4 | 5 | 6 | 7 |
| METRES | | | | | | | |

■ Broch period   ▨ Wheelhouse early   ▨ Passage house
▨ Aisled house   ▨ Wheelhouse late   □ Mediaeval and later

131 Plan of structures at Jarlshof, Shetland: the sequence at the site began with a broch, in whose courtyard first an aisled house (*A*) and then two wheelhouses (*W1*) and (*W2*) were built. A third wheelhouse (*W3*) was built inside the broch.

the same authors, to be called *Pre-Christian Ireland*. See also Raftery, 1951, and Evans, 1966, though the latter is rather a gazetteer of sites than any sort of textbook.

20. Some of the finest examples of brochs are to be seen in Shetland, at Clickhimin near Lerwick, and on Mousa; two others with parts of the walls unusually well preserved are near Glenelg (Inverness-shire). Dun Carloway, on Lewis (Hebrides), is also well preserved, and several brochs in Sutherland are also well worth visiting, though their walls are much reduced from their original height—for example, Dun Dornadilla, Carn Liath, Kintradwell and others, which are all easily accessible. At Clickhimin, a wheelhouse was built **131** inside the disused broch, and at Jarlshof, also in Shetland, wheelhouses were inserted into a broch courtyard. The Kilphedir wheelhouse in South Uist is another accessible one with interesting surviving structural details. Many brochs and wheelhouses in a fragmentary state can be seen in the western and northern isles. A useful source of information on sites to visit is Feachem, 1963, which includes a gazetteer of all kinds of monuments. See also Hamilton, 1956; a report by Mr Hamilton on his excavations at Clickhimin will be published very shortly. See also MacKie, 1965. Further references are quoted in all these sources.

21. For Colchester, see Hawkes and Hull, 1946; for Prae Wood, see Wheeler and Wheeler, 1936; for Bagendon, see Clifford *et al.*, 1961.

22. There are good examples from Bigbury Camp, Kent, Lord's Bridge, Cambridgeshire, Colchester, Essex, and Llyn Cerrig Bach, Anglesey. (See for example Fox, Sir C., 1946, pp. 84–5.)

23. See Birchall, 1965.

24. See Clarke, R. R., 1954. Not all the torcs were complete, but a study of the fragments showed that over fifty were represented.

7 Prehistory: the modern approach

There is still an all too frequent tendency for the archaeologist to be popularly regarded as a professional treasure hunter. The prehistorian would be similarly classified, and few people would bother to set him in a separate category. And those who take such a view of him are also inclined to suppose that his sole function is to excavate, and that his equipment, his badge of office almost, is nothing more sophisticated than a spade. If this were ever generally true, even in the distant past of the development of archaeology, it has long ceased to be so, and is getting further from the truth as each year passes.

Long and even bitter may be the academic arguments as to whether archaeology, as a teaching subject, should be classified with the Arts or with the Sciences, but there can be few prehistoric archaeologists who would not be glad to be called scientists in the broader sense of the word, and to hear it said that they approach their subject in a highly scientific manner, hand in glove with the scholars of many other scientific disciplines. As for excavation, that is no more than just one of many aids to the performance of the main task: the study, interpretation and exposition of the events of prehistory. In excavation, too, it would be fair to say that the spade itself is now often the least used of all the digging or earth-removing implements at the site.[1]

This book is not directly concerned with the methods and techniques of archaeological excavation, but it should be noted in passing that excavation itself is a scientific procedure, which should be carried out with an awareness of the requirements of any other scientific disciplines which may later be called in to deal with various aspects of the finds. It is the purpose of this final chapter to give some idea of the modern scientific approach in prehistoric archaeology, and of the tremendous extent of the combination between archaeology and other disciplines in approaching and solving some of the problems of prehistory. It is not possible to describe the various techniques mentioned in detail; in the case of some, space permits little more than the mention of their names. None is as simple and straightforward as the present account may make it seem, and all must be approached carefully and critically by the prehistorian, if he is to obtain a correct reading of the results they can offer him. The examples which appear here are of course only a selection, drawn from a fairly wide variety of fields in the natural sciences. References are quoted as far as possible, to enable the reader to study more fully any of the methods here referred to, and also to help him fill in at least some of the gaps.[2]

Pride of place is given to the study of chronology, which is of paramount importance to prehistory, since it is the measurement of time which provides the depth, and hence much of the meaning, for the narrative picture to which the previous chapters have been devoted. The next few pages indicate just a few of the ways in which the prehistorian can hope to establish the chronology of his sites and finds. It is only too obvious that a limitless amount of work remains to be done in this whole field for every period of prehistory, though some periods are clearly much worse off than others; if some of the gaps which remain seem discouraging, it is stimulating to glance in the other direction to see how far the science of chronology has come since the early nineteenth century, when C. J. Thomsen and others took the first tentative steps to bring order out of chaos (cf. Chapter 1).

'Order' in fact is a major part of what chronology means to the prehistorian: an order of events, calibrated by the measurement of time. Dating in the prehistoric period can be of two kinds: absolute or relative. By absolute dating is meant the assigning of an actual date, measured in years, to an object or site; relative dating is the assessment of its age in relation to other objects or sites. Thus it is absolute dating if the archæologist states that according to the radiocarbon evidence the latest level at site A must date from approximately 2300 B.C., but it is relative dating if he says that on grounds of the contained pottery and the typology of the flint artifacts, the latest level at site A must be rather younger than such and such a level at site B. In this second case, it might of course so happen that the level in question at site B had an independent absolute date, in which case a reasonable guess could perhaps be made at the date in years of the level at site A. But this, being only a deduction, would not alter the fact that site A had really only been relatively dated.

Obviously, absolute dating is highly desirable, but it is simply not always obtainable, and relative dating may be extremely useful. Thomsen was indulging in relative dating when he postulated the Three Ages, in which the Bronze Age was older than the Iron Age, and the Stone Age older than the Bronze Age; this proved to be a key to the whole basic problem of how to study prehistory.

224

Quite apart from the contributions of his colleagues in other disciplines, two cherished studies of his own are absolutely vital to the archaeologist in establishing a relative chronology: stratigraphy and typology.

The principle of stratigraphy is a golden rule of all excavation. The simplest example that can be given of how stratigraphy works has already been referred to in passing in Chapter 1: in an undisturbed sequence of horizontal strata, the lowest one must always be the oldest, and the highest one the youngest. This is mere common sense: the layers were deposited in chronological order from the bottom upwards, in fact, and since they are horizontal, the relative chronology of any objects that might occur in them would be very easily fixed merely by noting their depths below the surface.

In practice, of course, archaeological stratigraphy is much more complicated. The simple sequence of undisturbed horizontal layers is extremely rare. Contortions and inversions occur; ditches and pits are dug through earlier occupation levels, and the spoil from them is perhaps spread indiscriminately over the area around, after which they might become filled up again only slowly over a long period, possibly with intermittent cleaning out. Buildings collapse or are destroyed, and new ones are built up, partly or wholly on the same site. Ancient and modern animal burrowing, or the growth of tree roots, cause small objects to find their way down from their original containing level into an earlier one. But the rules of stratigraphy remain firm, and it is a matter of reading with minute care the sections revealed in the walls of **132** each archaeological trench to establish exactly what is the order of layers over the whole site. The order that holds good for the layers, in general holds good for the objects found properly *in situ* in them—though it must be remembered that not all the objects will necessarily have been new when they became

225

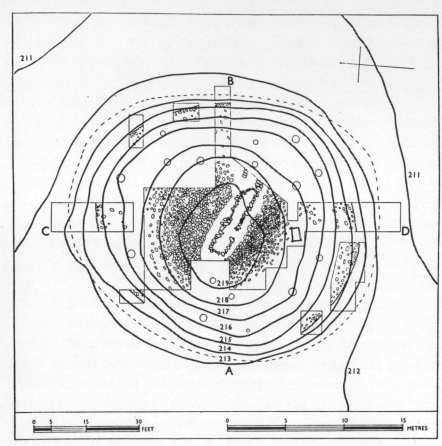

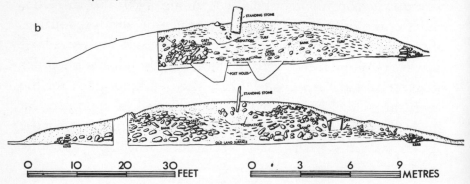

132 Archaeological plan (*a*) and sections (*b*), of a barrow excavation at Pitnacree, Perthshire, Scotland, to illustrate the care taken in recording a site during excavation. For details of the site and the excavation, see Coles and Simpson, 1965.

incorporated in the layer. After all, a penny bearing the head of Queen Victoria could easily fall from the pocket of a workman digging a trench today, and if some future archaeologist were to assume that the date on the coin automatically dated the digging of the trench, he might be making an error of more than a whole century.[3]

The question of typology has to be approached with similar care. Here, the principle is that objects of a given class can often be placed in order of age, simply on grounds of their style, technology and refinement, in so far as they form part of a sequence of types evolving in some understandable direction. Some examples of this have already been quoted: one famous one is the sequence of metal axe types in the Late Neolithic and Bronze Age, from the early flat copper ones through side-flanged types and palstaves to socketed axes. Here the evolution of the sequence appears largely to have been directed towards achieving efficiency in hafting. Another case mentioned was the gradual increase in refinement of Acheulian handaxes over a really vast period of time, again offering a typological sequence.[4] At Olduvai Gorge and a few other sites or groups of sites the evolving handaxe typology was admirably supported by the evidence of the stratigraphic succession.

Typology is always more satisfactory when thus supported, because it must be kept in mind that not every typological sequence necessarily proceeds in terms of straightforward technological improvement; there is, for instance, the possibility of devolution and degeneration. For example, the very last phase of Magdalenian art lacks the vitality and brilliance of its immediate predecessor, and the art, such as it is, of the Azilians, who may well have been direct descendants of the actual Magdalenian population, is a miserable sequel. On typological grounds alone, if there were no stratigraphy (that is, considering the naturalistic and

99

45

227

representational qualities of the art, and such technological features as the use in the cave art of perspective and of polychrome rather than monochrome painting), anyone who refused to admit the possibility of degeneration would be forced to place these cultural stages in the reverse order.[5] Another often quoted example, from a much later period, is the degeneration and indeed disintegration of the original designs of the Macedonian coins which were copied by barbarian cultures: successive barbarian reproductions of them get further and further from the fine originals, instead of closer and closer. So, typological sequence is not by any means synonymous with improvement as a hard and fast rule, and the archaeologist is right to approach unsupported purely typological evidence with deep suspicion. Functional variation can also cut across typological development in a most disruptive way.

The combination of typology and stratigraphy is a different matter, however, and offers the archaeologist the best means of placing a number of sites in their correct chronological order, in the absence of absolute dating. In some cases the stratigraphy involved is not only archaeological—i.e. not merely the occupation horizons, pits and ditches, building and destruction levels, and other artificial parts of a sequence. During the whole Palaeolithic Period, for example, the purely natural levels may be vital, as when they offer evidence that can securely link them to some specific climatic event of the Pleistocene sequence. Thus, at the Acheulian site of Hoxne, Suffolk, the artifacts occurred in an interglacial lake sediment, sandwiched between boulder clay deposits which were identifiable as belonging to the Mindel and Riss glaciations.[6] And the typology of the Hoxne handaxes agrees well with that of those from other sites of 'Great Interglacial' (Mindel-Riss) date.

Or again, a sequence of sites can be built up, by using the

occurrence in different places of deposits which represent the same climatic event. Another Lower Palaeolithic example will illustrate this: the latest Pleistocene deposit in the sequence at Barnfield Pit, Swanscombe, is a gravel which was demonstrably formed during cold conditions, and is attributable to the on-coming of the Riss glaciation. At nearby Baker's Hole, on a lower terrace level, Levalloisian artifacts were covered by a chalky deposit which is again of 'cold' origin, and which has been attributed to the very same cold phase. The relative dating of the Levalloisian site at Baker's Hole, in terms of the Swanscombe sequence, can accordingly be very closely fixed, and here the typology is of great interest, because the classic Early Levalloisian of Baker's Hole is something quite different from the Late Middle Acheulian which was the latest industry at Barnfield Pit.[7]

Some archaeological dating methods have both relative and absolute aspects. An example is the occurrence in barbarian contexts of traded objects from civilised cultures, like the Mycenaean objects which reached north-west Europe during the Bronze Age. In the relative sense, such finds demonstrate con-temporaneity between the barbarian recipients of the exotic objects, and that phase of the civilised culture responsible for the trading of them, if not for their manufacture. But since in the case of the civilised cultures the absolute chronology is often quite well known, the fact of contemporaneity may permit the extension of an absolute date to that particular phase of the barbarian culture. Even if there may be a certain time-lag involved, at least a terminus date of some sort should be forthcoming. For example, in some Scottish Iron Age sites beyond the frontier of Roman Britain, occasional fragments of Roman pottery acquired by the natives turn up, and can be assigned to vessels which could not have been made before such and such a date.[8] The Iron Age level where they were found accordingly cannot

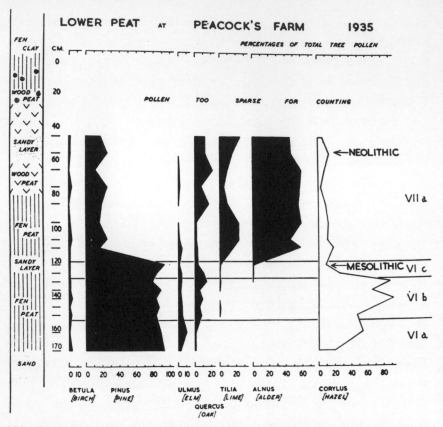

LOWER PEAT AT **PEACOCK'S FARM** 1935

PERCENTAGES OF TOTAL TREE POLLEN

POLLEN TOO SPARSE FOR COUNTING

←NEOLITHIC

VII a

←MESOLITHIC VI c

VI b

VI a

BETULA [BIRCH] PINUS [PINE] ULMUS [ELM] TILIA [LIME] ALNUS [ALDER] CORYLUS [HAZEL] QUERCUS [OAK]

133 Zoned tree pollen sequence diagram from peat deposits at Peacock's Farm, Shippea Hill, Cambs., showing changing vegetation. The positions of Mesolithic and Neolithic occupations of the site are indicated. For details of the site and the excavation, see Clark, J. G. D., 1955.

be earlier than that date, and one can perhaps hazard a guess on other grounds as to how much later it might be.

One of the uses of pollen analysis (other aspects of which are mentioned later in the chapter) also falls somewhere between the absolute and relative aspects of chronology. The identification of the pollen grains contained in a deposit, and the calculation of the amounts of each type of pollen present, enable the deposit in question to be assigned to a certain vegetational phase or

230

zone—the Late Glacial and Post-Glacial periods provide the best examples, although there are plenty of sites where pollen of much older date has been preserved: Hoxne and Clacton-on-Sea (the ancient Thames channel) are British examples of Lower Palaeolithic sites where pollen of Great Interglacial (Mindel-Riss) age occurred.

Thus a number of sites could be placed in order of relative age simply by pollen analysis, if identifiable pollen were present in sufficient quantity at all of them. The absolute dating aspect comes in because there are now sufficient absolute dates known (by methods described later in the chapter) for many of the pollen zones themselves (cf. Table 4), so that the assigning of a site to a definite pollen zone can sometimes be equivalent to giving it an approximate date in years within certain limits, making due allowance for such factors as the local variations in dating of the stages. So, if pollen from an epi-palaeolithic habitation site is identified as belonging to, say, a late part of the Allerød oscillation, Zone II, it will be known that Zone II dates roughly between 10,000 B.C. and 8800 B.C., and that this particular occupation appears to be late within that period.

There are also dating methods borrowed from the natural sciences which are of purely relative chronological interest. Excellent examples are provided by a number of analytical methods of establishing the relative ages of fossil or supposedly fossil bones—relative, that is, to each other and also to bones known to be of modern origin. A specific use of these methods has been to show whether or not particular bones found in Pleistocene deposits were contemporary with them.[9] Such methods on the one hand helped to reveal the Piltdown hoax, and showed that the Galley Hill skeleton from Swanscombe, Kent, was really a burial of much later date, intrusive to the Pleistocene gravel with which it had been claimed as contem-

231

porary; on the other hand they confirmed that the skull fragments from Barnfield Pit, Swanscombe, were genuinely contemporary with the fauna and implements found in the same Mindel-Riss gravel, and they have been used to confirm the high antiquity of many other important hominid fossils.

In general, the more successful of these methods depend either on the increase with time in the quantity of certain elements present in the mineral matter of a fossil bone, or else on the decrease in certain components of its residual organic matter. Thus in normal circumstances the amounts of fluorine and uranium in a bone increase with the time over which it has lain in a deposit, while the nitrogen content decreases. Local factors may be important, and unfortunately there are too many variables for it to be possible to obtain absolute dates by straightforward measurement of the relevant quantities themselves.

These then are some of the principal ways in which relative dates may be established, and, as has been shown, it may sometimes, but certainly not always, be possible to gain an idea of absolute dating from them.

Absolute dating itself has many techniques, most of them borrowed from other sciences, and each of them applicable only to certain objects or kinds of material, or in certain special circumstances.[10] A few leading examples are described in the next paragraphs.

The best known method, and the one which has supplied easily the most dates, including almost all those used in this book, is that of radiocarbon dating.[11] The method depends on two simple principles: first, all living organisms (animal or vegetable) contain carbon, of which a fixed proportion is radioactive; secondly, after death, no new carbon is received into the organism, and the radioactive carbon already there decays at a constant and measurable rate. Thus, by calculating the amount of radioactive

134 Part of the Radiocarbon Dating Laboratory at the British Museum, London

carbon left in suitable organic remains uncovered by the archaeologist, it should be possible to determine how much time has passed since the death of the organism.

The 'half-life' of C^{14}, the radioactive carbon isotope upon whose existence the method depends, has been variously calculated, but the most accurate figure yet obtained is 5730 ± 40 years. The half-life is the length of time which has elapsed when one half of a radioactive substance has decayed, but it should be borne in mind that during the following 5730 years what decays is not *the whole* of the remaining amount of radioactive carbon, but *half* of the remaining amount, and so on. In theory, therefore, the whole amount never actually vanishes, but from the practical point of view it becomes immeasurably small after a while, which is why the radiocarbon dating method cannot at the moment be used to obtain dates older than about 60,000–70,000 B.C. A few Mousterian dates have been calculated, and

233

even some Acheulian ones in Africa, where there is locally a very late survival of the culture; there are plenty of Upper Palaeolithic dates, too, but the bulk of the readings obtained by the radiocarbon method are for the later periods of prehistory.

Radiocarbon dates are given with a statistically determined probable error, stated as plus or minus so many years. This is inherent in the processing of the samples and the counting of the remanent radioactivity, and sometimes in the samples themselves, according to their origin and the risk of their being contaminated. The true date of any sample has only a finite chance of falling within the extremes represented by the calculated date plus and minus its quoted probable error, although too many archaeologists show a tendency to forget about this, and quote only the central figure without qualification.

There are many possible sources of fallibility in the radiocarbon method, ranging from lack of agreement about the exact half-life to the disturbing effects of nuclear weapon explosions which artificially increase the atmospheric content of C^{14}, and may therefore cause contamination. But in spite of all this, the numerous dates obtained up to now have remained pretty consistent within single archaeological periods or cultures, have usually come out in the correct order whenever there is a stratigraphical check on the samples used, and have on many occasions agreed reasonably well with any absolute dates which are known on other grounds, for example from historical sources. Doubtless improvements will continue to be made to the technology of radiocarbon dating, and therefore to its results, but it seems unlikely that the whole mass of dates already published will ever be proved wrong by more than an acceptably small percentage, or that the general validity of the method will be disproved.[12]

The lack of a widely applicable chronometric dating method for periods older than the extreme range of the radiocarbon method is crucial, so far as the Lower and Middle Palaeolithic periods are concerned. There are various radioactive decay methods which can date geological strata whose age is counted in tens of millions or even hundreds of millions of years, but these have so far proved of little use to the student of early prehistory with one main exception: the potassium-argon method.

The principles of this method are in some ways broadly comparable to those of radiocarbon dating. Potassium, which is a very common element in the earth's crust, and occurs in most minerals, contains a small but constant proportion of radioactive potassium (K^{40}). This decays slowly, and two products are formed: the Calcium isotope Ca^{40} and the Argon isotope A^{40}, the latter in a suitably small proportion. The amount of A^{40} in a potassium-rich mineral or rock sample is quite readily measurable, and by comparison of this amount with the potassium content of the same mineral or rock, the time required to produce such a quantity of A^{40} by decay of K^{40} can be calculated. While the method is at its best when applied to rather earlier periods, its use can occasionally be extended to the earlier parts of the Pleistocene. This depends on the presence in Pleistocene deposits of suitable potassium-rich minerals and rocks of contemporary (usually volcanic) origin, which have remained unaltered. It is unfortunately rare to find these conveniently in association with human industries, although this was the position at Olduvai Gorge.[13]

Far more potassium-argon dates are required before the degree of accuracy of this method for dating Pleistocene sites can be assessed, but meanwhile prehistorians are indebted to it for most of the few indications they have of the ultimate antiquity of man, and of the absolute age of some few events in the earlier parts of the Pleistocene sequence. (See also, however, the brief description of 'fission track dating' given below, and cf. Chapter 2, above, page 41 and note 7.)

If a generally applicable dating method is lacking for the earlier parts of the Pleistocene, the absolute chronology of its closing stages—the withdrawal of the Würm ice-sheets—is known in remarkable detail. This is due to the special nature of the sedimentary clay deposits formed at the bottom of the melt-water lakes along the margins of the dwindling ice-sheets. These sedimentary clays consist of superimposed thin regular laminations, and it was shown that each clay band corresponds to the deposition at the bottom of the lake of particles washed out from under the ice-sheet in the melt-water of a single year. These layers, called varves,[14] could be easily counted wherever they were exposed in quarries or cuttings into the former lake bed, now of course dry land. Since certain years produced distinctively thick or thin varves, because greater or less melting took place in response to a warmer or colder summer, it was possible to select 'marker' varves and trace them from one quarry to the next. Thus gradually the entire sequence has been counted for the whole ice withdrawal, as represented in various areas, the most successful results having been obtained in Sweden. The varve deposits over the whole former lake bed overlap each other

135 An exposure of varved clay, glacial Lake Hackensack, northern New Jersey

rather like tiles on a roof, because as the ice-sheets withdrew northwards, so the position of the melt-water lake along their margins moved back with them.

It was thus possible to date in actual years the various withdrawal stages of the ice, and to show for example that the great Scandinavian ice-sheet split into two in the melting process in the year 6839 B.C. Although these varve dates are never directly associated with human artifacts, since man did not live as near the ice-sheet as the melt-water lake, they are invaluable to prehistorians because they give absolute dates to the same Late-Glacial and early Post-Glacial stages which the pollen studies farther south can identify in their own way. And each varve can be used also to show exactly where the edge of the ice-sheet was at the time when it was formed; it is, of course, the position of the ice-sheet that affects the positions of the various vegetation zones farther south. Incidentally, the agreement between the varve dates and the radiocarbon dates for the various stages is close, and this was one of the early vindications of the radiocarbon method.

There is another absolute dating method which is occasionally useful to prehistorians, which is somewhat similar in principle to the varve dating. This involves the annual growth-rings in trees, and is known as dendrochronology. Like the varves, the tree-rings are a 'natural clock', since one ring is formed in each single year; as in the case of varves, so certain 'marker' growth rings can be picked out, corresponding to a year that was in some way exceptional. By counting growth-rings, and using the 'marker' ones to establish connections between one wood sample and another, it has been possible in a few areas to build up a strictly local sequence, starting with trees still growing today, and proceeding backwards through timbers used in buildings of historic age to the remains of timbers which occur on the sites of prehistoric buildings. It will be fairly obvious, however, that all the necessary conditions for the use of this method are only rarely fulfilled, and another limiting factor from the point of view of the prehistorian is the infrequency of timber survival in even the late prehistoric period.[15]

Two more absolute dating methods will be briefly described which are of comparatively recent archaeological application. The first is the estimation of the age of pottery by a technique known as thermoluminescence dating.[16] This method is still in the experimental stages, and the principles on which it depends are too complicated to describe here in detail. Broadly speaking, however, all pottery is bound to contain a small number of radioactive impurities; also, the structure of fired pottery is at least in part crystalline. The emission of alpha-particles from the radioactive constituents leads to the displacement of electrons, which become trapped in flaws in the crystal structure. The number of trapped electrons increases with the length of time since the pottery was fired, assuming it is not subjected meanwhile to excessive heat or to any other conditions which could upset the process.

In the laboratory, it is possible to release the trapped electrons from a powdered sample of pottery by rapid, violent heating under carefully controlled conditions. Their release is accompanied by an emission of light—hence the name of the method; the quantity of light emitted is measurable, and is directly related to the age of the pottery, though it is of course necessary to calculate other things like the rate of alpha-particle emission in the sample, since this will depend on the contained radioactive impurities, which naturally vary considerably.

If the thermoluminescence method, which has not yet by any means been fully developed or tested, can be proved properly valid, and refined as necessary for archaeological use, there will

238

be the remarkable prospect of obtaining absolute dates for the pottery found in most normal circumstances, and since pottery is one of the most frequent archaeological finds in later prehistoric periods, the contribution to the dating of prehistory would be impressive.

The final method selected for description here is the dating of artificial or natural (volcanic) glass by the fission track method.[17] This depends on the fact that the glass substances often contain uranium, which is subject to radioactive decay at a known and constant rate. Volcanic glass such as obsidian, for example, contains uranium in a quantity of the order of one or two parts per million. The spontaneous fission of uranium atoms during the decay process produces actual scored 'fission tracks', which can be seen and counted when a sample is examined microscopically. The age of the sample is proportional to the quantity of

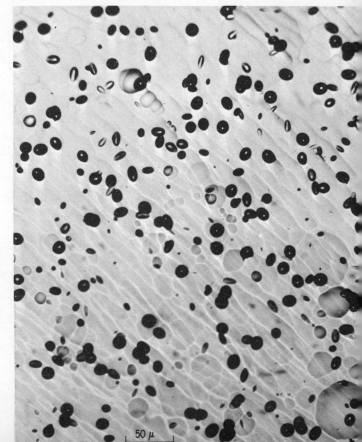

136
Fission track etch pits in an irradiated piece of natural glass (obsidian) from a Mesolithic blade, Gamble's Cave II, Elmenteita, Kenya

50 μ

fission tracks and the uranium content of the sample, and the age calculated is that of the formation of the glass, or the last time it was heated above a certain critical temperature. Thus natural glasses 20–40 million years old have been dated by this method, but it can also be used for artificial glass whose age is to be counted only in hundreds of years. A sample from an African obsidian dagger was tested, and it was found that the dagger had been exposed to violent heat about 4000 years ago. Of particular interest is the age of 2.03 ± 0.28 million years, calculated by the fission track method for natural glass in the volcanic deposits of Bed 1 at Olduvai Gorge (cf. page 235 above). When the respective margins of error are taken into consideration, this reading offers an exciting general confirmation of the high date determined for this bed by the potassium-argon method.

Enough has now been said in this chapter to give some idea of the variety of ways in which dates of one sort or another can be obtained for prehistory, and to show how far it is necessary to go beyond purely archaeological techniques to obtain them. Many more examples could be given, especially of relative dating methods. For instance, almost any effect on surviving animal or vegetable remains, or even on topography, whose direct relationship to climatic factors can be understood, may contain information relevant to the relative dating of Palaeolithic or Mesolithic sites. Such ultimately climatic effects may be exemplified as diversely as by general effects like the extinction of whole animal species through prolonged unfavourable conditions, or the formation of totally different and characteristic soils in the same area in warmer or colder or wetter or drier climates; or by such specialised effects as the differing ratio of the oxygen isotopes O^{18} and O^{16} in the calcium carbonate of the shells of the contemporary tiny foraminifera living in the surface water of the oceans, according to the temperature variations of the sea water.[18]

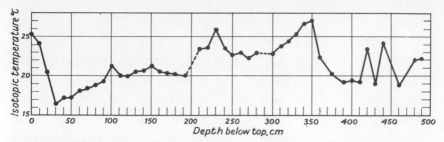

137 Temperature fluctuations in a deep sea core from the equatorial Atlantic, calculated from the ratio of the oxygen isotopes O^{16} and O^{18} in the calcium carbonate of foraminifera

These particular effects just mentioned relate, of course, to the glacial, interglacial and interstadial phases of the Pleistocene, which is why they are of chronological importance. The causes of the glaciations, which are not generally agreed, have also been studied from this point of view; thus M. Milankovitch worked out an absolute chronology for the Pleistocene Period based on the theory that the fluctuations of temperature and climate were the result of variations in solar radiation reaching the earth, and that the date of occurrence of these variations could be calculated on astronomical grounds. The figures he produced have not been universally accepted, though there is a most interesting comparison between some of the fluctuations in his 'radiation curve' and the Pleistocene climatic fluctuations recognised from other evidence.[19]

But the solving of the problems of chronology is not the only field in which the prehistoric archaeologist finds himself so deeply indebted to his colleagues in other branches of scientific study. The remainder of this chapter is devoted to a brief survey of some of the other aspects of his work in which similar methodological progress has been made. Examples will be given of new scientific approaches to the discovery of sites, to the study of ancient environments, and to the detailed study of different kinds

241

of artifacts. Where no special references are quoted, it may be assumed that a subject is well enough covered, and a bibliography provided, in the works already mentioned in the notes relating to earlier parts of this chapter.

Gone are the days when archaeologists dug only into obvious surviving monuments, such as the earth mounds of prominent barrows, or perhaps the ramparts of hill-forts, or in places where frequent finds had been made on the surface of the ground. Present digs often take place where there is little or nothing for the untrained eye to see on the surface. One of the major aids to the discovery of sites of this kind has been the adaptation of aerial reconnaissance and photography to archaeological purposes.

Buried walls and ancient banks and ditches, for example, leave clear traces when a wheat crop grows up in the field below

138 Archaeological air photography: crop-marks near Cassington, Oxon., showing part of a Late Iron Age defensive ditch (30 feet broad) and several ring ditches, which include Beaker and Middle Bronze Age barrow circles

whose surface they lie. In the shallow soil above masonry foundations, the crop grows poorly; in the deeper and richer soil marking the course of a filled ditch, the corn flourishes, standing taller and perhaps thicker; in conditions of drought, it will be the last to become parched, while that above the wall will be the first. Such differential growth in the field is unlikely when viewed from ground level to resolve itself into a clear pattern, but, seen from the air in optimum conditions, the shadows and the differences of colour stand out instantly to reveal a plan of **84, 138** the main structural features of the site, or of a whole palimpsest of sites. Thousands of sites of prehistoric and later periods have been discovered, in Britain alone, in this way.[20] The most recent suggestion is that satellite-based air reconnaissance, including such techniques as infra-red photography, might be of use to archaeologists and might reveal underwater or jungle-buried sites![21]

On the ground, too, much can be done before actual excavation begins, by resistivity surveying and the use of a proton magnetometer or similar instrument, quite apart from simpler expedients like the use of mine-detectors to reveal buried metal objects.

In the simplest terms, resistivity surveying depends on the fact that a mass of soil or rock of a suitable nature can conduct electricity flowing between two electrodes. If the mass of soil is homogeneous, the current behaves in a given 'normal' manner, but this becomes distorted if there are buried features anomalous in that they are either more or less 'resistive' than the soil mass. Thus the presence of such features as masonry structures or buried pits and ditches can be detected.

The proton magnetometer operates on a different principle, **139** namely by detecting anomalies or discontinuities in the earth's magnetic field, caused by the presence of buried fired structures or pits and ditches or masonry. It can also, of course, detect

139 A proton magnetometer in use: prospecting for Etruscan tombs, Tarquinia, Italy, 1961

buried iron objects. The fired structures, such as kilns and ovens, or even in fact areas of severely burnt earth, create a magnetic anomaly because clay or soil containing iron oxide, when it is heated to a certain critical temperature (about 675° C), retains on cooling a 'thermo-remanent magnetism' aligned to the contemporary magnetic field of the earth, which will have been different from that of today.[22] The buried pits, ditches and masonry, on the other hand, present a contrast with their surroundings in magnetic susceptibility.

The use of such techniques can be of the greatest assistance to an archaeologist in planning a dig, since a resistivity or magnetometer survey at a site can locate major features and indicate their general size and shape, before any removal of earth takes place, and the trenches can be located accordingly. Nor do scientific aids to the archaeologist necessarily cease when the actual digging begins: as an extreme example of the kind of assistance that can be forthcoming may be cited the use of closed-circuit television in the excavation of a ritual shaft almost 100 feet deep and only 6 feet wide, discovered beneath a Late Bronze Age pond-barrow at Normanton Gorse, Wilsford (Wiltshire).[23]

Finally, as regards the discovery of sites, and field-work, if that particular term can properly be used in this case, mention must be made of the rapidly growing subject of marine archaeology. Although there has in the past been much pure treasure hunting in ancient shipwrecks, if not plain looting, under the name of important archaeological work, a scientific and serious approach is rapidly becoming widespread. Prehistoric wrecks 107, 140

140 Marine archaeology: careful archaeological recording under water, during the excavation of a Byzantine wreck of the seventh century off the island of Yassi Ada, near Bodrum, Turkey

can provide priceless information, like that of the Bronze Age merchant ship with a cargo of copper ingots, which went down off Cape Gelidonya in south-west Turkey, around 1200 B.C. Space unfortunately does not permit a discussion here of the special techniques of submarine archaeological excavation, and there are many possibilities apart from the examination of ancient wrecks.[24]

The term 'environmental archaeology' has come into use to describe another field in which co-operation between archaeology and various branches of the natural sciences has been especially fruitful. The study of ancient environments is vital to any understanding of prehistoric peoples and economies, and there are now many ways in which environmental information can be obtained. Geological studies are an obvious one, particularly in connection with the Palaeolithic and Mesolithic periods, and enough examples have been given in the earlier parts of this book.

One of the most productive of the environmental studies has certainly been pollen analysis, which is a specialist botanical study rather than an archaeological one. This has already been mentioned for its part in helping to fix chronology, but that might be regarded as a secondary use. The survival of identifiable pollen grains in many ancient deposits in quite extraordinary quantities means that an ancient habitat can be vividly reconstructed, and light cast upon such matters as climate and temperature, natural food supplies for man and beast, and the availability of land for settlement. In the later prehistoric periods, too, the pollen record often shows the influence of man on the landscape—for example, when a sudden decline in tree pollen can be interpreted as caused by forest clearance, or when various effects of herd grazing or crop growing can be recognised. Apart from the microscopic study of pollen, the examination of larger plant

133

remains and surviving wood by the botanist is also important.

Two further fields which can provide information of this same general kind are the study of faunal remains and the study of soils. The faunal record from an archaeological site is clearly an eloquent witness to the ancient environment, especially if it does not consist solely of food animals selectively hunted. Certain kinds of animal are specialised to live in certain environments: the pig as a forest dweller and the horse for open country are classic examples. Then there are climatic specialisations: adaptations to warmer or colder and wetter or drier conditions. One does not today look for the warmth-loving hippopotamus in an arctic environment, or the reindeer in a tropical one. In Pleistocene faunas, differently adapted species of elephant or rhinoceros, for example, may alternate at the same latitude as a reflection of alternating warm and cold climates—which represent, of course, stages of the glacial and interglacial sequence. The cold-loving mammoth is known to have had a coat anything up to two feet thick. These examples are extreme ones, and it is the whole faunal record from a given site of whatever period that provides the best environmental evidence, not just selected species from it. In some circumstances the microfaunal remains, the mice, voles, and others, may be more sensitive indicators of climate and environment than those of larger animals. Molluscan remains can also be studied with important results, and bird-bones are another specialised branch of faunal studies. It is also usually possible for the faunal expert to distinguish between the bones of domesticated and wild species, a diagnosis which may be of both environmental and cultural interest.[25] These are only a few aspects of faunal studies.

The study of soils from archaeological sites is another important source of environmental information. Quite different kinds of soil form in different climates, by the weathering of the local rocks or other geological deposits, the precise nature of the latter also being an important factor. Other strata form in other ways: the deposition of loess dust in periglacial conditions, the settling of volcanic ash, or the formation of sedimentary clays on the bed of a temporary lake, are examples. The study of sedimentation processes in caves is a special branch of this general kind of study, and is of course highly relevant to the environmental archaeology of the Palaeolithic Period. While differing soils themselves reflect differing climatic conditions at the time of their formation, they are also important environmentally in that they support or inhibit different kinds of vegetation. The nature of the trees, wild food plants or crops which a soil will grow, makes for a favourable or unfavourable habitat for particular human and animal populations. The soil scientist and his close colleagues can also help considerably in the interpretation of archaeological as well as natural stratigraphy, by reporting on the deposits filling ditches and pits, for example, or layers which include burnt material.

The last main heading in this chapter is the specialist study of archaeological finds. This is extremely wide ranging, and involves co-operation between the archaeologist and workers in a host of other fields. It will already be apparent that an excavation report will often contain appended separate reports on such things as the bone, shell, plant and wood remains found at the site, but not much has yet been said of artifacts and inorganic finds, although passing mention of particular techniques of study has been made in earlier chapters.

Artifacts of stone and metal are often particularly rewarding subjects of study. The petrological examination of rock fragments used in tool-making, or even in building, can often lead to the
78, 79 identification of their sources and may reveal surprising facts

248

about prehistoric travel and trade. The fact that the Stonehenge 'bluestones' were brought to Wiltshire from the Preseli mountains in south Wales is perhaps the most famous example, but the identification of stone axe factory sites in Britain and elsewhere, from the microscopic examination of rock samples taken from actual implements, has produced a much greater quantity of information (cf. page 136 above). The trade in obsidian in the Near East in Neolithic times has also been studied in a broadly similar manner with interesting results.[26]

Metallurgical analyses of samples from copper, bronze, gold or iron objects can sometimes lead to similar results, but are often concerned with other kinds of information. Optical emission spectroscopy is a technique which has been used with considerable success in analysing the composition of the metals and alloys used by prehistoric smiths. The results of such analyses can cast light on, among other things, the processes used in preparing the metals, and how efficient they were. Another line of research has been into the methods of manufacture of the metal implements. In this case the examination, usually under a microscope, of the structure in a suitably prepared section of the implement, can reveal whether it has been cast in a mould, cold hammered or annealed.

Pottery is another subject to which microscopic analysis can sometimes be applied with striking success: the fabric is minutely examined, and it is occasionally possible to identify at least in general terms the geographical source of either the clay or the added tempering matter of grit, shell or whatever was used. Other more sophisticated analytical methods for pottery also exist, several of them described in the appropriate reference works quoted in the notes following this chapter.

Even the examination of flint implements, one of the oldest pastimes of the prehistoric archaeologist, has not escaped the influence of the microscope. Little progress, admittedly, has been made in tracing the raw material of flint artifacts to specific sources, after the style of the studies of the stone axe raw materials, or obsidian, and in any case flint tools are often enough made from material transported in pebble form by rivers or glaciers many miles from its genuine place of origin. But brilliant work by Dr S. A. Semenov in the U.S.S.R. has led to the identification and interpretation of wear and utilisation traces on a wide range of flint implements, in considerable detail, sometimes revealing not merely that a tool was used as a knife or scraper, but showing what kind of material it was used to cut or scrape.[27] Semenov has also worked on implements of other kinds of stone, and of bone and ivory, and he has studied the evidence for techniques of manufacture, as well as the utilisation traces. It is to be hoped that his lead will be increasingly followed in other areas.

As suggested above, then, a modern major excavation report is unusual if it does not include a number of specialist contributions, as well as the directing archaeologist's account of the dig and his interpretation of the results. Even a small site, or the find of a single important object, may be so treated.[28] But such specialist reports are, of course, additional to the purely archaeological description of the artifacts found—the lengthy typological classifications of the pottery and flints, or the detailed descriptions of the metalwork. Even here, however, the archaeologist is no longer left completely to his own traditional resources. One of the most dynamic, if not revolutionary, recent advances in the archaeological world has been the widespread adoption of statistical and mathematical methods of analysing and comparing archaeological material—methods often geared to the use of a computer.

While isolated examples of a statistical approach can be found in archaeological reports written several decades ago, it is only comparatively recently that there has been any general acceptance

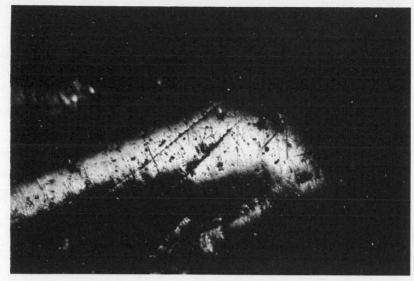

141 Traces of wear and utilisation on the working edges of flint implements:

    a. Late Palaeolithic end-scraper from Ali Tappeh, Behshahr, N.E. Iran, magnified × 100

    b. Neolithic or Bronze Age scraper, British (provenance unknown), magnified × 5

In both pictures, the preferred orientation of the scratches and wear marks is approximately at right angles to the axis of the working edge.

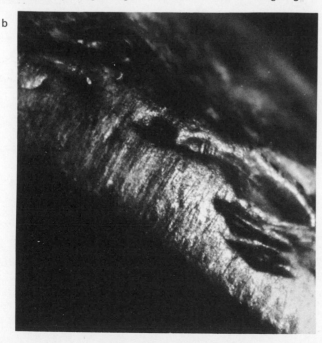

of the desirability of presenting all data as a series of precise objective and quantitative statements, instead of imprecise and relative generalisations, however inspired the latter might be. The use of what the uninitiated (amongst whom the writer includes himself) might regard as 'mild' statistics is becoming very wide-spread—frequency diagrams, histograms, means, standard deviations and 'tests of significance' for observed quantitative differences between artifact groups. But more sophisticated statistical methods—multifactorial analyses of one sort or another—are also gaining popularity, although the number of archaeologists who can understand them and operate them for themselves is still extremely limited. So here again there is much scope for co-operation between archaeologists and other specialists, in this case statisticians.

A pioneering study in Britain was that of D. L. Clarke, who used a system of matrix analysis—a multifactorial method—to assist a classification of British Beaker pottery. A computer was used in this experiment; there were between seven and eight hundred complete or reconstructable beakers, apart from several thousand sherds, and each beaker was described according to a list of thirty-nine objective variables or traits, which were mainly concerned with shape or decoration. The computer was successfully programmed to reveal significantly recurrent groups of these traits after all the information about all the beakers had been fed into it—in other words, to pick out what valid groups there might be in the whole British Beaker series, and to show something of their relationships and probable order in time.[29]

A more recent piece of work of considerable interest and methodological importance has been the successful use of 'average-link cluster analysis' and of a multidimensional scaling method, in classifying brooches from an Iron Age cemetery site at Münsingen, Switzerland, where there were various valid independent archaeological checks on what the 'correct' results were likely to be.[30] In America, work on archaeological problems using sophisticated statistical methods has been carried out by L. R. Binford, among others, including an example already referred to (see note 11 in Chapter 2). In France, the work of Professor F. Bordes on Lower and Middle Palaeolithic assemblages has long made use of numerical and quantitative methods, though of a simpler kind than the examples just mentioned.

Everywhere, and in all fields of archaeology, this still relatively new approach is gradually becoming a matter of course.[31] But it must not be thought that a computer is an instant push-button genius, or even a rather cumbersome magic wand. The machines do only exactly what they are told to do, no more and no less, and they do not originate methods of study: one cannot feed in yards of data tape in ordinary language, with a programme tape which merely bears the words 'find me the answer'. The present writer's own minor incursion into the world of computerised prehistory will illustrate this. The problem was only a very simple one: the working out by the computer of various means, standard devia-

142 'Still life with handaxes, 1968'. Two Middle Acheulian handaxes with some of the paraphernalia of metrical and statistical analysis, including slide rule, sliding callipers, computer tapes for data and program, print-out of a data tape and frequency graphs.

tions, frequencies and tests of significance in respect of thirty-eight groups of British handaxes—a total of towards 5000 implements was involved.[32] The computer itself took well under an hour to produce its neatly typed answers to the several thousand calculations. But the preparation of the data tapes in computer language, and the checking of them, plus the devising, testing and adjusting of appropriate programmes, even with expert assistance, took over fifteen weeks—not to mention several years spent on the actual collection of the data. However, to perform the same calculations by hand would have taken many months, quite apart from driving one mad!

This final chapter has touched on a wide range of subjects in a comparatively short space, and may well have left the reader somewhat dazed. If so, he is only sharing the reaction of many archaeologists to the scientific upheaval in their subject over the past ten or twenty years. Wide gaps have been left in the ground covered: little or nothing has been said for example about the use of experimental studies in elucidating ancient methods and techniques, or about the conservation of antiquities, or about the special role of physical anthropology, or of photography other than air photography—or a host of other subjects. But perhaps enough has been said, and enough references given, to justify the chapter's title.

To call such a chapter 'The Modern Approach' is asking for trouble, of course, but if it has already acquired an out-of-date look during the time the book has been in the press, this will merely illustrate further the whole point it has sought to make: the study of prehistory is very much moving with the times. We have not yet reached the stage where new text-books are automatically out of date in a month, and even the publication of crowded weekly journals cannot keep pace with research results.

But everyone can feel the power of the current acceleration in the study of prehistory, and no one need doubt that the subject is progressing along a path that is scientific in the best sense of the word.

NOTES

1. The subject of excavation, with all its modern methods and techniques, is outside the scope of this book. Properly directed and executed, an excavation is now a scientific research project carried out with infinite precision, and the publication of a major excavation report is no less exacting than the work in the field. It is for such reasons that a spade is too clumsy for all but the preliminary earth movement at most sites: a small pointed trowel is the most used implement, but delicate operations, such as the excavation and cleaning up of a skeleton or a delicate find prior to photography *in situ*, may be performed with such tools as a paint brush, a tooth pick and a darning needle, only a few cubic inches of earth perhaps being removed in a whole day's anxious and concentrated work. It must be remembered that almost every excavation involves the *only* opportunity to examine unique evidence which is thereby destroyed— not the artifacts themselves which are found, but their precise archaeological context. Hence the need for every care, and the presentation of a proper record **132** of what was seen and what was done.

The mention of excavation may well awaken in some readers the desire to participate in a dig. In Britain, they can do no better than get in touch with the Council for British Archaeology, and subscribe to its *Calendar of Excavations*, published monthly during each spring and summer, and costing only a few shillings. The *Calendar* lists forthcoming digs and indicates their requirements for volunteer helpers, stating whether training is offered and giving other essential information. The Council's present address is 8 St Andrew's Place, London N.W.1, and the present price of the *Calendar* is 7s 6d (1968).

2. Two basic sources for further reading are Brothwell and Higgs, eds, 1963, and Pyddoke, ed., 1963. The former is much the larger of the two books, which overlap in many respects, and are complementary in others; they contain between them an extensive supply of further references. De Laet, 1957, should also be consulted. The main general scientific and archaeological journals also contain information regularly; *Archaeometry* (published by the Oxford University Research Laboratory for Archaeology and the History of Art) specialises in various aspects of the field. The journal *Antiquity* is one which often carries at

least a note about new methods from the archaeological point of view soon after they are introduced. Books on more specific subjects, which are likely to be at least in part suitable at an introductory level, include those listed below, though not all the subjects with which they deal can be discussed in the present chapter: Aitken, 1961; Biek, 1963; Butzer, 1964; Cornwall, 1956; Cornwall, 1958; Dimbleby, 1967; Heizer and Cook, eds, 1960; Hodges, 1964; Rosenfeld, 1965; Tylecote, 1962; Zeuner, 1958.

3. Difficulties of just such a kind arise on archaeological sites when some object that was perhaps an heirloom is found in an occupation or rubbish deposit. The best guide of this kind to the age of the deposit must be the *newest* object properly belonging to it, not the oldest. In the case of the Victorian penny from the workman's pocket, it would really only establish that the trench could not have been dug *before* the date on the coin. No doubt the condition of the coin would strongly suggest that it had been in circulation for many years. When Roman Imperial or Belgic coins, for example, occur in prehistoric contexts, they lack the convenient feature of an actual date, and must be dated to the known reign of the emperor or king, though in the case of the Roman coins such things as the details of the inscription may permit a closer estimate of the year of issue. The next step is to consider how long they were likely to have been in circulation, and how they agree with the evidence of the other objects found with them.

4. The word 'type' is much misused and much argued about in archaeology, so that one hardly dares to use it, or the derivative 'typology'. It is certainly true that in both the examples here quoted, the main sequence is in terms of technological improvement and increased functional efficiency. Referring loosely to the typical product at each stage as a 'type' does not worry the present writer, who merely hopes the reader will forgive him if he feels it to be necessary.

5. However, it must not be forgotten that it is a subjective judgement to assume that what most people regard as the finest achievements, aesthetically, of Magdalenian art really are 'better' or 'more advanced' than those of the culture's last and supposedly degenerate phase. The Magdalenians themselves might have preferred the latter. Do the best examples of modern abstract painting and sculpture, of 'pop art' or 'action painting', represent a decline from, say, the masterpieces of High Renaissance painting and sculpture? Or have we instead ascended to some higher, rarified level of art far above the comprehension of the Renaissance masters? However much one might wish to give a simple, emphatic and immediate reply to such questions, they are not always so easily answered if approached with strict objectivity. Art does not in general improve or deteriorate technologically in the manner of functional artifacts, for all its

obvious changes of style. But it will still be found involved in the typological sequences of prehistoric archaeology, rightly or wrongly.

6. See West and McBurney, 1954.

7. Cf. Wymer, 1961, pp. 4–7, and other references quoted there.

8. Certain kinds of Roman pottery are very accurately datable. An example is Samian Ware, items of which often bear an identifiable potter's stamp on the base: the dates between which many of the potters worked are known, but similar considerations to those mentioned in n. 3 may apply.

9. Dr K. P. Oakley has described these methods on several occasions—see for example Brothwell and Higgs, eds, 1963, pp. 24–34, and other references quoted there; also Pyddoke, ed., 1963, 111–19.

10. 'Chronometric dating' is another name, increasingly found. Some of the works quoted in n. 2 above incorporate brief reviews of absolute dating methods in general, e.g. Zeuner, 1958 and Butzer, 1964. Another book to do this, mainly for the Pleistocene Period, is Oakley, 1966.

11. Brief accounts of the basic principles of the radiocarbon method are available in several of the source books already quoted for this chapter, and indeed in many popular archaeological books. The discoverer of the method was Professor W. F. Libby, whose own exposition of it can be read in Libby, 1955. The journal *Radiocarbon*, published annually by the *American Journal of Science* (Yale University), is another useful source of information, though its main function is the publication of dates obtained by laboratories all over the world.

12. Some of the basic sources of error are mentioned (with a good bibliography of references) by E. H. Willis in Brothwell and Higgs, eds, 1963, pp. 35–46. See also Stuiver and Suess, 1966 (with numerous references), Dyck, 1967 and Walton, 1967. It has recently become evident that at certain times during the past, for reasons which are not yet fully understood, the correspondence between one 'radiocarbon year' and one calendar year has not been exact.

13. See Leakey, 1966–7, I, pp. 86–91. The method in general is well explained in brief in Brothwell and Higgs, eds, 1963, pp. 72–84, with further references.

14. Two of several accessible references which offer further information on the varve method, and references, are Zeuner, 1958, pp. 20–45, and Oakley, 1966, pp. 77–80. A lively account of the work of Baron de Geer, the Swedish inventor of the varve method, will be found in Bibby, 1957, ch. 12.

15. For dendrochronology, see for example Brothwell and Higgs, eds, 1963, pp. 162–76, and references quoted. The most extensive application of the method to prehistoric material has been in America. For a recently published example in another area, admittedly not in the prehistoric period, see *Novgorod the*

Great (Thompson, 1967), 23–34: immense quantities of timber survived in waterlogged deposits in this important Russian medieval city, including superimposed timber streets; dendrochronology was used with great success.

16. Not much is yet published on this subject. A brief account of the method will be found in Brothwell and Higgs, eds, 1963, pp. 90–2.

17. See the weekly journal, *New Scientist*, as follows: vol. XXI, pp. 406–8 (13 Feb. 1964); vol. XXV, pp. 690–1.(18 Mar. 1965) and vol XXVI, p. 81 (8 Apr. 1965); also the weekly journal, *Nature*, vol. CCV p. 1138 (13 Mar. 1965). The main work on fission-track dating has been done by Drs R. L. Fleischer, P. B. Price, and R. M. Walker, of the General Electric Research Laboratory, Schenectady, New York.

18. The shells of the foraminifera become incorporated in the fine ooze deposits which cover much of the ocean bed; samples are taken by boring into undisturbed areas of these sediments, and are studied as 'deep sea cores'. Radiocarbon dating can be applied to organic material in the cores. See Brothwell and Higgs, eds, 1963, pp. 99–107, and references quoted.

19. See Zeuner, 1958, especially pp. 134–45. Brief accounts occur in various of the works already quoted in this chapter, e.g. de Laet, 1957, pp. 71–2, and Butzer, 1964, pp. 35–7.

20. One of the most important earlier books was Crawford and Keiller, 1928. One of the most recent is St Joseph, ed., 1966: the subject-matter is not confined to archaeology, but see Ch. 10, pp. 113–26 especially. Much further information will be gained from most numbers of the quarterly periodical *Antiquity* over the last ten years or so, latterly including regular reports and illustrations of new discoveries by Dr St Joseph.

21. See *Antiquity*, XLI, no. 63, Sep., 1967, pp. 225–7.

22. The principle of thermo-remanent magnetism can also be used in a method of dating fired structures and even pottery (in certain special circumstances). See Brothwell and Higgs,·eds, 1963, pp. 59–71, and other references quoted there.

23. See Ashbee, 1963.

24. See Taylor, ed., 1965. A description of the Cape Gelidonya find is included in this book, and there are good illustrations.

25. A comparable line of study is the identification of ancient cultivated plants, particularly the early wheats and barleys, and this is certainly an environmental study. A readily accessible source for further reference is Dr Hans Helbaek's article 'Palaeo-Ethnobotany' in Brothwell and Higgs, eds, 1963, pp. 177–85. For domestic animals, see Zeuner, 1963.

26. See Cann and Renfrew, 1964, and also Renfrew *et al.*, 1966.

27. See Semenov, 1964.

28. The reader can illustrate this point for himself by reference to any recent number of one of the leading archaeological journals. To take a single instance at random: see Coles *et al.*, 1964.

29. An interim report on this work is given by Dr Clarke in Clarke, D. L., 1962. A major book by him entitled *Analytical Archaeology* will be published in 1968 by Methuen.

30. See Hodson, *et al.*, 1966.

31. See Heizer and Cook, eds, 1960. Another important paper is Tugby, 1965.

32. An interim report on the research project in question appeared in Roe, 1964; a follow-up article, including an account of the computer work and the general results has been prepared and will be published shortly in the same journal (1968).

Bibliography

The place of publication is London unless otherwise stated

AITKEN, M. J. 1961, *Physics and Archaeology*, Interscience Publishers, London and New York.

ALIMEN, H. 1957, *The Prehistory of Africa*, translated from the French by A. H. Brodrick, Hutchinson.

ALLEN, D. 1961, 'The Origins of Coinage in Britain', in Frere, ed., pp. 97–308.

APSIMON, A. 1954, 'Dagger Graves in the "Wessex" Bronze Age', in *Tenth Annual Report of the University of London Institute of Archaeology*, 37–62.

ASHBEE, P. 1958, 'The Fussell's Lodge Long Barrow', in *Antiquity*, XXXII 106–11.

— 1960, *The Bronze Age Round Barrow in Britain*, Phoenix House.

— 1963, 'The Wilsford Shaft', in *Antiquity*, XXXVII 116–20.

— 1966, 'The Fussell's Lodge Barrow Excavations', in *Archaeologia*, C 1–80, Society of Antiquaries of London.

ATKINSON, R. J. C. 1960, *Stonehenge*, Pelican.

—, PIGGOTT, C. M., and SANDARS, N. K., 1951, *Excavations at Dorchester, Oxon.*, Oxford, Ashmolean Museum.

BALOUT, L., BIBERSON, P., and TIXIER, J., 1967, 'L'Acheuléen de Ternifine (Algérie), Gisement de l'Atlanthrope', in *L'Anthropologie*, LXXI, nos 3-4, 217-38.

BERGGREN, W. A., PHILLIPS, J. D., BERTELS, A., and WALL, D. 1967, 'Late Pliocene-Pleistocene Stratigraphy in Deep Sea Cores from the South-Central North Atlantic', in *Nature*, CCXVI (21 Oct 1967) 253-5.

BERSU, G. 1940, 'Excavations at Little Woodbury, Wiltshire', in *Proceedings of the Prehistoric Society*, VI 30-111.

BIBBY, G. 1957, *The Testimony of the Spade*, Collins, and also Collins's Fontana Library (paperbacks) series, 1962.

BIEK, L. 1963, *Archaeology and the Microscope*, Lutterworth.

BINFORD, L. R. and BINFORD, S. 1966, 'A Preliminary Analysis of Functional Variability in the Mousterian of Levallois Facies', in *Recent Studies in Paleoanthropology*, pp. 238-95 (ed. J. D. Clark and F. C. Howell, *American Anthropologist*, LXVIII, 2, part 2, Apr 1966).

BIRCHALL, A. 1965, 'The Aylesford-Swarling Culture: The Problem of the Belgae Reconsidered', in *Proceedings of the Prehistoric Society*, XXXI 241-367.

BISHOP, W. W. and CLARK, J. D., eds, 1968, *Background to Evolution in Africa*, University of Chicago Press.

BORDES, F. 1953, 'Essai de classification des industries "moustériennes"', in *Bulletin de la Société Préhistorique Française*, L 226-35.

— 1961, 'Mousterian Cultures in France', in *Science*, CXXXIV 803-10.

BOULE, M. and VALLOIS, H. V. 1957, *Fossil Man*, English translation by Michael Bullock of the revised and enlarged French 4th ed., Thames & Hudson.

BRAIDWOOD, R. J., HOWE, B. *et al.* 1960, *Prehistoric Investigations in Iraqi Kurdistan*, University of Chicago Press, being no. 31

in the series Studies in Ancient Oriental Civilisation, published by the Oriental Institute of the University of Chicago.

BRAIDWOOD, R. J. and WILLEY, G. R., eds, 1962, *Courses toward Urban Life*, Edinburgh U.P., being no. 32 in the series Viking Fund publications in Anthropology.

BRAILSFORD, J. W. 1949, 'Excavations at Little Woodbury: Part IV, Supplementary Excavation 1947; Part V, The Small Finds', in *Proceedings of the Prehistoric Society*, XV 156–68.

— and JACKSON, J. W. 1948, 'Excavations at Little Woodbury, Wiltshire (1938–39): Part II, The Pottery; Part III, The Animal Remains', in *Proceedings of the Prehistoric Society*, XIV 1–23.

BREUIL, H. 1952, *Four Hundred Centuries of Cave Art*, Centre d'Études et de Documentation Préhistorique, Montignac; English trans. 1952.

BREWSTER, T. C. M. 1963, *The Excavation of · Staple Howe*, The East Riding Archaeological Research Committee, Malton, Yorkshire.

BRITTON, D. 1960, 'The Isleham Hoard, Cambridgeshire', in *Antiquity*, XXXIV 279–82 and plates XXXVI-XXXVII.

— 1963, 'Traditions of Metal-working in the Later Neolithic and Early Bronze Age of Britain, Part I', in *Proceedings of the Prehistoric Society*, XXIX 258–325.

BROTHWELL, D. R. 1961, 'The People of Mount Carmel', in *Proceedings of the Prehistoric Society*, XXVII 155–9.

— and HIGGS, E. S., eds, 1963, *Science in Archaeology*, Thames & Hudson.

BULLEID, A. and GRAY, H. ST G. 1911–17, *The Glastonbury Lake Village*, vol. I, 1911, and vol. II, 1917, Glastonbury Antiquarian Society.

— 1948–53, *The Meare Lake Village*, vol. I, 1948, and vol. II, 1953, privately printed.

BUNCH, B. and FELL, C. I. 1949, 'A Stone-Axe Factory at Pike of Stickle, Great Langdale, Westmorland', in *Proceedings of the Prehistoric Society*, XV 1–20.

BURSTOW, G. P. and HOLLEYMAN, G. A. 1957, 'The Late Bronze Age Settlement on Itford Hill, Sussex', in *Proceedings of the Prehistoric Society*, XXIII 167–212.

BUTZER, K. W. 1964, *Environment and Archaeology, an Introduction to Pleistocene Geography*, Aldine Publishing Co, Chicago.

CANN, J. R. and RENFREW, A. C. 1964, 'The Characterisation of Obsidian and its application to the Mediterranean Region', in *Proceedings of the Prehistoric Society*, XXX 111–33.

CERAM, C. W. 1952, *Gods, Graves and Scholars*, English ed., Gollancz and Sidgwick & Jackson.

CHADWICK, J. 1961, *The Decipherment of Linear B*, Pelican.

CHARLESWORTH, J. K., 1957, *The Quaternary Era, with Special Reference to its Glaciation*, 2 vols, Arnold.

CHENG TÊ-K'UN 1959, *Archaeology in China*, vol. 1: *Prehistoric China*, Heffer, Cambridge.

CHILDE, V. G. 1929, *The Danube in Prehistory*, Oxford, Clarendon Press.

— 1931, *Skara Brae, a Pictish Village in Orkney*, Kegan Paul, Trench, Trubner.

— 1951a, *Social Evolution*, Watts.

— 1951b, 'The First Wagons and Carts from the Tigris to the Severn', in *Proceedings of the Prehistoric Society*, XVII 177–94.

— 1952, *New Light on the Most Ancient East*, Routledge.

— 1957, *The Dawn of European Civilisation*, 6th ed., revised, Routledge.

— 1958, *The Prehistory of European Society*, Pelican.

CLARK, J. D. 1959, *The Prehistory of Southern Africa*, Pelican.

CLARK, J. G. D. 1932, *The Mesolithic Age in Britain*, Cambridge U.P.

— 1936, *The Mesolithic Settlement of Northern Europe*, Cambridge U.P.

— 1948, 'The Development of Fishing in Prehistoric Europe', in *Antiquaries Journal*, XXVIII 45–85.

— 1950, 'The Earliest Settlement of the West Baltic Area in the Light of Recent Research', in *Proceedings of the Prehistoric Society*, XVI 87–100.

— 1952, *Prehistoric Europe: The Economic Basis*, Methuen.

— 1954, *Excavations at Star Carr: an Early Mesolithic Site at Seamer, near Scarborough, Yorkshire*, Cambridge U.P.

— 1955, 'A Microlithic Industry from the Cambridgeshire Fenland, and other Industries of Sauveterrian Affinities from Britain', in *Proceedings of the Prehistoric Society*, XXI 3–20.

— 1957, *Archaeology and Society*, 3rd ed., Methuen; also in Methuen's University Paperbacks series, 1960.

— 1958, 'Blade and Trapeze Industries of the European Stone Age', in *Proceedings of the Prehistoric Society*, XXIV 24–42.

— 1962, *World Prehistory: an Outline*, Cambridge U.P.

— 1963, 'Neolithic Bows from Somerset, England, and the Prehistory of Archery in North-West Europe', in *Proceedings of the Prehistoric Society*, XXIX 50–98.

— 1965, 'Radiocarbon Dating and the Expansion of Farming Culture from the Near East over Europe', in *Proceedings of the Prehistoric Society*, XXXI 58–73.

— 1966, 'The Invasion Hypothesis in British Archaeology', in *Antiquity*, XL (Sep 1966) 172–89.

— 1967, *The Stone Age Hunters*, Library of the Early Civilisations, Thames & Hudson.

— and FELL, C. I. 1953, 'The Early Iron Age Site at Micklemoor Hill, West Harling, Norfolk, and its Pottery', in *Proceedings of the Prehistoric Society*, XIX 1–41.

— and GODWIN, H. 1962, 'The Neolithic in the Cambridgeshire Fens', in *Antiquity*, XXXVI 10–23.

— and PIGGOTT, S. 1965, *Prehistoric Societies*, The History of Human Society series, general ed. J. H. Plumb, Hutchinson.

CLARKE, D. L. 1962, 'Matrix Analysis and Archaeology with reference to British Beaker Pottery', in *Proceedings of the Prehistoric Society*, XXVIII 371–82.

CLARKE, R. R. 1954, 'The Early Iron Age Treasure from Snettisham, Norfolk', in *Proceedings of the Prehistoric Society*, XX 27–86.

— 1960, *East Anglia*, Ancient Peoples and Places series, Thames & Hudson.

CLIFFORD, E. M. *et al.*, 1961, *Bagendon: A Belgic Oppidum. A Record of the Excavations of 1954–1956*, Heffer, Cambridge.

COGHLAN, H. H. and CASE, H. J. 1957, 'Early Metallurgy of Copper in Ireland and Britain', in *Proceedings of the Prehistoric Society*, XXIII 91–123.

COLE, S. 1961, *The Neolithic Revolution*, British Museum (Natural History).

— 1964, *The Prehistory of East Africa*, revised ed., Weidenfeld & Nicolson; originally published by Pelican, 1954.

COLES, J. M. 1963, 'Irish Bronze Age Horns and their relations with Northern Europe', in *Proceedings of the Prehistoric Society*, XXIX 326–56.

— COUTTS, H., and RYDER, M. L. 1964, 'A Late Bronze Age Find from Pyotdykes, Angus, Scotland, with associated Gold, Cloth, Leather and Wood Remains', in *Proceedings of the Prehistoric Society*, XXX 186–98.

— and SIMPSON, D. D. A. 1965, 'The Excavation of a Neolithic Round Barrow at Pitnacree, Perthshire, Scotland', in *Proceedings of the Prehistoric Society*, XXXI 34–57.

CORNWALL, I. W., 1956, *Bones for the Archaeologist*, Phoenix House.

— 1958, *Soils for the Archaeologist*, Phoenix House.

COX, A., DALRYMPLE, G. B. and DOELL, R. R. 1967, 'Reversals of the Earth's Magnetic Field', in *Scientific American*, CCXVI 2 (Feb 1967) 44–54.

CRAWFORD, O. G. S. and KEILLER, A. 1928, *Wessex From The Air*, Oxford U.P.

CUNNINGTON, M. E. 1923, *The Early Iron Age Inhabited Site at All Cannings Cross Farm, Wiltshire. A Description of the Excavations and Objects found by Mr and Mrs B. H. Cunnington, 1911–1922*, George Simpson, Devizes.

DANIEL, G. E. 1943, *The Three Ages*, Cambridge U.P.

— 1950a, *A Hundred Years of Archaeology*, Duckworth.

— 1950b, *The Prehistoric Chamber Tombs of England and Wales*, Cambridge U.P.

— 1958, *The Megalith Builders of Western Europe*, Pelican.

— 1960, *The Prehistoric Chamber Tombs of France. A Geographical, Morphological and Chronological Survey*, Thames & Hudson.

— 1962, *The Idea of Prehistory*, The New Thinkers Library series, Watts.

— 1967a, *The Origins and Growth of Archaeology*, Pelican.

— 1967b, 'Northmen and Southmen', a note in *Antiquity*, XLI (Dec 1967) 313–17.

DAY, M. 1965, *Guide to Fossil Man: A Handbook of Human Palaeontology*, Cassell.

DEHN, W. 1958, 'Die Heuneburg an der oberen Donau und ihre Wehranlagen', in *Neue Ausgrabungen in Deutschland*, pp. 127–45, published by the Römisch-Germanische Kommission des Deutschen Archäologischen Instituts zu Frankfurt-a-M; Gebr. Mann, Berlin.

DIMBLEBY, G. W. 1967, *Plants and Archaeology*, John Baker.

DYCK, W. 1967, 'Recent Developments in Radiocarbon Dating and their Implications for Geochronology and Archaeology', in *Current Anthropology*, VIII, 4 (Oct 1967) 349–52.

EOGAN, G. 1964, 'The Later Bronze Age in Ireland in the light of recent research', in *Proceedings of the Prehistoric Society*, XXX 268–351.

— 1967, 'The Knowth (Co. Meath) Excavations', in *Antiquity*, XLI (Dec 1967) 302–4 and plates XXXVIII–XLIII.

— 1968, 'Excavations at Knowth, Co. Meath, 1962–1965', in *Proceedings of the Royal Irish Academy*, 66, Section C, no. 4, 299–400.

EVANS, E. E. 1966, *Prehistoric and Early Christian Ireland: A Guide*, Batsford.

EVENS, E. D., GRINSELL, L. V., PIGGOTT, S. and WALLIS, F. S. 1962, 'Fourth Report of the Sub-Committee of the South Western Group of Museums and Art Galleries (England) on the Petrological Identification of Stone Axes', in *Proceedings of the Prehistoric Society*, XXVIII 209–66.

FEACHEM, R. W. 1963, *Prehistoric Scotland*, Batsford.

FLINT, R. F. 1957, *Glacial and Pleistocene Geology*, John Wiley, New York, and Chapman & Hall, London.

FOX, Lady A. 1964, *South West England*, Ancient Peoples and Places series, Thames & Hudson.

FOX, SIR C. 1946, *A Find of the Early Iron Age from Llyn Cerrig Bach, Anglesey*, National Museum of Wales, Cardiff.

— 1958, *Pattern and Purpose: A Study of Early Celtic Art in Britain*, National Museum of Wales, Cardiff.

— 1959, *Life and Death in the Bronze Age: An Archaeologist's Field Work*, Routledge.

FREEMAN, L. G., Jr. 1966, 'The Nature of Mousterian Facies in Cantabrian Spain', in *Recent Studies in Paleoanthropology*, pp. 230–7 (ed. J. D. Clark and F. C. Howell, *American Anthropologist*,

LXVIII 2, part 2, Apr 1966).

FRERE, S. S., ed. 1961, *Problems of the Iron Age in Southern Britain*, published as *Occasional Paper No. 11* by the University of London Institute of Archaeology.

GARROD, D. A. E. 1926, *The Upper Palaeolithic Age in Britain*, Oxford, Clarendon Press.

— 1957 'The Natufian Culture. The Life and Economy of a Mesolithic People in the Near East', in *Proceedings of the British Academy*, XLIII 211–27.

— 1962, 'The Middle Palaeolithic of the Near East and the Problem of Mount Carmel Man', in *Journal of the Royal Anthropological Institute*, XCII 232–51.

GIMBUTAS, M. 1965, *Bronze Age Cultures in Central and Eastern Europe*, Mouton.

GOLOMSHTOK, E. A. 1938, 'The Old Stone Age in European Russia', *Transactions of the American Philosophical Society*, new series, XXIX, Philadelphia.

GRAZIOSI, P. 1960, *Palaeolithic Art*, English translation, Faber, 1960.

GRIGOR'EV, G. P. 1967, 'A New Reconstruction of the Above-Ground Dwelling of Kostenki', *Current Anthropology*, VIII, 4 (Oct 1967) 344–8.

GRINSELL, L. V. 1953, *The Ancient Burial Mounds of Britain*, 2nd ed., revised, Methuen.

GURNEY, O. R. 1952, *The Hittites*, Pelican.

HAMILTON, J. R. C. 1956, *Excavations at Jarlshof, Shetland* (*Ministry of Works Archaeological Reports, No. 1*, H.M.S.O., Edinburgh).

HAMMEN, T. C. VAN DER, MAARLEVELD, G. C., VOGEL, J. C. and ZAGWIJN, W. H. 1967, 'Stratigraphy, climatic succession and radiocarbon dating of the Last Glacial in the Netherlands', in *Geologie en Mijnbouw*, XLVI 3 (Mar 1967) 79–95.

HAWKES, C. F. C. 1931, 'Hill Forts', in *Antiquity*, v 60–97.

— 1940, *The Prehistoric Foundations of Europe to the Mycenaean Age*, Methuen.

— and HULL, M. R. 1946, *Camulodunum*, Reports of the Research Committee of the Society of Antiquaries of London, no. 14, Oxford U.P.

HAWKINS, G. 1965, *Stonehenge Decoded*, Souvenir Press.

HEIZER, R. F. and COOK, S. F., eds, 1960, *The Application of Quantitative Methods in Archaeology*, Viking Fund Publications in Anthropology, no. 28, Quadrangle Books, Chicago, and Tavistock Publications, London.

HENCKEN, T. C. 1938, 'The Excavation of the Iron Age Camp on Bredon Hill, Gloucestershire, 1935–1937', in *Archaeological Journal*, XLV I–III.

HENSHALL, A. S. 1963, *The Chambered Tombs of Scotland*, Edinburgh U.P., vol. I 1963, vol. II forthcoming.

HIGGS, E. S. 1961, 'Some Pleistocene Faunas of the Mediterranean Coastal Areas', in *Proceedings of the Prehistoric Society*, XXVII 144–54.

HODGES, H. M. W. 1964, *Artifacts*, John Baker.

HODSON, F. R. 1964, 'Cultural Grouping within the British Pre-Roman Iron Age', in *Proceedings of the Prehistoric Society*, XXX 99–110.

—, SNEATH, P. H. A. and DORAN, J. E. 1966, 'Some Experiments in the Numerical Analysis of Archaeological Data', in *Biometrika*, LIII 3 and 4 311–24.

HOWELL, F. C. 1966, 'Observations on the Earlier Phases of the European Lower Palaeolithic', in *Recent Studies in Paleoanthropology*, pp. 88–201 (ed. J. D. Clark and F. C. Howell, *American Anthropologist*, LXVIII 2, part 2, Apr 1966).

— and CLARK, J. D. 1963, 'Acheulian Hunter-Gatherers of Sub-Saharan Africa', in *African Ecology and Human Evolution*, pp. 458–533, ed. F. C. Howell and F. Bourlière; published by the Aldine Publishing Co., Chicago, as no. 36 in the series Viking Fund Publications in Anthropology.

HUDSON, K. 1963, *Industrial Archaeology*, John Baker; Methuen's University Paperbacks series 1965.

HUTCHINSON, R. W. 1962, *Prehistoric Crete*, Pelican.

JACOBSTHAL, P. 1944, *Early Celtic Art*, Oxford U.P.

JOFFROY, R. 1954, *Le Trésor de Vix, Côte d'Or*, Monuments et Mémoires (Fondation E. Piot), 48, 1; Presses Universitaires de France, Paris.

— 1958 *Les Sépultures à Char du Premier Âge du Fer en France*, J. Pichard et Cie, Paris.

— and BRETZ-MAHLER, D. 1959, 'Les Tombes à Char de la Tène dans l'Est de la France', in *Gallia*, XVII 5–35.

KENDRICK, T. D. 1928, *The Druids*, Methuen.

KENYON, K. M. 1957, *Digging Up Jericho*, Ernest Benn.

— 1965, *Archaeology in the Holy Land*, 2nd ed., Ernest Benn, 1960; also in Methuen's University Paperbacks series, 1965.

KIMMIG, W. and GERSBACH, E. 1966, 'Die neuen Ausgrabungen auf der Heuneburg', in *Germania*, XLIV 102–36.

KLÍMA, B. 1954, 'Palaeolithic Huts at Dolní Věstonice', in *Antiquity*, XXVIII 4–14.

— 1962, 'The First Ground-Plan of an Upper Palaeolithic Loess Settlement in Middle Europe and its Meaning', in Braidwood and Willey, eds, pp. 193–210.

KLINDT-JENSEN, O. 1957, *Denmark Before the Vikings*, Thames & Hudson. Ancient Peoples and Places series.

KOENIGSWALD, G. H. R. VON 1962, *The Evolution of Man*, Ann Arbor Science Library, University of Michigan.

KOSTREWSKI, J. 1938, 'Biskupin: an Early Iron Age Village in Western Poland', in *Antiquity*, XII 311–17.

270

KRÄMER, W. 1958, 'Manching, ein vindelikisches Oppidum an der Donau', in *Neue Ausgrabungen in Deutschland*, pp. 175–202 (published by the Römisch-Germanische Kommission des Deutschen Archäologischen Instituts zu Frankfurt-a-M; Gebr. Mann, Berlin).

— 1960, 'The Oppidum of Manching', in *Antiquity*, XXXIV 191–200.

KROMER, K. 1959, *Das Gräberfeld von Hallstatt*, Association Internationale d'Archéológie Classique; Sansoni, Firenze.

— 1963 *Hallstatt: Die Salzhandelsmetropole des ersten Jahrtausends vor Christus in den Alpen*, Naturhistorisches Museum, Prähistorische Abteilung, Vienna.

LAET, S. J. DE 1957, *Archaeology and its Problems*, Phoenix House; trans. Ruth Daniel.

LEAKEY, L. S. B. 1951, *Olduvai Gorge*, Cambridge U.P.

—, ed. 1966–7, *Olduvai Gorge*, Cambridge U.P., vol. I, 1966, and vol. II, 1967. For the latter, see also Tobias, 1967*a*.

LEAKEY, M. D. 1968, 'Preliminary Survey of the Cultural Material from Beds I and II, Olduvai Gorge, Tanzania', in Bishop, W. W. and Clark, J. D., eds, pp. 417–46.

LE GROS CLARK, W. E. 1958, *History of the Primates*, 6th ed. British Museum (Natural History).

LEROI-GOURAND, A. 1968, *The Art of Prehistoric Man in Western Europe*, Thames & Hudson, 1968, being an English trans. by Norbert Guterman of the author's *Préhistoire de l'Art Occidental*, Editions d'Art Lucien Mazenod, Paris, 1965.

LETHBRIDGE, T. C. 1953, 'Burial of an Iron Age Warrior at Snailwell', in the *Proceedings of the Cambridge Antiquarian Society*, XLVII 25–37.

LIBBY, W. F. 1955, *Radiocarbon Dating*, 2nd ed., University of Chicago Press.

LONGWORTH, I. H. 1961, 'The Origins and Development of the Primary Series in the Collared Urn Tradition in England and Wales', in *Proceedings of the Prehistoric Society*, XXVII 263–306.

LYNCH, T. F. 1966, 'The "Lower Perigordian" in French Archaeology', in *Proceedings of the Prehistoric Society*, XXXII 156–98.

McBURNEY, C. B. M. 1950, 'The Geographical Study of the Older Palaeolithic Stages in Europe', in *Proceedings of the Prehistoric Society*, XVI 163–83.

— 1959, 'First Season's Fieldwork on British Upper Palaeolithic Cave Deposits', in *Proceedings of the Prehistoric Society*, XXV 260–9.

— 1960, *The Stone Age of Northern Africa*, Pelican.

— 1964, 'The Old Stone Age in Wales', in *Prehistoric and Early Wales*, ed. I. Ll. Foster and G. E. Daniel, and published by Routledge in the Studies in Ancient History series, general editor F. T. Wainwright.

— 1967, *The Haua Fteah (Cyrenaica) and the Stone Age of the South East Mediterranean*, Cambridge U.P.

MACE, A. 1959, 'An Upper Palaeolithic Open-site at Hengistbury Head, Christchurch, Hants', in *Proceedings of the Prehistoric Society*, XXV 233–59.

MACKIE, E. W. 1965, 'The Origin and Development of the Broch and Wheelhouse Building Cultures of the Scottish Iron Age', in *Proceedings of the Prehistoric Society*, XXXI 93–146.

MANBY, T. G. 1963, 'The Excavation of the Willerby Wold Long Barrow, East Riding of Yorkshire', in *Proceedings of the Prehistoric Society*, XXIX 173–205.

— 1966, 'Cresswellian Site at Brigham, East Yorkshire', in *Antiquaries Journal*, XLVI 211–28.

MARINATOS, S. N. 1960, *Crete and Mycenae*, Thames & Hudson; photographs by M. Hirmer; trans. J. Boardman.

MEGAW, J. V. S., THOMAS, A. C. and WAILES, B. 1961, 'The Bronze Age Settlement at Gwithian, Cornwall: Preliminary Report on the Evidence for Early Agriculture', in *Proceedings of the West Cornwall Field Club*, II.

MELLAART, J. 1965, *Earliest Civilisations of the Near East*, Library of the Early Civilisations, Thames & Hudson.

— 1967, *Çatal Hüyük, a Neolithic Town in Anatolia*, Thames & Hudson.

MORGAN, F. DE M. 1959, 'The Excavation of a Long Barrow at Nutbane, Hants', in *Proceedings of the Prehistoric Society*, XXV 15–51.

MOVIUS, H. L., Jr. 1960, 'Radiocarbon Dates and Upper Palaeolithic Archaeology in Central and Western Europe', in *Current Anthropology*, I 335–91.

MÜLLER-KARPE, H. 1966, *Handbuch der Vorgeschichte: Band I, Altsteinzeit*, C. H. Beck, München.

MYLONAS, G. E. 1966, *Mycenae and the Mycenaean Age*, Princetown U.P.

NEUSTUPNÝ, E. and NEUSTUPNÝ, J. 1961, *Czechoslovakia before the Slavs*, Ancient Peoples and Places series, Thames & Hudson.

OAKLEY, K. P. 1965, *Man the Toolmaker*, 5th ed., British Museum (Natural History).

— 1966, *Frameworks for Dating Fossil Man*, 2nd ed., Weidenfeld & Nicholson.

OKLADNIKOV, A. P. 1962, 'The Temperate Zone of Continental Asia', in Braidwood and Willey, eds, pp. 267–87.

Ó RÍORDÁIN, S. P. and DANIEL, G. E. 1964, *New Grange and the Bend of the Boyne*, Ancient Peoples and Places series, Thames & Hudson.

OVEY, C. D., ed., 1964, *The Swanscombe Skull, A Survey of Research on a Pleistocene Site*, Royal Anthropological Institute of Great Britain and Ireland, published as *Occasional Paper no. 20*.

DE PAOR, M. and DE PAOR, L. 1958, *Early Christian Ireland*, Ancient Peoples and Places series, Thames & Hudson.

PÉQUART, M. and PÉQUART, ST J. 1937, *Téviec. Station-nécropole mésolithique du Morbihan*, published as Mémoire 18 of the series *Archives de l'Institut de paléontologie humaine*, Paris.

— 1954, *Hoëdic. Deuxième station-nécropole du mésolithique côtier Armoricain*, de Sikkel, Antwerp.

PIGGOTT, S. 1950, *William Stukely*, Oxford, Clarendon Press.

— 1954, *The Neolithic Cultures of the British Isles*, Cambridge U.P.

— 1959, *Approach to Archaeology*, Black, 1959 and Pelican, 1966.

— 1961, *Prehistoric India to 1000 B.C.*, Pelican.

— 1962, *The West Kennet Long Barrow: Excavations 1955–56*, published as no. 4 in the series *Ministry of Works Archaeological Reports*, H.M.S.O., London.

— 1963 'Abercromby and After: the British Beaker Cultures Re-examined', in *Culture and Environment: Essays in Honour of Sir Cyril Fox*, pp. 53–91, ed. I. Ll. Foster and L. Alcock, Routledge.

— 1965, *Ancient Europe from the Beginnings of Agriculture to Classical Antiquity*, Edinburgh U.P.

— ed. 1961, *The Dawn of Civilisation*, Thames & Hudson.

POWELL, T. G. E. 1958, *The Celts*, Ancient Peoples and Places series, Thames & Hudson.

— 1966, *Prehistoric Art*, Thames & Hudson.

PYDDOKE, E. 1964, *What is Archaeology?* John Baker.

— ed. 1963, *The Scientist and Archaeology*, Phoenix House, London, and Roy Publishers, New York.

RAFTERY, J. 1951, *Prehistoric Ireland*, Batsford.

RENFREW, A. C. 1967, 'Colonialism and Megalithismus', in *Antiquity*, XLI (Dec 1967) 276–87.

—, DIXON, J. E. and CANN, J. R. 1966, 'Obsidian and Early Cultural Contact in the Near East', in *Proceedings of the*

Prehistoric Society, XXXII 1–29.

RIEK, G. 1962, *Der Hohmichele: ein Fürstengrabhügel der späten Hallstattzeit bei der Heuneburg*, with a contribution by H. J. Hundt. Published by the Römisch-Germanische Kommission des Deutschen Archäologischen Instituts zu Frankfurt-a-M, as *Heuneburgstudien* 1; Walter de Gruyter, Berlin.

RIVET, A. L. F., ed. 1966, *The Iron Age in Northern Britain*, Edinburgh U.P.

ROCHE, J. 1960, *Le gisement mésolithique de Moita do Sebastião, Muge, Portugal*, Instituto de Alta Cultura, Lisbon.

ROE, D. A. 1964, 'The British Lower and Middle Palaeolithic: Some Problems, Methods of Study and Preliminary Results', in *Proceedings of the Prehistoric Society*, XXX 245–67.

ROSENFELD, A. 1965, *The Inorganic Raw Materials of Antiquity*, Weidenfeld & Nicholson.

ROWNTREE, A., ed. 1931, *History of Scarborough*, Dent.

RUST, A. 1937, *Das altsteinzeitliche Rentierjägerlager Meiendorf*, Wachholtz, Neumünster.

— 1943, *Die alt- und mittelsteinzeitlichen Funde von Stellmoor*, Wachholtz, Neumünster.

ST JOSEPH, J. K. S., ed. 1966, *The Uses of Air Photography*, John Baker.

SCHWABEDISSEN, H. 1954, *Die Federmesser-Gruppen des nordwesteuropäischen Flachlandes zur Ausbreitung des Spät-Magdalénien*, Wachholtz, Neumünster.

SEMENOV, S. A. 1964, *Prehistoric Technology: an Experimental Study of the Oldest Tools and Artifacts from traces of Manufacture and Wear*, translated and with a preface by M. W. Thompson; Cory, Adams & Mackay.

SMITH, I. F., ed. 1965, *Windmill Hill and Avebury: Excavations by Alexander Keiller 1925–39*, Oxford, Clarendon Press.

SMITH, P. E. L. 1966, *Le Solutréen en France*, Publications de L'Institut de Préhistoire de L'Université de Bordeaux, Mémoire No. 5, Imprimeries Delmas, Bordeaux.

SMITH, R. A. 1911, 'A Palaeolithic Industry at Northfleet, Kent', in *Archaeologia* (published by the Society of Antiquaries of London) LXII, part 2, 515–32.

SONNEVILLE-BORDES, D. DE 1960, *Le Paléolithique Supérieur en Périgord*, Imprimeries Delmas, Bordeaux.

STEAD, I. M. 1965, *The La Tène Cultures of Eastern Yorkshire*, The Yorkshire Philosophical Society.

STEKELIS, M. 1966, *The Lower Pleistocene of the Central Jordan Valley: Excavations at Ubeidiya, 1960–1963*, Israel Academy of Sciences and Humanities, Jerusalem.

STONE, J. F. S. 1941, 'The Deverel-Rimbury Settlement on Thorny Down, Winterbourne Gunner, S. Wilts', in *Proceedings of the Prehistoric Society*, VII 114–33.

STUIVER, M. and SUESS, H. E. 1966, 'On the Relationship between Radiocarbon Dates and True Sample Ages', in *Radiocarbon*, VIII 534–40.

TAYLOR, J. DU PLAT, ed., 1965, *Marine Archaeology*, ed. Joan du Plat Taylor for the Confédération Mondiale des Activités Subaquatiques, Hutchinson.

TAYLOUR, LORD WILLIAM 1964, *The Mycenaeans*, Ancient Peoples and Places series, Thames & Hudson.

THOMAS, A. C. 1958, *Gwithian: Ten Years' Work*, West Cornwall Field Club, published by the Excavation Staff, Gwithian, Cornwall.

THOMPSON, M. W. 1954, 'Azilian Harpoons', in *Proceedings of the Prehistoric Society*, XX 193–211.

— 1967, *Novgorod the Great: Excavations at the Medieval City directed by A. V. Artsikhovsky and B. A. Kolchin*, compiled and written by M. W. Thompson, Evelyn, Adams & Mackay.

TOBIAS, P. V. 1967a, *The Cranium of Australopithecus (Zinjanthropus) Boisei*, being vol. 2 of *Olduvai Gorge*: see Leakey, L. S. B., ed. 1966–7.

— 1967b, 'Cultural Hominization among the Earliest African Pleistocene Hominids', in *Proceedings of the Prehistoric Society*, XXXIII 367–76.

TUGBY, D. J. 1965, 'Archaeological Objectives and Statistical Methods: a Frontier in Archaeology', in *American Antiquity*, XXXI 1–16.

TYLECOTE, R. F. 1962, *Metallurgy in Archaeology*, Arnold.

UCKO, P. J. and ROSENFELD, A. 1967, *Palaeolithic Cave Art*, World University Library series, Weidenfeld & Nicolson.

VOGEL, J. C. and HAMMEN, T. C. VAN DER 1967, 'The Denekamp and Paudorf Interstadials', in *Geologie en Mijnbouw*, XLVI 5 (May 1967) 188–94.

WAALS, J. D. VAN DER 1964, *Prehistoric Disc Wheels in the Netherlands*, J. B. Wolters, Groningen.

WAINWRIGHT, G. J. 1968, 'Durrington Walls: a Ceremonial Enclosure of the 2nd Millennium B.C.', in *Antiquity*, XLII (Mar 1968) 20–6.

WALKER, D. and SIEVEKING, A. DE G. 1962, 'The Palaeolithic Industry of Kota Tampan, Malaya', in *Proceedings of the Prehistoric Society*, XXVIII 103–39.

WALTON, A. 1967, 'Radiocarbon Dating and Methods of Low-Level Counting', in *Antiquity*, XLI (Dec 1967) 317–18.

WATSON, W. 1956, *Flint Implements*, 2nd ed., British Museum. A new edition will be published by the Museum in 1968.

WEINER, J. S. 1955, *The Piltdown Forgery*, Oxford U.P.

WEST, R. G. and McBURNEY, C. B. M. 1954, 'The Quaternary Deposits at Hoxne, Suffolk, and their Archaeology', in *Proceedings of the Prehistoric Society*, XX 131–54.

WHEELER, R. E. M. 1943, *Maiden Castle, Dorset*, Reports of the

Research Committee of the Society of Antiquaries of London, no. 12; Oxford U.P.

— and WHEELER, T. V. 1936, *Verulamium: A Belgic and Two Roman Cities*, Reports of the Research Committee of the Society of Antiquaries of London, no. 11; Oxford U.P.

WOLSELEY, G. R. and SMITH, R. A. 1924, 'Discoveries near Cissbury', in *Antiquaries Journal*, IV 347–59.

WOLSELEY, G. R., SMITH, R. A. and HAWLEY, W. 1927, 'Prehistoric and Roman Settlements on Park Brow', in *Archaeologia*, published by the Society of Antiquaries of London, LXXVI 1–40.

WYMER, J. 1961, 'The Lower Palaeolithic Succession in the Thames Valley and the date of the Ancient Channel between Caversham and Henley, Oxon', in *Proceedings of the Prehistoric Society*, XXVII 1–27.

ZEUNER, F. E. 1958, *Dating the Past*, 4th ed., Methuen.

— 1959, *The Pleistocene Period*, Hutchinson.

— 1963, *A History of Domesticated Animals*, Hutchinson.

278

Index